T0373357

BISON BOOKS

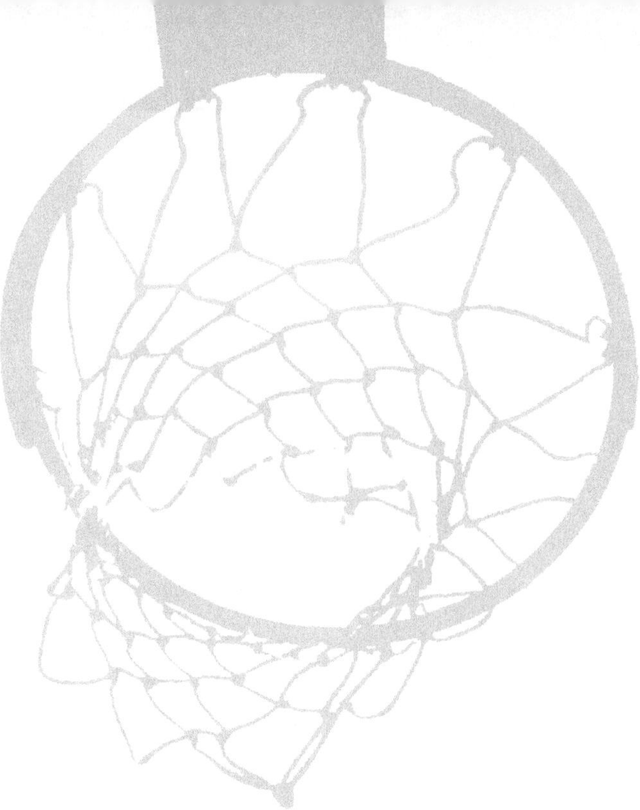

UNIVERSITY OF NEBRASKA PRESS • LINCOLN AND LONDON

Under the Boards

The Cultural Revolution in Basketball

JEFFREY LANE

© 2007 by Jeffrey Lane. All rights reserved
Manufactured in the United States of America
∞

"Ten Crack Commandments" words and music by Khary Kimani Turner, Chris Martin, and Christopher Wallace. © 1997 EMI April Music Inc., Weblife, Hertzrentatune, Gifted Pearl Music, and Justin Combs Publishing Co., Inc. All rights controlled and administered by EMI April Music, Inc. All rights reserved. International copyright secured. Used by permission.

Libray of Congress Cataloging-in-Publication Data
Lane, Jeffrey, 1979–
Under the boards : the cultural revolution in basketball / Jeffrey Lane.
p. cm.
Includes bibliographical references.
ISBN-13: 978-0-8032-8053-3 (pbk. : alk. paper)
ISBN-10: 0-8032-8053-x (pbk. : alk. paper)
1. Basketball—Social aspects—United States. 2. Basketball—United States—History—20th century. 3. Basketball players—United States—Social life and customs. I. Title.
GV889.26.L36 2007
796.3230973—dc22 2006029803

Designed and set in Scala by A. Shahan.

To my mother and father,
for believing in me with
loving devotion and utter
conviction so powerful
that I became a believer too.

CONTENTS

ILLUSTRATIONS

ACKNOWLEDGMENTS

I offer heartfelt thanks to my mother and father for their constant support, encouragement, and love, not just with this project but with all things and at all moments, and for generously making sure that I had what I needed to get this book written; my father again for his dutiful, contemplative reading of each and every word of this book; his illuminating input; and his grammar and language wizardry; my loving godparents, Sheila and Brett, for always believing in me and in this book; their infectious enthusiasm for life and learning; and for connecting me with wonderful, helpful people; my agent, Dan Carlinsky, for believing in my potential as a writer and pushing me to get there, teaching me about the book business and taking a chance on the project; Rob Taylor, acquiring editor at the University of Nebraska Press, for his confidence in me and commitment to the book; my project editor, Ann F. Baker, for her supportiveness of a first-time author; my copyeditor, Bojana Ristich, for her rigorous and sophisticated refinement of the manuscript; the University of Nebraska Press for taking on and investing in the project; my family and friends, not all of whom I'll name here but to all of whom I'm grateful—you all contributed to this project in one way or another: Pauline, Michael, Natalie, Roy, Zach, Sam, Craig, Eddie, Ian, Jon, Bones and Bones, Team Hot, Suzie, Eli, McGoey, Molly, Evan, Billy, Matt P., Krin, Gavin, Stu (I wish he were here to celebrate with me), Danny, the Grossmans, my crews—HCES/HS, Wesleyan, Gonzalez, and Shockamania; Mary Ann Clawson and Charles Lemert of the Wesleyan University Sociology Department for inculcating a love of the discipline and for their guidance in the embryonic stages before I even realized that I was writing a book; my caring, sharp principal readers: Joan Bryant (who helped get this book in gear in the early stages), Christopher Hayes, Judy Polumbaum, Kristofer Rutman, Bob Segal, Jessica Seidman, and Matthew Stimmel (a helluva roommate too); Todd Boyd and Nelson George for providing a well of inspiring, provocative writing from which to learn and draw upon; Ghostface Killah, Biggie, and Jay-Z, and Chris Rock for the creative stimulation and for breaking things down; Tom Blatchford, Jeff Cohen, Tom Konchalski, Jackie MacMullan, Tony Rosa, Dan Shaughnessy, and Jeff Twiss for their thoughts, candor, and expertise during our interviews; Harvey Araton for his valuable input on the Larry Bird chapter; the Indiana University Media Department for generously providing photos and information; the family at Diner in South Williamsburg, Brooklyn, for (first) great company and (second) grub and caffeine; the Atlas Café on Brooklyn's Havemeyer Street and DT/UT in Manhattan for the high-speed Internet and good vibes; Emily for all that she has contributed to the book and, more than that, to my life; the Osler family for taking good care of me during my stay in Cambridge/Boston; Ruth Witmer at the *Indiana Daily Student*, Mike Schreiber, Angelika Jauch at *imago*, and Jaime Calsyn at *Icon Sports Media* for providing brilliant photos and for looking out for me; and, of course, God and the sport that I love.

INTRODUCTION

Best-selling mystery novelist Lisa Scottoline's 2005 *Devil's Corner* begins with a black male teenager, his hair in cornrows, holding a Glock handgun to the head of the main character, a female lawyer. The teen offender, a product of the Philadelphia ghetto, wears Iversons (Reebok-produced sneakers named after the ballplayer Allen Iverson), baggy jeans, and "a red satin Sixers jacket." Scottoline probably selected this look for her character because it would likely bring forth a familiar mental picture of a street thug in her readers' minds.

This stock image of a hoodlum fits with, and even helps explain, the depraved act being perpetrated. By aligning the teen's physical appearance with controversial Sixers star guard Allen Iverson, the author seals the connection between the character and criminality: the invented gun-wielding delinquent and Iverson, who has been arrested multiple times—including at least once on a gun charge—share the same hairstyle, sneakers, jeans' style, and team apparel and allegiance.

Precisely because many people reflexively associate both hip-hop fashion and Allen Iverson with unlawfulness, the National Basketball Association (NBA) no longer permits its players to dress in the way described above. Prior to the implementation of an off-court dress code for the 2005–06 season, the league's mostly young and black athletes usually dressed in one of two ways over the last decade or so: hip-hop casual or hip-hop corporate. NBA chic meant that a player either looked like a wealthier, bejeweled version of Scottoline's fictional troublemaker or went instead with a snazzy, custom-fitted dress suit accented by shiny accessories — diamond earrings, watches with bezels, designer shades. A player with a sense of humor and notion of self-grandeur — someone like seven-foot-one Shaquille O'Neal of the Miami Heat—might, as a playful nod to his flamboyant predecessors who played in the funk- and Afro-centric American Basketball Association (ABA) days, throw in a top hat, cane, or loud suit color. With the announcement of the dress code, hip-hop corporate now pervades but in a toned-down, censored form: no chains or pendants outside the shirt; no headwear or sunglasses indoors; and—though they aren't explicitly mentioned—no canes.

NBA players who prefer the outlawed new-money hip-hop look celebrate an aesthetic they helped popularize along with a conspicuous cast of movers and shakers from the inner cities nationwide; they have ascended income brackets by legal or illegal means such as sports, entertainment (e.g., rap music), drugs, and gangsterism. In the interwoven circles of rap music, basketball, and drug culture, the hangouts, automobiles, ideology, jargon, and sexual partners of each group are frequently one and the same. For example, "Me against the World," a well-liked rap song by Tupac "2Pac" Shakur, functions also as a self-reliance mantra for embattled young black men and is a commonly found tattoo on hoopsters' bodies. Moreover, the notorious boss of Death Row Records, Marion "Suge" Knight, a major player in the Los Angeles underworld, is believed by many to have orchestrated Shakur's killing.

Although hip-hop had become institutionalized in the NBA as a meaningful part of players' lives and a commercial force essential to the NBA's standing in popular culture, the league, always careful in its handling of the genre, plainly changed its relationship to it. After a series of disparaging incidents—most glaringly a 2004 brawl in Detroit during which players on the Indiana Pacers tussled violently with the Pistons' fans on national television—the league took a stand against hip-hop. With fan and player welfare, legal responsibility, and (most important) image at stake, the NBA introduced a series of housecleaning reforms for players—including random in-season drug testing, age limits, and mandatory etiquette workshops during the preseason. Featured in the league's list of quality-of-life and safety adjustments was a ban on oversized jeans.

According to this logic, clothes were part of the problem. The NBA therefore needed to ban all banable symbols of hip-hop (prohibiting tattoos would certainly prove more difficult) because there was something treacherous about these items that was either impelling wearers to behave like criminals or impelling spectators to see the items as symptoms of a broader disorder and destructiveness.

Standout player Tim Duncan of the San Antonio Spurs didn't understand why the NBA had infused clothing with such transcendent meaning. In an unlikely incendiary quip, Duncan, the league's quietest and least hip-hop superstar, called the NBA dress code "retarded." Duncan doesn't dress hip-hop cool; he dresses comfortably, without actively using his clothing to make a statement. His outfit was now a concern, but for what purpose? Was he one person in a blazer and khakis and another in a low-hanging Jesus piece and do-rag? Clothing doesn't actually make the man as advertisers and fashion magazines allege, does it? There's no known correlation between fashion sense and common sense.

But there's something more complicated going on here.

The New York Police Department profiles the city's most successful rappers. It's no secret that a section was created in the department to map out the rap world and monitor these musicians through secret surveillance. In 2004, Court TV's thesmokinggun.com posted portions of a five-hundred-page dossier of mug shots, rap sheets, and incident reports of hip-hop heavyweights like Jay-Z, 50 Cent, and Ja Rule. The folder's thickness reflects the alarming fact that most of the popular rappers in the area have criminal records (some for serious charges, some for lesser ones; some before and some after rappers had become famous).

Such tracking by the police is an obvious attack on hip-hop and a seeming breach of civil rights. Yet defeating this probe is probably not the first personal liberties cause most people would champion, nor is such internal intelligence irrational from the police perspective. Big-name rappers have an unusually powerful cultural position and can influence world events, yet at the same time they are frequently figures of dubious legal standing: they often bait police with insults and threats or start beefs with rival rappers that have been known to unfold violently. Many rappers openly maintain ties to organized crime and street gangs, and drug dealing routinely finances rap label start-ups.

In a controversial book, *Out of Bounds: Inside the NBA's Culture of Rape, Violence and Crime*, Jeff Benedict found that 40 percent of NBA players active during the 2001–02 season had criminal records. (The statistic was based on documents available for 177 of the 417 American-born players listed on team rosters.) While one can debate the merits of Benedict's research—he doesn't distinguish between a player's being investigated and his being convicted, for example—and the accuracy of his findings given his small sample size, it is nonetheless obvious that the NBA has to confront criminality, the victims of which, specifically and sadly, are often women. Although NBA commissioner David Stern was critical of Benedict's work, the NBA has essentially reacted to the connection between hip-hop and the criminal culture in the same way as the New York Police Department. Because a substantial proportion of both rappers and ballplayers has been in trouble with the law, these two groups currently find themselves the targets of sweeping reactionary measures and, in the case of NBA players, a movement to separate them from their most obvious association with hip-hop: their clothing fashion.

Doesn't it behoove the NBA to more closely monitor the product it's selling and to protect its image? After all, it is a business, and a sound business controls image and makes money while limiting liability.

From the NBA's vantage point, it doesn't matter if a connection exists between baggy clothing and criminality. According to Virginia Postrel, author of *The Substance of Style*, now more than ever consumers make purchases based on their aesthetic response to a product. Whether it is the lead performer in a play or an espresso machine, a customer invests in items that have the "right" appearance because of the values that customer intrinsically attaches to them. In an arena where many ticket buyers are higher-income white men in their mid-forties, the goal of the NBA as a business is to cater to the tastes of such ticket buyers and to attract companies advertising products aimed at this demographic. If these consumers, cognizant of their reactions or not, see a criminal when they see Carmelo Anthony of the Denver Nuggets on the sidelines in a flat-brimmed New Era cap, oversized white T-shirt, and droopy jeans, then it makes business sense to adjust his appearance.

In acting as a profit-minded enterprise, does the NBA advance a racist conflation between hip-hop clothing and violence that is not only unfounded but that also antagonizes the black labor force responsible for much of its financial success? Is the NBA affirming a devastating stereotype of the black male as a societal menace? Then again, isn't hip-hop in all of its incarnations—fashion surely included—about being provocative and undermining authority? Are the players, as Benedict's findings can be used to suggest, doing it to themselves? Regardless, the NBA is clearly guilty of having it both ways: it chastises players for looking or acting "too street" while it manipulates and sells their street-bred swagger for all its worth and cashes in on the celebration of its players and iconography in mainstream hip-hop. The NBA prohibits players from wearing trendy throwback jerseys during postgame press conferences but outfits them for games in uniform reissues to model an expanding inventory of merchandised apparel. The NBA can thank the rap world, from which it's rapidly distancing itself, for making retro team gear a fashion epidemic.

Ironically, the NBA, acting like an out-of-touch parent, weighed in too late with its announcement of a dress code and missed not only the boat but also the point: hip-hop polices its own fashion. Hip-hop's self-determined, always evolving style sense was already moving in a fresh direction long before the NBA worked the dress code into the new Collective Bargaining Agreement in the summer of 2005. Hip-hop trendsetters like Outkast, P. Diddy, and Jay-Z, applauded in such men's magazines as *Esquire* for their visionary understanding of high-end fashion, had already been telling their followers, at least for a couple of years, to put away the big jerseys and "go dressier," more sophisticated, more businesslike (but, of course, to do so with flavor). California-based Élevée Fine Clothing estimated recently that it had been customizing suits for 50 percent of the NBA *before* the league-mandated fashion makeover.

There's a major difference between black fashion leaders guiding a change in the preferred look of young black men and a white authority structure determining what is and is not permissible. Moreover, with more than eighty foreign-born players on team rosters at the start of the 2005–06 season, new looks and trends were naturally arriving through the sport's globalization.

The dress code and issues related to it have absolutely nothing to do with the game of basketball—the on-court parts of the sport, the in-game action. Unlike rule changes like the addition of a three-point line or permitting a zone defense, the dress code is designed exclusively to change what happens off the court—that is, its purpose is to affect image. Image is what much of basketball is about—looking good, bad, safe, edgy, cool, tough—and the manipulation, ownership, and selling of image is the contested terrain between the league and its players. The overall image of basketball has changed dramatically over the last thirty years or so. Since the 1970s, both amateur and professional men's basketball have become enormously more important and interesting. Basketball is America's most exciting sport not because of its dynastic teams, sublimely talented players, or most thrilling buzzer-beaters, but because of the emergence of a transcendent culture of the game, complete with values and symbols; aesthetics and styles; and economic, political, and racial dynamics. Race in basketball, still basically a black and white category, is a particularly rich and revelatory subject, encompassing (among other things) tensions between black players and white owners and managers; the peculiarity of white minds—commentators and writers—thinking and talking about black bodies; the definitions and self-fulfilling expectations of black and white masculinity; and the overt and latent prejudices and fetishes of fired-up fans.

In addition to reflecting trends in society, the culture of basketball influences the everyday. Regular people shadow ballplayers in numerous ways—in dress: jerseys, warm-ups, and Air Jordans have become street clothes; in talk: "finish strong," "fourth-quarter mentality," and "I can take that guy" are part of the general vocabulary; in thinking: a free-agent attitude pervades the workplace and little showmen perform in the classroom; and in views of the future: the ubiquitous but illusory hoop dream is a practical goal for young people.

Focusing primarily on the NBA, in this book I explore six case studies that collectively tell the true, gritty story of basketball's last thirty-plus years. These highlight the players, coaches, institutions, and events that have shaped the culture and politics of basketball while impacting and reflecting American life and popular culture. Taken together, these accounts show how and why basketball has changed, how it takes from and gives to the rest of our culture, and where it all leads.

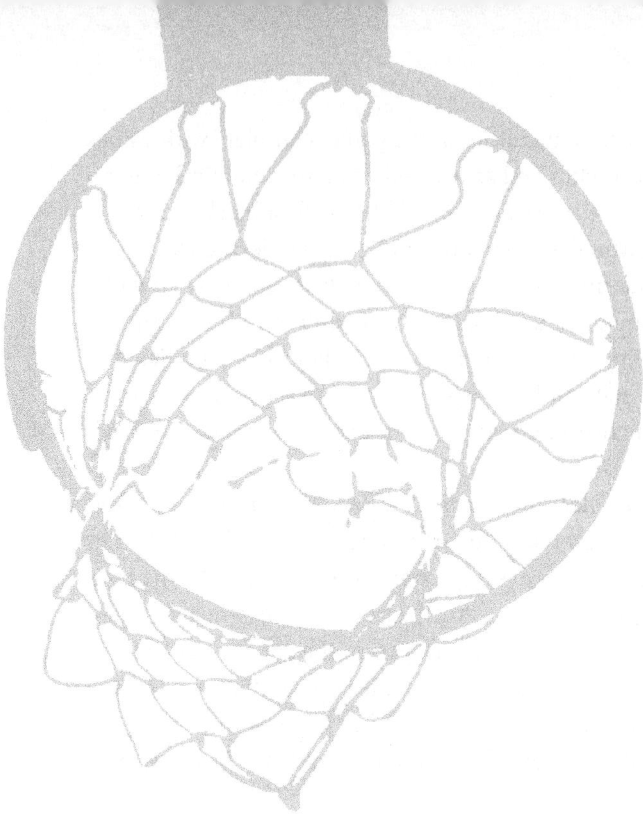

Under the Boards

1. Jay-Z protégé and Roc-A-Fella/Def Jam rapper Freeway, in a vintage Michael Jordan jersey, poses in front of Keith Haring's *Crack Is Wack* mural in Manhattan. After his 2000 arrest for selling drugs, which came on the heels of his rap debut on a Jay-Z track, the North Philadelphia hustler switched his energy into music. © Mike Schreiber, Michael Schreiber Photography.

1 Can't Knock the Hustle

Individualism in Hip-Hop, Hoops, and the Drug Culture

There are two non-music-driven threads that I think play crucial roles in the story of hip hop, by both affecting and reflecting it: drugs and basketball. It's no coincidence that hip hop germinated in the economics of Ronald Reagan's America and that rap seemed to draw on the same strength and vitality that crack sapped. On any given inner-city day, drug dealers—who commit crimes, make money, and influence wardrobes—ply their destructive trade within feet of basketball courts where dreams of public glory, mad loot, and innovative, idiosyncratic style are dearly held. Sometimes the dealers and the players are the same people . . . torn between hoop dreams and immediate green. Sometimes they are friends, both stars in their local 'hood.

Nelson George, from *Hip Hop America*

About 6.5 percent of Cadillac buyers are black, but 19 percent of Escalade buyers are black. Six players on the Golden State Warriors professional basketball team have an Escalade. Of the six top draft picks for the Green Bay Packers and Denver Broncos football teams, five bought Escalades with their new riches.

At least 10 rap songs, including one by Jennifer Lopez, mention Escalade. In music videos and live performances, rappers often drive Escalades.

Cadillac dealers say they sometimes toss teenagers out of showrooms because they spend too much time fawning over Escalades after school.

Earle Eldridge, *USA Today*, October 23, 2001

Hip-hop music, the NBA, and crack dealing became central parts of the American consciousness in the 1980s. In black ghettos nationwide, disenfranchised youth channeled their energies into one or more of these three worlds in the hopes of rising above poverty and transforming their invisible existence into a life of glamour, excitement, and wealth. Today, hip-hop, the NBA, and drug dealing (no longer confined to crack but encompassing a range of less lethal products) drive much of American popular culture while specifically defining both possibility and cool for young black males stuck in the 'hood. Making hip-hop music, playing professional basketball, or selling drugs is particularly thrilling in that each represents not simply a way out, but also a way in: access to a fantasy world of fame, cash, and suddenly interested women. No time need be wasted toiling in the mundane or dealing with the hardships of being poor while slowly earning money through boring, low-level work.

The story of a high-profile rap star/NBA player/neighborhood drug lord (choose one) sitting in the VIP section of an exclusive night club is sold as quickly on the block as it is on television. Facing the desperation of ghetto living and contemporary black culture's obsession with quick wealth, black teenagers often blindly chase the dream of making it big in hip-hop, basketball, or drugs. For the overwhelming majority, it's a foolish endeavor. The risks are dangerously high and the probability of breaking through is painfully low. But in the absence of other models of success, black teenagers still go for the basketball model or the rap model or the crack model because in many cases they are able to reconcile the recklessness and the absurdity. Young black males often recast themselves as participants in a game rather than everyday people living in the real world. Instead of a real-life pursuit, the dream is a game to be played.

As in any game, there are rules and strategies, winners and losers. The "true" players—those who have made it—have beaten the competition. In pursuing their dream the young seekers decided somewhere along the line that while almost all of the other black boys following the same goal will fail, they will succeed. And the winners in the rap game, the NBA game, and the crack game have all learned that the road to success is taken alone. Savage individualism, an unshakable and absolute faith in and commitment to self, is the only way to the top.

A 2003 issue of *Rolling Stone* features an article on hip-hop superstar 50 Cent, with a black-and-white shot of the rapper squeezing imaginary gun triggers with both index fingers. The accompanying caption—"When 50 signed his contract, his first purchase was crack"—is a reference to how the former drug dealer spent his $5,000 cash advance from Columbia Records. In the photo, 50 has on a headband with an NBA logo. A month before the issue came out, 50 was busted outside of a New York City nightclub after police found two handguns in his SUV. At the time of the arrest, 50 was dressed for layup lines in New York Knicks warm-ups.

The incestuous relationship of hip-hop, basketball, and the drug culture cannot be overstated. A typical hip-hop video features a rap star outfitted in contemporary or vintage NBA gear—jersey, warm-ups, headband—boasting of a distinguished drug-dealing past and a penchant for smoking marijuana. Sometimes basketball stars even make cameos: Los Angeles Lakers forward Lamar Odom, who has violated the NBA's drug policy, dances nonchalantly in rapper Jadakiss's "Knock Yourself Out." In rapper Mike Jones's 2005 hit video for "Flossin'," fellow Houston luminary and Rockets star guard Tracy McGrady leans against an expensive car, checking out the girls in the neighborhood and approvingly flashing Jones a peace sign. The five-foot-nine Jones went from standout high school guard to successful drug dealer to record label owner and chart-topping lyricist. Chris Webber and Allen Iverson, Philadelphia 76ers teammates and two of basketball's biggest names, have each recorded rap albums, and each has been arrested for marijuana possession. Rap pioneer Snoop Dogg, who contends that he was once recruited to play hoops by the University of Nevada–Las Vegas (UNLV, a perennial NBA feeding ground), was recently named "Man of the Year" by *High Times*.

No one at UNLV has ever substantiated Snoop's claim. In the fall of 2005, Snoop led the "Save Tookie" campaign, aimed at sparing the life of California death row inmate Stanley "Tookie" Williams, who in 1971 founded the Crips, a notorious Los Angeles drug mob, before authoring from his cell children's books on the hazards of gangbanging.

In the mid-1990s, Tupac Shakur, arguably the most cherished figure in hip-hop, starred in *Above the Rim*, a film about a promising Georgetown recruit who teeters between hoop dreams and hustling. Shakur plays a neighborhood drug boss who tries to lure a talented high schooler (played by Duane Martin) over to the criminal side by getting him to play on a hoops team he assembles for a local tournament. The tournament is modeled after the legendary blacktop showdowns at Rucker Park in New York City's upper Manhattan.

Rucker Park has been the site of the famed Entertainers Basketball Classic (EBC) since the early 1980s, and it hosted some of the most celebrated street basketball matchups decades before that. Founded by rappers, the EBC is New York City's flagship summer hoops league, bringing together elite amateur and professional talent. Athletes battle for bragging rights before an overheated, raucous crowd egged on by megaphoned announcers calling for a "scrubstitution" to replace "coach's son." Rap impresarios from Suge Knight to Sean "Puffy" Combs (now Diddy) to Jay-Z, a former pusher, have sponsored EBC squads at one time or another.

The EBC is all about street credibility. Legendary EBC coach Tony Rosa explains, "You've got NBA guys there because they want to be known in the 'hood. An NBA player . . . goes from city to city and the connection with the fans feels so distant—the fans are white, most of the players are black—I'm sure they love the adulation but there's something about the 'hood: everybody wants to be known in the 'hood. Kobe came through; Shaq came through because it's important to them." Like the streetballers pining for an NBA contract and the cash and validity that come with it, the NBA players want the coveted of-the-people legitimacy that the local street heroes enjoy. Why else would the pros violate their contracts, risk career-threatening injuries, or—even worse—suffer the monumental embarrassment of being outplayed on the notoriously uncontrolled blacktop? What happens on the block is forever meaningful to the streets' native sons, even if they've moved on to NBA careers and sprawling suburban estates.

Rappers, too, coming to the tournament quickly learn where they stand in the 'hood. Jermaine Dupri, a top-selling record producer who wisely raps only occasionally, found out the hard way that his style was too pop, too pretty for the hard-core Rucker contingent. Said Rosa, "'Hood fans: they know when you're real and when you're not, they know when you're fronting and when you're not."

On a recent summer day at the EBC, Dupri, who took his street acceptance as a given, aggressively joined in the local banter, heckling, coaching, and riding the refs from the sidelines. The fans exposed Dupri as a phony playing to the crowd. They rode him mercilessly for his tight white T-shirt, calling for the garment's return to its rightful owner, rapper Bow Wow, Dupri's pint-sized teenaged protégé. One creative attendee put a baby's shirt on a stick and passed it over to Dupri for the producer to put on. Clearly Dupri misplayed his first visit to the tournament. According to Rosa, "instead of just sitting there and relaxing and enjoying everything, he wanted to play coach . . . . Those people, they let you know whether they like you or not. Other [rap] people got good receptions."

Nearly every mainstream rap song routinely references basketball or some part of the drug culture. Some rap lyrics mention known basketball players. On his hit single, "Hot in Herre," Nelly propositions a girl to dance on his basement strippers' pole and then, if she's not into the idea, dismisses the request as "kidding like Jason" (that is, Nets point guard Jason Kidd). Jay-Z, on a track from *The Black Album*, aspires to stack his money so high that it trumps the expanse of six-foot-seven Scottie Pippen's wingspan. The seemingly endlessly extending limbs of the former Chicago Bulls forward helped make him one of the better defenders of his day.

Other rap lyrics reference heated hoops rivalries. Phife Dawg, one third of A Tribe Called Quest, warns rival MCs that he'll take their "heart[s]," just as Michael Jordan did to an outmatched John Starks during the historic but completely one-sided 1990s playoffs between the Bulls and the Knicks. Rappers frequently invoke moments of infamy in basketball history to make a point. Jay-Z equates his competitors with former University of Kentucky center Sam Bowie and himself with Jordan, recalling the 1984 draft debacle during which the short-sighted Portland Trail Blazers notoriously passed on Jordan (who went third) and took the bigger but less talented Bowie as their second pick. Rap duo Mobb Deep, in violent hyperbole, claims to have strangled more people "than Sprewell."

Drug-related allusions similarly abound. There are dreamy scenarios of stoner wishes (Nas shares his fantasy for the legalization of marijuana in "If I Ruled the World [Imagine That])," declarations of devoted drug consumption (the Beatnuts are so persistent in their weed smoking that "like a stewardess," they're always "high"), and boastful proclamations of drug-selling feats (Biggie brags that he outsold Johnson and Johnson in his days of allegedly dealing "powder").

The worlds of basketball, rap music, and drug dealing have co-opted each other's vocabularies. "Selling out" is missing a layup, going pop, or ratting someone out to the cops. A "baller" might be an adept basketball player, an accomplished rapper, or a crack dealer with a thriving business. Those playing ball, making records, or expanding their street clientele are "hustlin'," "playin'," or "slingin'"; they're "gettin' theirs." A "dime" is an assist in basketball, a perfect female (i.e., Bo Derek "10") in hip-hop parlance, or the quantity/price of a bag of dope on the street. To "lock down" can mean to prevent an opponent from scoring in basketball, or to incarcerate, or to lose one's independence at the hands of a controlling girlfriend or boyfriend.

In basketball, encounters between opposing players or teams are increasingly described in the macho terminology of the drug trade or contemporary rap music. When the Lakers swept the Nets in the

2002 NBA championship, the Lakers "did it to 'em." The Nets "got done," "served," "punked." When Doug Christie missed badly on a pivotal three-point attempt at the end of game seven of the 2002 Lakers-Sacramento Kings playoffs, a "shook" Christie "played himself." He "sold (out)." When Michael Jordan crossed over Byron Russell and pulled up for an impeccable jumper in the closing seconds of Chicago's victory over the Utah Jazz in the 1998 championships, Jordan "wet" a 15-footer right in Russell's "eye." In this moment, Jordan made Russell, if not the entire Jazz club, his "son."

There's an aesthetic to drug dealing—a particular tackiness and conspicuousness designed to tell the entire neighborhood that "while y'all are still poor, I'm rich." The image of the neighborhood drug boss festooned with expensive jewelry and driving a behemoth luxury SUV while the rest of the block is taking the train is simultaneously repulsive and irresistible. It's an image that announces an individual's ascent while scoffing at the failures of the rest of the pack. Contemporary basketball and rap music internalize and celebrate this in-your-face mentality and self-aggrandizing swagger.

Contemporary basketball is a game of sudden explosive outbursts. The dunk, the crossover, and the blocked shot are all displays of individual athletic prowess that render an opponent, if not an entire opposing team, temporarily helpless. The premium placed on humiliating the opposition, however, has never been higher. Players routinely attach an element of defilement to their dunks and one-on-one moves. The commitment to thoroughly and theatrically humble one's competitor is pumped up by the hip-hop culture's veneration of all things fast and furious, all things gangster (*The Sopranos*) and gangsta (*Oz*).

The genre of relentlessly flamboyant, "fuck-you" basketball is a major force in pop culture. Upstart sneaker giant AND 1, as well as several production companies, has released numerous highlight videos piecing together the finest and most brutal displays of showmanship and otherworldly athleticism in amateur basketball. Taken from streetball games, high school contests, amateur tournaments, or other venues—and sometimes the producers cheat and stage games—these videos celebrate the best in opponent degradation: dribbling the ball off a defender's face, making the man guarding you trip over his own feet and fall violently to the pavement, sending an opponent's shot over the park fence and into oncoming traffic.

Coach Ron Naclerio of Cardozo High School in Queens, New York, coached a summer club team featuring Rafer Alston, a Harlem-bred point guard better known on the New York City streets as Skip to My Lou. The nickname was spawned from the title of Alston's signature playground move, in which he skips down the court—keeping his legs as straight as possible as he kicks them out one at time in an exaggerated motion—while nonchalantly bouncing the ball ahead of him. Sometimes he will dribble like this right up to the defense, baiting his defender to swipe at the seemingly neglected ball, and then fluidly pulling it in and blowing by the now off-balance opponent. Currently a professional with the Miami Heat, Alston rose to national prominence while still an amateur by becoming the first basketball player to sign a shoe contract without having an NBA contract. Naclerio shot video of Alston playing indoors and outdoors, on different teams, and simply "doing his thing" with the basketball, including his patented Skip to My Lou dribble. He gave the video to AND 1. According to the sneaker company, the tape floated around the office, to the delight of awed employees and visitors. When a group of NBA players (among them Larry Hughes and Rex Chapman) came to shoot a television commercial, they were offered tapes and video games, including the Alston video, to pass the down time. They watched Alston's moves over and over again and then took to the court to improvise upon Alston's jukes while the cameras rolled.

Through the Alston video an anonymous sneaker business forged its identity. AND 1 positioned itself as a renegade company with the same rawness and swagger as the respect-deprived streetball players and the lower-profile, showboating NBA players initially celebrated in its ads. Borrowing from the format of skating and surfing videos—homemade highlight clips matched to thematically or stylistically appropriate music—AND 1 made its first video based on the Alston submission. It generated street buzz by giving it out gratis to hoops camps and clinics, DJs and people in the record industry, ballplayers, and networking types in relevant industries. The video "broke" when the shoe chain Foot Action offered it as a gift with purchases of any sneakers or apparel. The purchased items quickly became secondary to the freebies, and Foot Action rapidly unloaded its inventory of videos. Some videos reemerged on eBay and at Dr. Jay's, a jeans and sneakers department store on 125th Street in Harlem, where they sold under the table for $25. Soon AND 1 needed more footage and more streetball stars; eventually demand spawned an AND 1 national tour, later made into a documentary-style show by ESPN, with its own cast of reality stars.

The same mixed tape formula used by AND 1 has long been a staple marketing tool for rappers looking to generate enough underground buzz to pique a record company's interest. Eminem and 50 Cent are two of the most famous rappers to parlay mixed tapes distribution into major label distribution. To coincide with the release of 50's semi-autobiographical movie *Get Rich or Die Tryin'*, MTV Books released 50's memoir, *From Pieces to Weight: Once upon a Time in Southside Queens.* Both narratives highlight that 50's understanding of the music business grew out of his experience in the drug trade. 50, whose mother was also a drug dealer until rival pushers poisoned her with carbon monoxide when 50 was eight, dropped out of Andrew Jackson High School in New York City's Cambria Heights after the ninth grade to focus exclusively on selling drugs. He later developed what he had learned in the crack game as his business model for breaking into the music business. As a rapper, 50 attracted a following in the same way he had built his customer base of users. He writes in his memoir: "I knew the only way to get into any market is to give out free samples. I had to build up clientele before I could see a profit. I had to invest in my brand." Like AND 1 had given away a deliberately unpolished tape of Alston free-styling on the court, 50 built his name and fan base through the same grassroots, mixed-tape approach. Streetball's best known and most talented players now enjoy celebrity status and spots on basketball tours televised on ESPN2. No longer resigned to retelling tales about what they did to overconfident NBA players who ventured back to the old neighborhood, today's playground legends are so popular that they even have their own video games. In Activision's *Street Hoops*, players choose from a variety of blacktop icons, like Half Man/Half Amazing and Hot Sauce, whom they can then outfit in trendy hip-hop duds for their matchups. Gamers can even select jewelry and tattoos for their ballplayers. Programmed into each character is a repertoire of basketball wizardry and high-flying slams inspired by the signature moves of the streetballers.

Today's blacktop celebrities broadcast a very different version of novelty hoops from that which was made famous by basketball's oldest traveling show, the Harlem Globetrotters. While today the Trotters have returned to a serious brand of hoops, for decades they made a name for themselves by providing comic relief and family basketball fun—goofing on referees, flipping consecutive around-the-back passes on the break, and dribbling with various body parts. Although the Trotters would routinely embarrass the refs, as well as the lighter-skinned, slow-footed Washington Generals, who were their regular opponents, their show was decisively light-hearted and nonconfrontational. The Generals would play up their expressions of bewilderment and frustration, while the smiling Trotters, dressed in red, white, and blue, would wave to the kids in the audience after blowing past their defenders. Played in big arenas with lights and music, these games were packaged events and more circus show than competitive basketball.

The original Globetrotters were very different. In 1926, founder Abe Saperstein organized a team of former high school teammates from Chicago into a legitimate basketball squad that instantly became one of the elite, pre-NBA barnstorming clubs. Playing in temporarily converted armories and ballrooms against all-black rivals like the Harlem Rens and the Chicago Hottentots and later against all-white squads like the original Celtics and the South Philadelphia

Hebrew All-Stars (SPHAS), the Trotters played real-deal basketball at its highest level.

It wasn't until 1949 that the Trotters turned into a comedy troupe. Racism made the conversion an economic necessity since, as Nelson George explains, "the idea of five black men rolling into a Midwestern town, kicking ass, and getting paid could not have been the easiest sell ever."

Today's brand of touring basketball showmanship laughs in the face of the Trotters' accommodationist beginnings and recent clownishness. The basketball on AND 1's mixed tape collection isn't for the whole family; it's as profane as it is breathtaking. Players aren't weaving up the parquet floor of an air-conditioned arena to the tune of "Sweet Georgia Brown"; they're pounding the ball against the cracked pavement of a fenced-in park on a hot summer day while expletive-laced rap music blares from a boom box in the crowd. They are abusing one another with their personalized arsenal of ankle-breaking, "made-you-look" fakes and shakes. They are playing for street fame, to stand out, to build and bolster a rep.

Albeit in less edgy form, NBA players relish the same mano-a-mano approach and flamboyance, accenting their individual flair and athleticism by personalizing both offensive moves (Iverson's high-to-low crossover; Chris Webber's around-the-back dish; Michael Jordan's fadeaway jump shot) and rituals (Kobe Bryant's snobbish smirk and nostril flare after scoring; Dikembe Mutombo's post-rejection figure wave; Antoine Walker's wiggle after sinking a basket). Certain moves and gestures develop into easily recognizable signatures of particular players; they are emulated on playgrounds and pointed out by excited fans ("Here it comes!" "Here it is!" "That was it!"). Players who popularize particular moves are granted imagined government-protected ownership: Jordan's turnaround, fadeaway jumper, complete with distance-creating leg kick, became MJ's patented shot.

The offense of any professional team is designed to highlight the athleticism as well as the personal style and ingenuity of a team's best player or players. Through isolation plays and motion basketball, a team's offense grows out of one-on-one play. Like other forms of black artistry, the act of soloing, a statement and celebration of the individual, is absolutely central.

In hip-hop, rap music consists of a series of solos, generally separated by a song's chorus or hook. Whether a rap track features one artist or multiple artists, each verse represents a solo where all eyes and ears are focused on one MC. Rappers distinguish themselves from other artists by creating a flow—a voice and expositional style—uniquely their own. Music writer Kelefa Sanneh equates Jay-Z's multimillion dollar flow with "everyday speech." To "heighten the effect" of what he is saying, Jay punctuates his verses with "conversational tics—a little laugh in the middle of a line, or a pause, as if he were thinking something through."

To create a personalized sound, rappers draw upon a variety of literary and artistic tools, of which only a few are taught in English classes. A lyricist may rap at different speeds, vary the rhyme scheme, play with words (through alliteration, onomatopoeia, double entendre, etc.), stretch words, alter the pitch of his voice, exaggerate twangs and accents, produce sound effects, make up words, scream, whisper, mumble, and so on. Those perceived as imitating an artist's flow are denounced as "biters," "imitators," "wannabes," "sellouts," "punks," "fake thugs," "fugazi acts," and "copycats."

Like the pompous, confrontational basketball played today, most rap music is about one-upmanship and black male machismo. Rappers play a game of "I'm better than you" based on the usual measurements of manhood—who drives the most expensive car, makes the most money, sleeps with the most women. Added to this list are hip-hop indicators of "true" manliness—who sells the most records, smokes the best weed and rolls the fattest blunts, wears the gaudiest jewelry, and *really* doesn't "give a fuck" about life.

Rapper Nas, who occasionally uses the name of infamous Colombian drug lord Pablo Escobar as an alias, is one of many artists to specifically rap about the similarities between the "rap game" and the "crack game." To survive in either the (relatively) legitimate music world or the illegitimate drug world, players must learn the cold rules of the game. In the "Ten Crack Commandments," deceased rap legend Notorious B.I.G. (a.k.a. Biggie Smalls; real name: Christopher Wallace), in the pulp tradition of Iceberg Slim's attempt to systematize a pimping etiquette, outlines a ten-point plan for successful crack dealing:

> I been in this game for years, it made me an animal
> It's rules to this shit, I wrote me a manual.

Included in Biggie's handbook are the following:

the importance of hiding one's assets

> Never let no one know, how much dough you hold,
>   cause you know
> The chedda breed jealousy.

keeping one's business plans under wraps

> Never let 'em know your next move
> Don't you know bad boys move in silence or violence
> Take it from your highness.

and never taking an addict at his word

> That goddamn credit, dead it
> You think a crackhead payin' you back, shit forget it..

Those who abide by Biggie's code may live to be wealthy drug dealers; those who fail to follow the rules risk imprisonment or even death.

Biggie's "commandments" are mostly about trust—specifically the mistake of trusting anyone. The only person one can trust in the drug game is oneself. Rappers have long said the same for the music business. In "Check the Rhime Y'all," A Tribe Called Quest, as a caution to other rappers, refers to businesspeople in the music industry as categorically "shady." For years, rap artists have voiced their disgust over exploitative industry practices in their lyrics. Whether through convoluted contract language; the coercing of artists to work with a label's own team of managers, agents, and lawyers; or simply empty promises, record executives ensure that the label will receive the overwhelming bulk of the profits and that the artists will assume the overwhelming risk. This is why, according to Bert Padell, an accountant for many top music acts recently quoted in the *New York Times*, an artist who releases an album that generates $17 million walks away with only $70,000 before taxes. Even Biggie Smalls, according to his manager, Wayne Barrow, died without ever receiving a penny in royalties. If we take Barrow at his word, Biggie's contract with Bad Boy, the company that belongs to Biggie's former producer, mentor, and friend Sean "Diddy" Combs, was structured in such a way that the only cash Biggie took home was his cut from concerts.

The artists-versus-record-label mentality, the craving to outfox the foxes, emerges in the lyrics of some of rap music's most respected acts. On his album *Blueprint*, Jay-Z raps about "raping" the parent company of his former label, Roc-A-Fella, for as long as it takes to be personally worth $100 million. That Jay-Z and many other artists constantly refer to themselves as "hustlers" offers further insight into how rappers view themselves in relation to their industry. Indeed often rappers literally are relocated street hustlers, using their cunning and smarts to "get over" (i.e., make it) in a cutthroat, corrupt business. Having moved up the industry ladder to become president of Def Jam, Jay-Z graduated not from business school but—as he puts it—the "School of Hard Knocks."

To succeed in hip-hop, artists then can't just be good at making music; they also need business savvy. They must be able to manipulate the predatory record business to get what they want (to get paid). The same applies to basketball: it isn't enough to simply master the physical and mental parts of the sport; a player must learn the hustle—the financial side of the game—to excel in his industry. Given the amalgamation of hoops, hip-hop, and drugs into one dominant notion of black youth culture, black athletes are often influenced by or look directly to the rap game and drug world to make sense of the financial politics of professional basketball. The same desire to get over and the trust-no-one approach have redefined professional basketball.

Like rappers weary of conniving record executives or drug dealers suspicious of undercover police or rival pushers, ballplayers often maintain a distrustful distance from those within the basketball business—jealous teammates vying for the spotlight, tightfisted general managers and owners, paternalistic coaches pushing players to buy into a system. Anyone who is potentially hazardous to a player's pursuit of wealth constitutes a threat or possible roadblock—family members out for the player's riches; friends who have become hangers-on; and ex-girlfriends, groupies, or women in general. Today, National Football League (NFL) and NBA rookie camps feature lectures on the risks of lending money to friends, maintaining an entourage, or bedding a groupie. Professional athletes tell all sorts of horrifying tales of backstabbing uncles, family members who had once vanished but reemerge with treacherous intentions, and seductresses who poke holes in condoms or freeze used ones (exactly the portrait of women painted in mainstream rap). The key to riches, longevity, and presumably happiness is unyielding individualism—today's doctrine for young black athletes.

Since it's about "getting yours"—hip-hop speak for doing whatever it takes to attain wealth, status, and popularity in a dog-eat-dog world (i.e., the fast-paced, hyper-corporate realm of the NBA)—players today often separate themselves from any tangible connections to their teams or coaches. From a financial standpoint, this individualism appears rational: a player often must play somewhat selfishly and assert his separateness from broader allegiances in order to benefit from free agency, procure a major contract, join a desired franchise, or attract endorsement deals.

For a player to be viable in both the NBA marketplace (that is, a player whose team wants to keep him and other teams want to acquire him) and the broader marketplace (that is, a player who has become a celebrity whom companies seek out to pitch their products), he must have adequate opportunities to showcase himself. He must be able to consistently play enough minutes and take enough shots to establish himself as a legitimate star or at least a potential star. If he finds himself playing behind someone or is overshadowed by more established teammates who monopolize the spotlight, he must do whatever it takes to craft a better position. This often means asking to be traded or playing more selfishly.

In order to sign a contract that reflects his optimal market value, a player must demonstrate that he has no reservations about leaving his current team. The current team will fork over big bucks only when forced to contend with offers from other interested franchises. Players often speak publicly about wanting to join another club, or they talk with other teams to push their own clubs into outmatching prospective deals with competitors or those already on the table. With millions and millions of dollars at stake and a chance to live in the sort of extravagance that Jay-Z and Jermaine Dupri rap about, players aim to outhustle the most successful hustlers in the game of capitalism—businessmen who own their own sports teams. Wealth and fame are enticing to everyone, but to young and poor black men bombarded by images of hip-hop materialism, this is the big dance.

When Corey Maggette, who left Duke University after his freshman year, began his second season in the pros (in 2000–01) on his second team, the Los Angeles Clippers, after only fifteen games he was talking freely about leaving the team unless he got more minutes of playing time. After he had decided to stay with the Clippers, Maggette found himself on a team with ten other players heading for free agency over the next two summers, and he wantonly competed with his own teammates for minutes, television time, shot attempts, and, ultimately, dollars. According to *Sports Illustrated*, at a team meeting called by General Manager Elgin Baylor and Coach Alvin Gentry in the hopes of halting a six-game Clipper losing streak, several players confessed that they had made personal statistics a higher priority than winning. Ironically, Maggette became the star of the 2003–04 Clippers and was among the league leaders in scoring. The sort of civil war that transpired during the Clippers' 2002–03 season is common in the NBA.

The Philadelphia 76ers were fortunate to have drafted two extremely gifted guards, Allen Iverson and Jerry Stackhouse, in the late 1990s. Coexistence between them, however, promptly proved impossible, as both ambitious youngsters battled to be the "go-to" guy on the team's offense and to be seen in the front office as a franchise player—that is, a player around whom it is literally worth building a franchise. Rather than pooling their talents, Iverson and Stackhouse undermined one another's abilities by phasing each other out of the offense. As relations between them degenerated, the two even came to blows during a practice session. On another occasion, Iverson and Stackhouse's respective "crews" allegedly rumbled outside the Philadelphia 76ers practice facility. (Although both players deny that the rumble ever happened, the story has gone down in basketball folklore.) Unable to play together, the two separated twenty-two games into the 1997–98 season, when the Sixers traded Stackhouse (along with Eric Montross) to the Detroit Pistons. Iverson and Stackhouse (who was traded to the Washington Wizards and then again to the Dallas Mavericks) have achieved differing degrees of stardom as the original trade ultimately benefited both teams and both players.

Not too long ago the Toronto Raptors seemed to have the makings of a dynasty with a pair of basketball's most exciting and talented players, guard-forwards Vince Carter and Tracy McGrady. As childhood friends and self-dubbed "cousins" (there is no blood relationship), the two looked poised for a harmonious partnership as teammates. Yet tensions quickly arose, stemming undoubtedly from the desire of both players to be the Raptors' headline act. McGrady left Toronto and signed with the Orlando Magic. He explained why he had jumped ship in an interview with *SLAM* Magazine:

> When you're hearing the talk, "He's in his cousin's shadow," and all the crazy-ass talk, I'm like, man, I ain't in nobody's shadow, man. That's why. . . . Orlando was wide open. They

> didn't have a superstar player there, and I was like, that's home, and the door was wide open for me to come down here. I couldn't let that opportunity pass by me.

McGrady's individualism makes sense: he took the opportunity to be a franchise player when it presented itself. McGrady achieved superstardom in Orlando and signed a lifetime endorsement deal with sneaker giant Adidas.

After the Magic limped through an abysmal 2003–04 season, management sent McGrady to the Houston Rockets in a blockbuster deal before the start of the 2004–05 season. McGrady is a fan favorite, but unless he can lead the team to greatness (and not simply to the first-round of the playoffs), his superstar credibility will be called into question.

In the same *SLAM* interview, McGrady considers his evolution into NBA superstar as hardly evolutionary at all. He does not think that his development as a basketball player, his increasing comfort with the NBA game, his coaches and teammates, or his off-season workouts helped to him get there. He feels he has become a superstar because he cashed in on a golden opportunity—because he looked out for himself:

> Man, I'm telling you, I had this game in Toronto, man. I was just in a different system, and it wasn't my time to really shine. I wasn't the guy, the go-to guy. I was probably a third or fourth option there. But I've always had this game, it's just all about opportunities. I got the opportunity to do what I wanted to do here [in Orlando], just go out and lead my team. Just have the green light.

As perimeter players, Stackhouse and Iverson and McGrady and Carter were all more likely to vie for shot attempts and minutes than an inside-outside duo. Nonetheless, in-house competition and individualistic impulses routinely derail even inside-outside combos seemingly bound for greatness. The Shaquille O'Neal–Anfernee

"Penny" Hardaway tandem, destined to bring championship glory to the Orlando Magic in the 1990s, disintegrated shortly after the team's first trip to the NBA Finals. O'Neal's solidarity with his second team, the Los Angeles Lakers, was tenuous at best and resulted in the controversial dealing of O'Neal to the Miami Heat. In Los Angeles Shaq and shooting guard Kobe Bryant, whose collective talents made the Lakers a championship club, feuded for top billing, aired their grievances publicly, and accused one another of selfish play, thus jeopardizing the Lakers' success.

While maneuvering—"hustlin'"—through the callous business side of basketball may bring a player greater attention and wealth, he can get only so big by his lonesome. The sharpest players in the game know—and this knowledge separates the young bucks from the seasoned hustlers—how to spell team with an "I." Only players on great teams—teams that win championships—are considered truly great. Once a star player can accept that committing himself to his team's welfare may very well translate into self-interest, he is generally on the road to broader individual recognition. Winning teams play longer into the season, appear more frequently on television, and receive more press—in other words, they get the most exposure. Players receiving the most exposure earn the most money: companies pay for pitchmen who are highly visible. Most important, companies, like team owners, reserve the fattest contracts for proven winners.

Michael Jordan—MJ—probably the most individualistic player in hoops history, became the greatest player in history only after he had learned the value of a great team. A master of controlling his image and selling himself, Jordan began his career as a phenomenal player on a mediocre team. With time, he realized that to maximize his own success he had to improve his team as a whole. Thus Jordan pushed his teammates—during both practices and games—to play their hardest in order to make the Bulls better. It's no secret that Jordan ran the ball club and did so with an iron fist. Steve Kerr, who once left practice with a black eye, can attest to that fact. If Jordan's teammates put in the necessary effort, they were rewarded with a winning team and a chance to shoot the ball too. If they failed to comply, they were punished with Jordan's scorn.

MJ's commitment to himself never waned as he committed himself to the improvement of his team. His body language and interactions with his teammates always communicated separateness. It could be seen in the way he reacted when the Bulls won their titles; at the end of a deciding game, Jordan ran to embrace the game ball, not his teammates. Wrapped around the trophy or the ball, Jordan seemed to zone out in championship euphoria. In these moments, it always looked as though Jordan, the ball, and the championship trophy shared a linear relationship that had nothing to with MJ's competition or his teammates.

The paradox with which younger players must come to terms if they want to be legitimate superstars seems simple enough: by giving oneself over to the greater good of the team (albeit with careful calculation), one has a better chance of realizing one's personal desires—stardom, fame, endorsement deals, etc. Moreover, poor reputations and tumultuous personal histories have a way of disappearing when a player leads his team to success. When Allen Iverson took the Sixers to the championship series against the Lakers in 2001, Philly fans fell in love with a "thug." Latrell Sprewell, the picture of violence in sports, won over Knicks fans and resurrected his seemingly doomed career when he led the Knicks to the Eastern Conference championship in 1999.

This understanding of the importance of team generally comes with age. In the rap game, the wise and successful recognize the value of putting together a strong pack and cultivating new talent. 50 Cent has personally primed an entire crew of talent—rappers like Tony Yayo, Young Buck, and Lloyd Banks—and has paired them with already established acts stuck in creative or business ruts on other labels—for example, M.O.P. and Mobb Deep—to strengthen his G-Unit label. Rather than relying solely on individual stardom, which is generally accompanied by an expiration date in the music industry, 50 developed his skills as a talent scout and entrepreneur. He has partnered with nonmusic corporations to expand and diversify his business, attaching his name to clothing, films, books, sneakers, video games, and beverages. On the streets the same logic applies: look out for yourself while building an army and an empire. Hip-hop, pro basketball, and drug dealing are all games in which success is determined by an individual's ability to manipulate group situations for individual gain.

While drug dealing is the only enterprise of the three that's illegal, all three are high-risk businesses. Because drug dealing involves physical and legal gambles that do not threaten those chasing hoops or microphone dreams, it's commonly assumed that the trade-off for the perils is instant cash returns—that poor, uneducated people can earn lots of fast, untaxed cash money doing work that requires neither intelligence nor specific skills but simply two essential qualifications: desperation and audacity. Consequently, it's presumably easier to get rich as a drug dealer than a basketball player or a hip-hop artist. But in the best seller *Freakonomics*, co-author Steven D. Levitt demonstrates otherwise. Levitt starts with a good question: why do drug dealers still live with their mothers? The answer, he proves, is simple and no different from the reason most noncriminals live at home: they can't afford to move out. Contrary to popular belief, most drug dealers make crummy livings as low-level laborers in tightly regimented street gangs that control the neighborhoods in which the pushers deal. Like the poorly paid employees at the counters of local fast-food franchises, alongside whom they are too embarrassed to work, most dealers are stuck at the bottom of a typical capitalist conglomerate.

In his study—a collaborative effort with Sudhir Venkatsh, a brave University of Chicago sociology student who was embedded in a crack-dealing Chicago gang named the Black Disciples for a stretch in the 1990s—Levitt details the conventional pyramidal organization of a major drug consortium. The centralized leadership—a roughly twenty-member board of directors—sits atop the pyramid and controls several regional gangs, including the Black Disciples. Below the board is the gang leader of the Black Disciples, who presides over three officers—an enforcer in charge of protecting gang members, a treasurer who manages the gang's cash, and a runner who moves drugs and money between the gang and the supplier. Below the officers are the roughly fifty foot soldiers: street dealers on the Black Disciples' payroll. At the lowest rung, there are up to two hundred rank-and-file personnel; they are not paid, nor are they employees, but rather they pay dues to the gang in exchange for some participation in the gang's operations or permission to work their own rackets within gang territory. The gang leader, officers, foot soldiers, and rank and file comprise a regional syndicate that, along with many other similarly structured local syndicates, reports to the umbrella organization—the board of directors.

After paying out the board of directors' fees and covering his gang's costs of business (the most important element of which was the buying of drugs wholesale), the Black Disciples' leader, J.T., divvied up the net profits: each month he kept 45 percent for himself and paid out the remaining 55 percent to his employees. He divided roughly a quarter of the last amount equally among the three officers and then evenly split the balance among the fifty foot soldiers. For the foot soldiers, this worked out to a rate of $3.30 per hour. The low-level employees were living on a prayer rather than on the sort of wages necessary to move out of mom's basement. The rank and file, as indicated above, received nothing. Like unpaid interns working in desirable law firms or publishing houses, the rank and file saw their position as an opportunity—the proverbial foot in the door—that would, they hoped, lead to a promotion to foot soldier. While the rank and file aspired to be just foot soldiers, the foot soldiers aspired to become officers, the officers dreamed of becoming gang leaders, and the gang leader—the only one in the local syndicate who could actually afford to live large—hoped to one day get grandfathered in as a director and collect from all of the franchises.

Upward mobility proved extremely difficult in the Black Disciples; there were hardly any spots into which one could even conceivably move. In the NBA, there are 420 roster spots available on 30 teams. Three percent of the boys in this country who play high school basketball go on to play at some level in college; fewer than 1 percent play Division I. Approximately .03 percent of college players eventually get drafted by an NBA team. Players who are not drafted but are good enough to be paid to play hoops and want to leave more than a college legacy will toil through relatively obscure professional leagues around the globe, often holding on for an NBA offer that is unlikely to come. While the music industry does not conspire to retain a particular number of signed artists and it's impossible to calculate how many people pursue recording deals, it's nonetheless exceptionally difficult to land a record contract from a major label. Making it in the drug world is not any easier than making it in the two legal industries.

Being a foot soldier is far more hazardous than chasing a hoop dream or persevering as a starving artist. Selling drugs on the street is one of the most dangerous jobs in the country. A foot soldier leaves his house with a weapon and a drug stash to wait on a corner to do business with a junkie. He is an easy pickup for the police and—far worse—a stationary target for gun-toting members of rival gangs. All this for less than Burger King wages in an industry with even less mobility than that available to employees in the fast-food business.

Why then get into drug dealing? Depressed youth choose to sell drugs for two reasons: the sexiness of the drug dealer image and the ugliness of the alternative. Wealthy drug dealers are accorded eminent social standing in the 'hood; at the same time, ghetto youth are ashamed to work at minimum-wage jobs. During the second season of his *Comedy Central* show, Dave Chappelle joked about the stigma attached to taking a job flipping burgers. In a skit involving a McDonald's clone, WacArnold's, Chappelle's imaginary employee becomes the laughingstock of the neighborhood and eventually implodes. In American ghettos impoverished black men who do not sell drugs routinely congregate on street corners and would rather spend the day doing nothing than taking a low-paying, limited-mobility job.

The markers of wealth and success for young black males are in sports, hip-hop, and drugs—Escalades, bling, gorgeous arm candy—and replicate the stuff that juvenile dreams and male egos are made of. Like sports and music, drug dealing is a glamour profession: people want to work in this industry so badly that they will work for little or no pay and will take enormous risks. Of course, basketball and music offer plenty of positives that drug dealing does not. They are life-enriching activities that not only require self-discipline but also enhance self-esteem. They can also provide an opportunity for schooling that would not normally be available to the young participants.

But hoops, hip-hop, and drugs are dangerous dreams because they all have serious limitations. There is only a narrow space to break through, and success is unlikely in all three trades. Moreover, the three pursuits, as we have discussed above, have come to resemble one another too closely. As demonstrated by Terrance Howard's pimp/dealer/rapper character in *Hustle and Flow*, ghetto multitasking makes practical business and logistical sense and allows one to simultaneously try one's hand in different legal and illegal 'hood activities, thus increasing the chances of success. And because pimping, dealing, and rapping share the same values, skills, and language, it's easy to pursue more than one at a given moment or within a short time. But success is still a fantasy—a low-odds chase—and the pursuit is dangerous and easiest to stomach when thought of as a game instead of life.

2. Controversial Philadelphia 76ers leader Allen Iverson waited almost ten years into a stellar professional career before being selected to Team USA. Iverson's incendiary look and style of play are both despised and adored by fans. © imago/Ulmer.

2 Peddling the Street

Gangsta Wannabes, Allen Iverson, and Black Masculinity

When I was in high school in the mid-1990s, hip-hop had reached its apex of mainstream popularity. Puffy's Bad Boy record label gave hip-hop a popular music makeover while 2Pac and Snoop provided a more thuggish, West Coast alternative that was equally catchy and radio friendly. Rock music was buried in what came to be called hip-pop on the radio and on MTV. Youth fashion, values, and lingo came nearly exclusively from hip-hop. At my school, a laboratory school in Manhattan, the usual high school cliques divided the social scene: cool kids, jocks, nerds, punks, Goths, artsy kids, preppies, and hoods. Of course there was often overlap. A preppy guy, for example, could also be part of the arts scene because he played guitar, and if he was good enough to have a band—or if he just dated a hot girl—he could also be considered cool. With the exception of the punks and Goths, all of these groups were informed and remade—for better or worse—by hip-hop, the "it" force of the youth culture of the day. The catchall of hip-hop was where the greatest overlap occurred as we lived the title given to us: the hip-hop generation. My school was also mostly white and Asian.

We wore colorful rugby and polo shirts by Polo, Tommy Hilfiger, and Nautica because East Coast rappers wore them and routinely rhymed about how good they looked in these brands. We wore construction worker staples like Timberland work boots, Champion hooded sweatshirts, and Carhartt jackets. Apache, a one-hit wonder, gave the okay for girls to wear this stuff too with his early 1990s single "Gangsta Bitch"; it became standard female gear, along with slicked-back hair, hoop earrings, nameplate necklaces, and brown lipsticks. We bundled up in fleeces, down vests, and ski shells made by the North Face, or else we appeared in Starter team jackets for L.A. franchises—the Kings of the National Hockey League (NHL) or the NFL's Raiders—because these teams' black and silver colors and iconography were also those of gangs. The less brazen opted for team jackets bearing only one of the two colors forming the axis of street evil—for example, the silver (and blue) of the Dallas Cowboys or the black (and aqua) of the San Jose Sharks. We bought baggy jeans from Girbaud, Hugo Boss, and Guess and wore them with a fat belt and a beeper clipped to it because drug dealers and hip-hop artists communicated that way. The jeans were heavy and too big, so they sagged and left our underwear exposed. The term "wigger" (an imitator in the worst sense) circulated, and it offended both whites and blacks for different reasons. Underneath our shirts, wife-beaters—white A-shirts—held us snuggly. We all smelled the same. Snoop's post-bubble-bath routine included a dousing of Cool Water cologne, so we sprayed ourselves with Cool Water or Polo Sport or a "more sophisticated" Polo option. We accessorized with ski masks and goggles, visors and bandanas; even our backpacks, which were ubiquitously Jansport and then North Face, required accessorizing with as many straps as possible, little strips of leather or cord tied to the rings on the zippers. Stealing straps from other people's backpacks or from packs on sale at sporting goods stores became a devious after-school activity for even the nerdiest kids. The taking of these straps became the pettiest of the popular exercises in juvenile delinquency. Others included bombing (putting up graffiti tags with paint markers or aerosol cans); herbing (mugging or just roughing up other kids); shooting the fair one (fist fighting); and blazing or puffing or any one of a number of slang expressions that meant smoking marijuana.

There was sometimes a real meanness to the hip-hop vibe in New York in the 1990s. The comparatively lighter rap music of the 1980s gave way to the hostile subgenre of gangsta rap, launched with seminal albums like N.W.A.'s 1988 *Straight Outta Compton*, the D.O.C.'s 1989 *No One Can Do It Better*, and Dr. Dre's 1992 *The Chronic*. But my white and Asian classmates also got into other hip-hop-driven activities that were positive and noncriminal: freestyle rapping, slam poetry, dancing, stepping, and streetball.

At parties, the alcoholic beverage of choice was the same one celebrated in hip-hop that had long been poisoning ghettos nationwide: malt liquor, a low-grade beer in forty-ounce glass bottles known as "forties." It was sold under brand names such as St. Ides (a.k.a. Crooked I, mysteriously the strongest of the lot), Olde English (a.k.a. OE or Olde E or Old Gold), Colt 45 (shortened to Colt), Crazy Horse, and Private Stock. As I write this, I can hear Biggie stretching "tape popped" to rhyme with "Private Stock" on his 1994 career-starting hit single, "Juicy." The East Coasters generally went for OE, while St. Ides was bigger out West because of its popularity in West Coast rap. When they were imbibed covertly outdoors, "forties" were downed out of brown paper bags and playfully tipped out to offer sips in honor of imaginary deceased brethren whose lives had been cut short by the perils of the 'hood. Those who smoked chose Newports over other cigarette brands because they were the rappers' favorites and had a (factual) reputation as "black" cigarettes; Marlboros and Camels were "white" makes. As per instruction in rap songs, marijuana smokers "split blunts": they took cheap cigars (with brand names like Phillies, Swisher, White Owl, and Dutch Masters), dumped out the tobacco, replaced the brown leaves with green ones, rolled the cigars up again, and sealed them with saliva. Kids argued over which brand burned the most slowly and therefore maximized the blunt's "passability" and potency. Cognizant of how their products were being used, cigar companies started to offer an assortment of flavors with fruit or liquor themes like peach and cognac. Sweeteners—commonly added to food and drink so as to appeal to both younger and poorer people—were now being added to cigars. To eliminate the labor of splitting the blunt, companies also started to sell regular and flavored blunt wraps.

Getting in trouble, dressing provocatively, listening to music that is sure to offend parents, and bullying are timeless elements of youth culture that all fall under the category of deviance. For my generation hip-hop deviance was by far the most popular way to push the boundaries. It was an "insta-cool" formula, an entire set of rapper-approved activities and fashion styles matched to a list of brands to wear, drink, smoke, and spray on the body, and it was all based on what hip-hop told us black kids were into. Coolness was achieved through feeling and looking "black." As a result, the wannabe gangstas (that is, black gangsters) with the most black friends or the "crews" with the most minority members enjoyed the reputation of being the most legitimate. "Down" (i.e., cool) white kids became famous to their white peers because of their purportedly intimate connection to black ghetto life. Bolstering their notoriety through graffiti tags and appearances at particular theme nights at nightclubs catering to teens, these white kids became local legends, tough thugs, and desirable bachelors, though often only in the eyes of their same-colored peers. The particulars of New York City's geography, which sometimes result in a $4 million brownstone or luxury apartment complex being situated across the street from a housing project, facilitated the formation of crews across race and class lines. Moreover, some private schools included a greater number of black and Latino students than others. Crews and schools with larger nonwhite populations garnered broader respect. In the swanky Riverdale section of the Bronx, Fieldston School, with its greater minority population, outranked neighboring Riverdale County Day School in the street cred department.

The brands of the time that had been marked cool quickly realized that hip-hop was creating a new and massive stream of customers who were putting a unique twist on their products. The hip-hoppers took some of the rigidity out of preppy clothing by going big—wearing larger sizes, loud colors, and items with blatantly visible logos. The brand-consciousness of hip-hop music connected certain brands with money and status. The clothing companies simply sold the idea back to hip-hop fans that they were wearing big cash signs by making the brand references bigger and bigger. Hilfiger spelled out "Tommy" in huge block letters and stretched out its trademark red and white flags to cover entire shirts. The cuts of clothing became more generous too, often even deliberately droopy and clunky. Cheaper lines, like Chaps Ralph Lauren and Tommy Sport, were started to allow consumers on a budget to wear these names. Polo, with a longer and more firmly established following in WASP culture than Tommy Hilfiger or Nautica, opened a Polo Sport store across the street from its flagship Manhattan Ralph Lauren/Polo store on 72nd Street and Madison Avenue to sell edgier, younger, and urban (a.k.a. black), but still very expensive clothing.

Of course the white hip-hop kids with gangsta aspirations—dubbed the "Prep-School Gangsters" by Nancy Jo Sales in her *New York Magazine* cover story of the same title—didn't get their hip-hop fashion totally right. ("Prep-School Gangsters" refers to the wealthy but thuggish-looking kids on the Upper East and West Sides of Manhattan and not to the downtown groups, depicted in the movie *Kids*, that were causing havoc at the same time.) Easily drawn to the preppy brands popular with their parents, Prep-School Gangsters wore too much of the Polo and Hilfiger gear trendy among East Coast hip-hop acts like Grand Puba and A Tribe Called Quest. Moreover, they bought so much of the ridiculously expensive preppy stuff that they looked less and less like the poorer blacks they were trying to emulate and more and more like parodies of real gangstas. To guard against being labeled poseurs, the prep schoolers started to steal the gear that their parents could readily afford; this way they weren't technically buying their way in. The black hip-hop kids often wore more black and less expensive stuff, and sometimes they matched all of their clothing to a color scheme featuring two solid colors (frequently based on sports teams [as noted above], widely recognized high-status fashion items, and street gangs).

The most voyeuristic and overt example of white wannabes pursuing coolness through "visiting" blackness was the quirky New York City phenomenon of the boomer cab. Boomer cabs were private cars provided by several city taxi services and catering specifically to the prep school troublemaking set. They were black luxury sedans—usually Lincoln Town Cars—with tinted windows and a set of subwoofers in the back to pump out a soundtrack of loud, bass-heavy rap. They provided a concealed, supervision-free, and transient space for illicit activities and the right ambiance in which to roll and smoke blunts, down a "forty," and generally play the role of gangsta. In addition to shuttling kids to specific addresses as conventional cabs did, boomer cabs offered a unique touring service: a joy ride through the 'hood. With a knowledgeable, usually nonwhite driver, the comfort of an air-conditioned car, and the anonymity of tinted windows, the cabs took white kids through black neighborhoods and places with a particular contemporary or historical relevance in hip-hop: a housing project from which a certain rapper hailed, a favorite store like Dr. Jay's in Harlem, or perhaps farther uptown to Rucker Park, where (as noted in chapter 1) rappers started the EBC summer tournament in the early 1980s. The white kids in boomer cabs weren't simply seeing these places; they were pretending to be a part of them—to live them and to do so with rap-video swagger, with a blunt hanging from their lips while they nodded to the beat. What better way to absorb the geography, style, and decadence of hip-hop while avoiding the poverty, desolation, and destruction from which it derived?

A boomer cab ride was a brief and safe trip to the wild side, a way to feel tough and reckless without giving up anything or changing anything about one's life. It's most significant that this normal teenage desire to be "bad" is experienced through acting black according to the tenets of black life described and often extolled by hip-hop. In some ways, it's the least creative and most obvious way to act on the teenage spectrum of rebellion. A white teenager's acting the part of a black gangsta is an easy way to challenge parental expectations, throw off neighbors, and provoke teachers. Of course, none of the wannabes actually want the burden of being black; the taking on of blackness was conditional.

The need to act out subsides as teenagers become adults, but it never fully goes away. For adults it is a vicarious high to get into the sinister characters in a good mob movie. When the credits roll, one leaves the movie feeling mischievous and darker. Sometimes the viewer feels a passing desire to dress more sharply, talk more slickly, and move with stealth and style. Adults of all ages love to talk tough, show off their knowledge of expressions from the lexicon of cool disseminated by hip-hoppers and teenagers, dress younger, laugh at black comedians, watch black athletes, and adore and/or hate them (sometimes both at the same time). Blackness specifically still equals cool, even for white adults. The white, Oscar-winning actor Adrien Brody, approaching the age of forty, boasted in a hip-hop magazine about being down, claiming that as a kid he "went bombing in Brooklyn with Tupac."

In 1999, David Shields penned an unusual book, *Black Planet: Facing Race during an NBA Season*. The book was the painfully honest confession of a white basketball fan's profound, sometimes perverse obsession with the black players on the Seattle Supersonics. Shields, who trailed the team for a year for his study, admits that by identifying with his favorite player, trash-talking point guard Gary Payton, and sharing in Payton's brash style of play, he could " fantasize about being bad." Shields reveals that his infatuation with black players permeates all areas of his life, even—and this is where he's at his most twisted—one evening after a birthday dinner, when he and his wife "make love." Shields immediately rethinks his choice of words and clarifies what he believes took place in the bedroom: "that's not quite the right term—it's more like fucking: a rough physicality that I realize later is my attempt to imitate the athletes I spend so much time watching and thinking about."

The fetishism extends to Shields's white friends. At a Sonics home game, his neighbor Richard, commenting on the decreasing number of white jump shooters in the NBA, explains that "'when you go to play ball in the ghet-to, you gots to throw it down, not shoot it.'" Neighbor Richard's brand of commentary—an exaggerated reproduction of black speak described by Shields as a "shucking-and-jiving routine"—is commonplace when white fans consume hip-hop or basketball in exclusively white surroundings.

Over the summer of 2005, a proudly uncouth Randy Moss, the controversial all-pro wide receiver, pleased with his having deluded the NFL once again, told Bryant Gumbel on HBO's *Real Sports* that he had smoked marijuana during his NFL tenure. Moss's Raiders jersey became the number one seller the same month. (The Raiders were already the official bad-kid team of the league for their tradition of taking chances on controversial players; their smash-mouth brand of play; and their apparel, with its California gang associations.) The best-selling jersey surely requires plenty of white buyers following that desire to feel and look "bad," to take another temporary trip to the dark side, to hop in that boomer cab again.

The purchasing of jerseys is always based as much on politics as it is on geography. In 2001, in the post-Jordan era, the NBA Finals showcased two superstar guards on opposing teams: Kobe Bryant and Allen Iverson. The former was a league hero, and the latter was its antihero. Before his long fall from grace, Lakers shooting guard Bryant reveled in the role of Jordan's successor, while Sixers point guard Iverson renounced any label—good or bad—as an unwarranted attempt to apply a polish to his image. It was widely reported that when Iverson was a rookie, during a game between Philadelphia and Jordan's Chicago Bulls, he told Jordan that he didn't have to respect anybody in the league, His Airness included. During the 2002–03 season, Iverson's jersey outsold those of any other player with the exception of Kobe Bryant. The fans had chosen between hero and antihero.

There are of course no statistics on the racial breakdown of purchasers of Iverson jerseys, but for it to be a consistent best seller year in and year out—and it has regularly been in the top five—it is clear that there must be a major white contingent of purchasers. Purchasing a player's jersey is a meaningful decision for a fan.

Wearing clothing with someone else's name on it—clothing "belonging" to and originally designed for another person—is like putting on a costume and exchanging identities. It's also a provocative item in our sports-obsessed society: it demands that others evaluate the wearer based on the team and athlete that is represented. A Shaq jersey—a jersey that arguably "belongs" to the game's biggest crossover star—communicates a different message from an Iverson jersey. The former symbolizes pulling for the favorite, basketball fun, a celebration of one's own overgrown kid tendencies, and complicity with mainstream culture and with the NBA. The latter indicates support for the underdog, mischievously siding with a troublemaker, and staging one's own small-scale revolution. An Iverson jersey is official badass gear, recognized in pop culture in the same way as a Sex Pistols T-shirt or a Rolling Stones shirt with the signature lips emblem. But because it's only a costume, it's only a temporary trip to the dark side.

The breakneck, furious ascendancy of hip-hop through the 1990s made it a universal, cross-racial cultural tour de force. But both its popularity and intensity boiled over during 1996–97 (my senior year in high school). Hip-hop imploded. The coastal beef between label heads Suge Knight and Puffy Combs and their best-selling artists, Tupac Shakur and Christopher Wallace (a.k.a. Notorious B.I.G.), became real-life tragedy when 2Pac and then Biggie were gunned down in September 1996 and March 1997 respectively. Though both murders remain unsolved because of increasingly obvious police complicity, facts eventually pointed to Knight, a bona fide gangsta, as their most likely orchestrator. Knight's underworld standing in California extended so far above ground that it enabled him to play puppet master with both the Bloods, a Los Angeles street gang, and the Los Angeles Police Department (LAPD) and evidently get away with two murders. While drug gangs have traditionally provided the creative inspiration as well as the start-up cash for hip-hop labels on both coasts, the slayings of 2Pac and Biggie, inarguably the biggest hip-hop stars of the day and most likely of all time, sobered up aspiring gangstas, black and white alike. The deaths were a reminder of hip-hop's foundations in the street; at any point hip-hop could transcend its subsistence as art. 2Pac and Biggie may have understood the street, but they were artists, gangsta-rappers at moments in their careers, but never real gangstas. Suge Knight, on the other hand, was a gangsta.

The deaths of 2Pac and Biggie forced hip-hop even further into the American public's consciousness, presenting an apocalyptic view of the music and the culture in the process. While hip-hop was at the apex of its popularity, it was also at its scariest and most capricious. For those uninterested in hip-hop but already assuming the worst about rappers even before the murders—those believing that all rappers were every bit as violent and criminal-minded as they claimed to be in their lyrics—the fatal shootings served as graphic, absolute confirmation. For those knowledgeable of hip-hop who had assumed that rap was about headline-grabbing feuds and lyrics that were as lewd and grotesque as possible so as to stir up controversy, increase record sales, and make money, this was a reality check. Rap really could be as violent and ugly as it alleged.

Regardless of one's familiarity with hip-hop, the 2Pac-Biggie saga made it unequivocally clear that hip-hop existed on two planes: on the one hand, it was a cultural and commercial powerhouse that had captivated an enormous audience that ranged across the color spectrum; on the other hand, it was a combustible force bound to the underworld and the impoverished streets from which it had been spawned. In hip-hop, the NBA had a new cultural location, image, and marketing direction to carry it, as a gradually declining Jordan, who had made the NBA into a major international entity, headed toward retirement. Whether Commissioner Stern and the league brass desired such changes is uncertain, but it is extremely unlikely. For them the challenge of managing the infusion of hip-hop, which inaugurated the arrival of pro basketball's new class of young stars, was akin to playing with fire: handle it right and it would power the NBA into the new millennium; manage it wrong and it would burn down the house that Stern, Magic, Bird, and Jordan had built.

During this tumultuous, critical time for hip-hop, Iverson burst onto the NBA scene. As if ordained to fill the void left by the premature departures of the genre's two most influential icons, Iverson was basketball's hip-hop incarnate; he brandished a badass swagger and street cred far more provocative than any previously seen in the professional game. His biographer, Larry Platt, borrowed a description from Michael Eric Dyson, a revered critic of black culture, for the title of the introductory chapter: "Tupac with a Jumpshot." Indeed there were numerous significant similarities between the two. Tupac and Ive were both unusually handsome black men with big, revealing eyes and nearly identical small but strong physiques tattooed with messages affirming street life. Sometimes profane, other times gentle and sweet, and always grappling with their own vulnerabilities, they each made (and in Iverson's case continue to make) a point of speaking candidly in public, defying authority and other people's rules, and invoking people and experiences important to them—what they'd seen (the inside of a jail cell, the violent deaths of loved ones), where they were from, their families and hometown buddies. Whether on the microphone or on the court, both resembled stacks of dynamite detonating over and over again; their overflowing energy and talent manifested themselves in quick, explosive bursts of lyrical venom or athletic virtuosity. Iverson, however, brought the same incendiary attitude and brand of artistry that had earned 2Pac respect in the rap world to an NBA arena stocked with middle-aged white fans.

The buzz around Allen Iverson could be felt long before his NBA debut, less than two months after 2Pac's demise. For most hoops fans outside of Virginia, the introduction to Iverson came as word spread of an imprisoned two-sport high school star (football was his first love) in the midst of a racially charged legal drama. If freed and kept on the straight and narrow—so the media message went—he would go on to athletic greatness; if not, the streets that made him would mark his demise. His problems with the law gave him the ghetto credentials and scar of blackness that the gangsta wannabe set dreamed of, posed as if they owned, but would never actually want or know firsthand. At a bowling alley in Hampton, Virginia, in 1993, Iverson and some of his pals, all black, were involved in a violent and racially loaded brawl with a group of local whites. Each side claimed the other had instigated the brawl. When police arrived on the scene, they arrested only four black men—Iverson and three of his friends. Iverson was tried individually and found guilty of "maiming by mob"—a rare conviction originally and ironically designed to protect black men from lynchings by Klansmen; he was sentenced to fifteen years in prison with ten years suspended.

Iverson spent four months in jail before being pardoned by Virginia governor L. Douglas Wilder, the country's first black governor. Wilder explained: "While there is not sufficient evidence at the present time for me to grant the extraordinary relief inherent in a traditional pardon, there is sufficient doubt to merit that Allen Iverson be granted limited freedom and the opportunity to continue his education." Wilder required that Iverson finish his high school education, respect a curfew, and temporarily not play organized ball.

Two years later, in light of new video documentation and a fresh review of the case, Iverson's conviction was overturned for lack of evidence. Regardless, the incident functioned as the public's first conceptualization of Iverson. Depending on which reports they read and on their broader feelings on the justice system—not to mention their stance on Iverson's pardoning by a black governor—sports fans conceived of Iverson as either a "rebel survivor" or a "spoiled thug." The press barely mentioned that Iverson was cleared of the conviction once a video of the brawl was made admissible; most sportswriters referencing the incident have generally overlooked or omitted this important fact.

College coaches who had fervently pursued Iverson backed off once he went from blue-chip prospect to convicted felon; then Iverson's club (nonscholastic) team coach, "Boo" Williams, stepped in. A major player in the amateur basketball world, Williams reached out to John Thompson, a Georgetown coach known as a father figure for embattled black teenagers with prodigious basketball skills. Williams and Iverson's mother, Ann, pleaded their case to Thompson while Iverson was still incarcerated. Thompson agreed to take Iverson incumbent upon his release from prison, a permissible SAT score, and a satisfactory scholastic evaluation by Thompson's academic coordinator. Iverson met Thompson's stipulations, matriculated at Georgetown, and debuted in Hoya blue and gray in the fall of 1994. Iverson was now known to the basketball public as Thompson's most challenging and controversial protégé to date.

No one could contain Iverson in college—not opposing guards, weak-side defenders, Georgetown teammates, or even his coach. Before going pro after his sophomore year, for two electrifying seasons, AI (one of Iverson's many nicknames) blazed through defenders on offense and shut down opposing guards on defense, twice earning Big East Defensive Player of the Year honors. He accumulated over 1,500 points, 300 assists, and 200 steals while at Georgetown—impressive totals for even a four-year career. To the chagrin of Othella Harrington, the next in a line of touted Georgetown centers (among them Patrick Ewing and Alonzo Mourning) and with his coach's forced-hand blessing, Iverson converted the Hoyas' usually tightly controlled, bang-it-inside offense into a freewheeling one-man show led by a score-first point guard breaking traps with his dribble, heaving threes, and humbling wide-eyed defenders with assailing dunks. After a sophomore campaign in which Iverson averaged 25 points a game, drastically improved his three-point and overall field goal percentages, and raised his numbers in all other significant statistical categories, he declared himself eligible for the 1996 NBA draft. Iverson was so dominant in college, so divinely athletic and rich in potential, that the Philadelphia 76ers made him their number one draft pick. Generously listed at six feet and 165 pounds, Iverson was the shortest and lightest number one draft pick in NBA history and the first guard selected first overall since the six-foot-nine Earvin "Magic" Johnson in 1979.

The then lowly Sixers yearned for a new superstar to replace past greats like Charles Barkley, Julius "Dr. J" Erving, and Moses Malone, all of whom had revolutionized basketball in their own iconoclastic ways. Barkley, the undersized but thick and springy power forward, was the shortest player ever to capture a rebounding title (14.6 boards per game in 1986–87); before his rebirth as a neo-conservative with political aspirations, he routinely blasted Philly as a city and the Sixers as an organization for tendencies he considered racist. Before Barkley, Dr. J had brought ABA style to the NBA with his court innovations and acrobatics and a bountiful Afro that antedated Iverson's cornrows as a statement of black pride. The prolifically inside-scoring and rebounding Malone, drafted by the ABA's Utah Stars directly out of high school in 1974, showed the basketball world that high schoolers could successfully jump directly to the pros decades before the trend became common in the 1990s.

Philadelphia, then, was the right place for Iverson to stage his own hoops revolution, but the young upstart presented Sixers fans and hoops fans nationwide with a predicament. He was plainly and uniquely talented—destined only to get better with time—and yet he brandished a recklessness that seemed a fatal flaw that could do him and the Sixers in. Here was a trigger-happy floor leader with the body of a tenth-grade point guard, shooting without shame and fearlessly pursuing the rim, charging into the territory of men easily more than a foot taller and more than a hundred pounds heavier. Moreover, Iverson was unabashedly proud of his ghetto roots; he bore an unpolished look plainly derived from the streets and from jail culture, had the credentials of teen incarceration, and raised unsettling concerns that he had stymied his social and basketball maturation by leaving Georgetown early. As a rookie, Iverson could at times score at will, even reeling off five consecutive 40-point games during one supernatural stretch of play, but the Sixers were still a losing team. Was he good for the team and—more important—was he good for basketball?

Today Iverson's style is commonplace in the NBA, but when he first entered it, he pushed the league in a new and bold direction, accelerating the hip-hop makeover the league had begun incrementally before his arrival. In the hip-hop-infused 1990s, cheerleaders became "city dancers," grooving and gyrating to hip-pop in sassy fly girl outfits. Rap music blared from arena speakers during warm-ups, breaks in play, and even (unspeakably to some) select moments of game action. Uniform shorts extended progressively lower down the thigh, obscuring the rulebook-protected tops of the kneecaps; entire uniforms fit more loosely, and someone as thin as Iverson looked as if he were swimming in a sea of mesh fabric. Uniform designs, team logos, and colors became louder, bigger, brighter, and glossier, mirroring the cut and hues of hip-hop clothing and the shine and gleam of gold rope chains and diamond-covered accessories. The NBA began licensing hip-hop-themed products, most famously video games like NBA *Jam* and its sequels and spin-offs. The NBA Web site assembled downloadable highlight reels of in-your-face dunks and other manhood-dissing moves.

If the Ralph Lauren brand—the badge of old white money and preppy living—could go hip-hop, then the NBA, which had become younger and blacker, could do it too. Of course, the NBA's appropriated version of hip-hop was corny and watered down—not the Iverson style of hip-hop, laced with profanity and street grime, but Will Smith–style hip-hop, painted with a slick coat of Hollywood lacquer. Like the "Prep-School Gangsters," overdoing it with big red, white, and blue Tommy Hilfiger gear from Bloomingdale's, the NBA didn't get its hip-hop quite right either.

For the displeased followers of the sport, Iverson was difficult to swallow if not totally unpalatable; for many younger black fans, he was an inspirational role model—someone not much bigger than they and resembling the cool brothers in the neighborhood. For white kids who cast AI as their black rebel of choice and a personification of all they loved about hip-hop, he was very difficult to impersonate: this guy was just too real. Iverson's radical cornrows, which he first sported in his second pro season in 1997, immediately impacted hair decisions for young black people everywhere and for some of the more daring white folks. Three years after Iverson's cornrows debut, the *Wall Street Journal* tritely announced: "Cornrows for Men Exploded This Year into the Mainstream—NBA's Sprewell, Iverson Inspire Young Blacks, and Trend Spreads to Pop Culture." Sometimes imitation of black style can be logistically or socially dubious for white fans. White pop icons like singer Justin Timberlake and British soccer stud David Beckham boldly but only very briefly sported the hairdo; white hair doesn't lend itself to cornrows—it's not thick or resilient enough. Socially, a white adult with cornrows risks mockery from blacks and derision from whites. White fans who wanted to copy Iverson's style would have to settle for wearing his jersey.

A replication of Iverson's tattooed body—now inked more than twenty times over, with messages paying tribute to (among others) his deceased friends and old neighborhood—is similarly not feasible for the average white male fan. Copying Iverson's look was more difficult than buying or stealing the right hip-hop clothing; it couldn't be pulled off. For lusting white fans, this was another sobering reminder of the separation between them and Iverson. As they had realized in the case of hard-core rappers with real rap sheets and "thug life" tattoos, black ghetto living could never be experienced hands-on but could only be romanticized from a distance.

No matter what comes of it, Iverson has "kept it real." Many black players experience a tension between league expectations (being good role models, avoiding situations that may generate negative publicity, maintaining allegiance to the team, etc.) and "keepin' it real." Put simply, "keepin' it real" means doing exactly what one did before one became famous (to the closest possible degree)—retaining the same beliefs, allegiances, and behavior. "Keepin' it real" meant that a player who had become a star would not abandon the people he'd hung out with before he'd made it. If he'd smoked pot before he was drafted, he'd still smoke after landing on a pro team.

It should be mentioned that "keepin' it real" is both an exceedingly selective guideline and an increasingly banal expression. While stars may often remain close to their friends and family and continue certain behavior patterns even after they have made it, others will be left behind. If a player came from the projects, he will rarely (if ever) stay there once he enters the league. The "keepin' it real" idea has become hackneyed, co-opted long ago by the mainstream, worn out as slang, spoofed and manipulated so often that the term is now nearly passé and can mean almost anything. Recently I watched two buddies in a movie theater bathroom define the phrase anew. Upon completing their business, one guy washed up while the other headed for the door. "C'mon, man," said the first guy, with soap in hand. "What?" replied his nonwashing friend; "I'm keepin' it real."

Nonetheless, the term is a commanding force in basketball and in black culture in general, and it's one of the best ways to make sense of the politics of the NBA. In pro hoops, players "keep it real" by embracing the same sort of fashion statements (tattoos, cornrows, baggy clothes, certain designer labels, big jewelry), speech, and general demeanor that prevail in the black urban neighborhoods in which most of them were raised. Maintaining what sociologist Richard Majors calls the "cool pose" has become part of black male identity and authenticity: "[The 'cool pose' is] unique, expressive and conspicuous styles of demeanor, speech, gesture, clothing, hairstyle, walk, stance, and handshake [designed to] offset an imposed invisibility and provide a means to show the dominant culture (and the black male's peers) that the black male is strong and proud." Indeed, "keepin' it real" is such a persuasive force for younger black men—specifically basketball players and rappers—that young black guys often exaggerate their closeness to established emblems of this "realness."

Because of this pressure to appear "real," blacks who are not from the mean streets may represent themselves as coming from horrible areas and sharing a "street" mentality even if they are the products of privilege. In hip-hop music, the harder the background, the better and more legitimate the rap star. Biggie was never as poor or desperate or criminally inclined as his lyrics tell us. 50 Cent may claim in his music that he's permanently stoned and boozes regularly, but in real life he's neither a marijuana smoker nor a drinker. While their private lives may be at odds with their rap personas, they still feel the need to present themselves as conforming to narrow, now well-established guidelines of "black authenticity." In these instances, there's a wannabe element in all of us, regardless of race.

That listeners generally believe the music and may even be disappointed by the truth—for example, reading that 50 doesn't even like weed or hearing Biggie's mom talk about her son's safe home life—is a testament both to these rappers' skills and to our naiveté, ignorance, and even prejudices. Just because Biggie raps in the first person, we reflexively believe that he must have been a crack dealer. Rap music is (among other things) a more recent form of the black oral tradition, in which one's individual experience is no different from that of one's community. (Of course, as discussed in chapter 1, matters are complicated because many rappers do come from the gravest of home situations and have committed crimes, the most common of which is selling drugs.) In the rap world hardship is embellished. From being poor or working class one advances to starving and forced to rob, sell dope, or act criminally; from committing crimes and carrying a gun one jumps to using the firearm as a fearless felon, even committing murder (and maybe that of a police officer). Rappers get away with such exaggeration because of the accuracy and ferocity of their look, stance, and oration and the high probability that at least some of their brothers and sisters in the neighborhood have in fact lived their lyrics.

The nonblack wannabes of the Prep-School Gangster era desperately clawed for the same badge of authenticity upon which rappers built their careers. Although they looked like phonies right away—confused kids posing as toughs in their luxury buildings—they understood the desire and reasoning behind "keepin' it real." They badly wanted to feel strong and hardened, bound to something dangerous and exciting, and—most important—real. But this truth—this realness—was not their own.

Thus what fans have long been buying when they attended an NBA game, and what the NBA has been selling, is black masculinity. David Stern and the NBA walk a fine line, both peddling and curbing black authenticity, benefiting from it and reproaching the "cool pose," in order to create a product that is exciting but "safe" for white, middle-class consumption and corporate partners. In the 1990s, the NBA had succeeded in creating a tenuous but highly lucrative balance: it had fanned the fire while keeping the coals burning red hot. *Sports Illustrated* writer Phil Taylor remarked in 1997 that "one of the NBA's greatest accomplishments—essential to the way the league has flourished financially over the past two decades—is the way it has not only handled the race issue but also tamed it and used it to turn a profit." Encapsulated in Taylor's observation is the essence of how blackness and hip-hop are sold to white America—as an embraced but contained culture—as well as a validation of the NBA's efforts to effectively mediate the hip-hop explosion.

In effect, although a certain amount of deviance (from the white, middle-class norm) is not only tolerated by the league but also desired, too much flamboyance and recklessness can become problematic. The commercially viable equilibrium—this construction of blackness—is enforced by penalizing players perceived as "too street" or "too black." Penalties range from dress code violations (incurred either on or off the court) to taunting opponents; they take the form of fines, suspensions, and even symbolic gestures. Since the mid-1990s, the league has manipulated the markers of hip-hop culture in the NBA with increasing aggressiveness. Starting in 2005 with the new Collective Bargaining Agreement—which we will consider in depth in the next chapter—the league has controlled what players wear in public while on the NBA's clock and has conducted random in-season drug testing, which includes screening for marijuana, the previously ignored drug of choice for ballplayers and rappers alike.

The notion of "keepin' it real" is indelibly stamped onto Iverson's body. His most conspicuous tattoo announces a sort of motto for ghetto youth: "Only the strong survive." Another one proclaims his attachment to those closest to him, those who were with him before he made it: "tru cru."

Most of the media's (mis)understandings of Iverson's career up until the last few years, which have guided public impressions, have stemmed from their failure to see "keepin' it real" as a valid and influential ideology. When Iverson ran into legal problems at the start of his second season (1997–98)—the same year of the infamous cornrows—his vilification became both more apparent and more legitimately grounded: the media and the league now had fresh confirmation of his criminal tendencies. Iverson began the season with a suspension from the season opener after he was arrested and charged with carrying a concealed weapon and possessing marijuana. He was arrested after police pulled his car over in Virginia for speeding. One would expect that a star NBA player would deservedly receive negative publicity for getting arrested. However, much of what was written about Iverson was premised upon assumptions about his (lack of) character and psychological explanations. Dave Kindred, a white writer for the *Sporting News*, equated Iverson with "the most egregious of fools," referenced the bowling alley incident as evidence of a criminal past, and even rejected the public apology that Iverson issued after the arrest. Part of the apology was as follows: "I would like to . . . apologize to my family, my team and my fans for any embarrassment that this incident may have caused them. . . . I look at this as a learning experience and I hope to grow from it." Kindred's response: "Iverson calls it a LEARNING EXPERIENCE. It's a STONE DUMB CRIME . . . . Why should his family, teammates and fans be embarrassed? THEY DIDN'T GET ARRESTED, HE DID." A furious Kindred appears personally offended by Iverson's behavior and apparently insufficient apology. He calls Iverson a fool; the implication isn't that Iverson acted recklessly but that he was simply incapable of acting better. Then, either conveniently or because he never bothered to look into the case, Kindred leaves out that Iverson was cleared of all charges in the bowling alley incident.

Like Kindred's piece, virtually all of the articles that covered Iverson's 1997 arrest as more than just a news brief referenced the bowling alley incident as evidence of a pattern of criminality, and some analyzed it in psychological terms. Whereas *U.S. News and World Report* rationalized Iverson's arrest as the result of his "knack for finding trouble," many articles explained his behavior on an even more personal, sometimes vindictive level. Peter May, writing for the *Sporting News,* suggested that the arrest was a product of Iverson's incorrigibility. May wrote that Iverson "[wasn't] some virginal creature," and if he had had the capacity to learn from past experience, this never would have happened. Again contextualizing the incident as part of a criminal past premised upon the bowling alley event, black sportswriter Michael Wilbon, writing for the *Washington Post,* also pointed to Iverson's supposed predisposition for trouble as the inevitable result of his failure to listen to and learn from others. "There's no sense in preaching to Allen Iverson anymore," Wilbon claimed, since he just didn't listen.

As an athlete who always "keeps it real," Iverson has repeatedly demonstrated a resistance to traditional authority figures. However, the authors of the articles noted above seem to have mistaken Iverson's connection to this ideology for some sort of deep-seated psychological incapacity to learn from the past or listen to others. The media, in these instances, equated "keepin' it real" with an innate inability to conform to mainstream expectations rather than with the conscious and deliberate rebuttal of such expectations. The importance of age in determining Iverson's allegiance to a philosophy predicated upon being young, black, male, and from poverty was also overlooked in the process. Iverson was only twenty-two at the time of the speeding incident.

In contrast, William C. Rhoden, in a brief *New York Times* piece sympathetic to Iverson, claimed that Iverson's arrest on gun and marijuana charges was motivated by this model of black male authenticity rather than by a psychological shortcoming resulting in incorrigibility. Breaking a taboo of political correctness, Rhoden wrote what many had been thinking: some black athletes carry guns. Rhoden quoted Dr. Alvin Poussaint, a well-respected black professor of psychiatry at Harvard, who offered neither a psychiatric nor a psychological explanation: "If . . . [athletes] came up in a tough neighborhood it is not unusual that a lot of the guys are packing guns. When you talk to them about it they will tell you it's for protection. They had family members or friends robbed or shot."

In two additional *New York Times* pieces, Iverson's arrest specifically and his character in general are treated in two vastly different ways by two *New York Times* writers. In "Questions Follow Troubled Iverson," Ira Berkow, a white sports journalist, again drew upon the bowling alley incident as evidence of Iverson's predilection for trouble; he implicitly connected this tendency to Iverson's shameless desire to call attention to himself by (for example) tattooing his nickname, "The Answer," on his shoulder and writing it on various pieces of clothing. As noted, this sort of tattooing is commonly found on young black athletes, but Berkow, despite his tenure as a sportswriter, appeared stunned, if not appalled, by such unabashed broadcasting of a sports nickname.

While Berkow focused primarily on Iverson's character, *Times* columnist Mike Wise titled his piece "Image-Conscious NBA Suspends Iverson and Rider" and emphasized the league's desire to protect itself. Attention was channeled away from Iverson's character and past, and the arrest was contextualized as part of a series of events that had potentially damaged the NBA's reputation. Wise cited two occurrences in which the NBA had punished white individuals (Nets coach John Calipari and Heat announcer David Halberstam) for making racially disparaging remarks. Unlike Berkow, Wise chose not to offer a psychological analysis and left the bowling alley incident out of his article. As if responding to how others were bound to view Iverson (and even defending him), Wise highlighted the fact that white individuals had also made mistakes during the course of the season. Unlike Berkow, Wise seemed unsurprised and undisturbed by Iverson's link to black authenticity.

Iverson's commitment to "keepin' it real" and the controversy and publicity that followed made him a leader, if not *the* leader, of the hip-hop world by the late 1990s. For the same reasons, Iverson was a potentially huge commercial commodity but one that was hard to contain, predict, or partner with. Companies generally shied away from Iverson, leaving one of the world's biggest sports stars one of the least commercially visible. From his very arrival, the NBA began benefiting tremendously from Iverson's popularity and cultural standing, while it immediately began to manipulate and manage his image. Looking to maintain that line of reasonable deviance, the NBA has harnessed Iverson while celebrating and selling his edge.

Rebellion in American culture is a favorite theme in advertising and is not limited to hip-hop. The General Motors Corporation (GM) boldly committed to launching ten new Chevrolet cars and trucks over a twenty-month period in 2004 and 2005. To help sell the new vehicles it used an advertising campaign built around a familiar idea: "An American Revolution." GM wanted potential consumers to believe that they were being revolutionary by buying and driving one of the new automobiles. One pilot commercial combined a song by rapper Ice Cube with a new version of Steppenwolf's "Magic Carpet Ride" in the hopes of pushing a style of marketing that GM advertising executives called "acceptable rebellion."

As intended, the ads achieved just the right dosage of radical sentiment by pairing the two music selections of Ice Cube and Steppenwolf. Ice Cube had come 180 degrees since he started out as one-fifth of N.W.A. in the late 1980s, rapping about attacking racist cops on "Fuck tha Police." He then became a movie star, first appearing in political films like John Singleton's *Boyz n the Hood* and *Higher Learning* and then going on to silly movies like *Torque* and *Are We There Yet?* Today he's a mainstream commodity, but because of his edgy roots, he retains a certain degree of anti-establishment swagger. His rebelliousness is innocuous because he's moved in a safer direction and has presumably mellowed over the years. Steppenwolf made a name for itself singing raucous rock songs about what happened when one was "Born to Be Wild"; while "Magic Carpet Ride" may be about a drug bender, it was also an amusing song popular in the late 1960s that was sure to spark nostalgia among baby boomers buying new cars. Together, Steppenwolf and Ice Cube were a rock-rap marriage that still touched the revolutionary spirit of the counterculture 1960s and hardcore rap. But because the 1960s ended long ago and Ice Cube now acts in family comedies, the connection to rebel culture is tame. GM employs exactly the sort of calculated thinking used by the NBA.

Pursuing the same goal of "acceptable rebellion," the NBA very aggressively edited the potentially inflammatory elements of Iverson's look and even his game during the first part of AI's career. Indeed, the league targeted even the minutest of deviant fashion choices. In his rookie season, Iverson's black ankle braces elicited a scornful reaction because they obscured too much of the required white socks bearing the NBA logo. Nearly ten years before the implementation of the dress code at the outset of the 2005–06 season that saw thirteen players fined within the first month or so, Iverson's errant shorts landed him in hot water. The NBA first issued warnings and then fines for the shorts, which fell below the minimum of one inch above the knee. Wincing even as it praised the young star, the league complained to the 76ers when Iverson wore a then permissible (now banned) skullcap to accept his award as the 1996–97 Rookie of the Year. The league then declined to promote Iverson's winning of the distinction because of his appearance in what would have been the publicity photos.

Iverson's response to the league's bickering about his fashion was as follows: "Damn, these people want me to wear Italian suits all the time like Michael [Jordan] . . . want me to act like I'm 25, 26 or 27 years old. Well, I'm not that old yet. . . . Don't rush me."

Even Iverson's style of play was treated as emblematic of his broader disrespect for authority. His trademark crossover dribble, in which he dribbles with one hand and allows the ball to bounce almost up to his shoulders before rapidly bringing the ball down to his ankles and across his body into his other hand, was banned. The NBA asked referees to call Iverson for carrying, an infraction that is rarely enforced upon star players and whose disregard is generally tacitly accepted throughout the NBA. Usually a sudden increase in such calls is tied to a bigger-picture crackdown on a "destructive" trend in the game. Iverson's crossover, after all, had notoriously tripped up Michael Jordan during a heated regular season showdown during Iverson's rookie year. And indeed there was a cultural element to Iverson's reinvention of this standard offensive move. Academic Todd Boyd, who writes on basketball, hip-hop, and the intersection of the two, notes that blacks have always participated in a "tradition . . . of . . . redefining artifacts so as to make them specific and central to Black culture and experience," and he points to the deliberate altering of the pronunciation and spelling of words in rap music as a contemporary manifestation. Boyd gives the example of the word "thing" morphing into "thang" in rap lyrics to underscore the important difference between what is a "white thing" and what is a "black thang."

Iverson too shares in this long-established process of cultural transformation by taking the crossover dribble, a basic basketball maneuver, and altering its composition in accordance with the playground tradition and its defining tenets of flash, reinventing the game, and humbling the opposition.

The most overt editing of Iverson was a print censoring during the 1999–2000 season. In December 1999, the NBA released an issue of *Hoop*, the league's official publication, in which Iverson's diamond earring and some of his tattoos were digitally removed from the cover photo. Other tattoos were obscured by the strategic layering of text over them. This was not the first photo alteration of Iverson's physical appearance. In 1998, a tattoo on his left arm had been edited out of a photo in the NBA's *Inside Stuff* magazine.

Iverson's presence on the international stage has been censored as well. USA Basketball conspicuously omitted the star from the 2000 Dream Team. Selected in place of the quickest and probably the most exciting player in the NBA were Tom Gugliotta, a requisite white athlete with mediocre talent; Tim Hardaway, an overly ripened point guard with no legs left; and Vin Baker, an overweight, depressed, alcoholic forward. The National Team that had been assembled for the 1996 Olympics posed too much while breezing through its outmatched competition, so the United States wanted an older, less brazen team for 2000. Iverson didn't fit the bill. Finally, eight years into a career in which he had scored over 14,000 points, captured three scoring titles, won regular season and all-star game MVPs, and earned five All-NBA first- or second-team distinctions, Iverson was selected for the 2004 Olympics Games in Athens. But even getting on the 2004 team proved arduous: Iverson called Vice President of USA Basketball Stu Jackson to plead his case. Jackson begrudgingly acquiesced, adding Iverson at the last minute.

In March 2006, despite Iverson's excellent showing in his lone Olympic appearance and a 2005–06 season in which he averaged a career-best 33 points per game, along with seven assists, USA Basketball again passed on him. It is almost unfathomable, but twenty-one other NBA players and two college standouts were invited to compete for spots on the U.S. National Team for the 2006 world championships in Saitama, Japan, and the 2008 Olympics in Beijing.

While publicly castigating Iverson for his physical appearance, fashion sense, and style of play, the league has been taking notes all along. The NBA recently began licensing black socks with NBA logos for players to wear during games. The Sixers promptly made over their uniforms and team colors: road uniforms became glossy, all-black getups, with a gold basketball shooting across the front of the jersey like a pendant swinging from a hip-hopper's neck. The NBA's merchandised gear has turned baggier and flashier; the league sells oversized $300-plus retro jerseys from Mitchell and Ness, a Philadelphia-based clothing company that is partnered with the NBA and specializes in licensed recreations of old sports uniforms. Iverson knew about the uniform maker long before its institutionalization in hip-hop culture and routinely wore Mitchell and Ness clothing during press conferences.

A few years ago the NBA store on Fifth Avenue in New York City created a temporary Iverson wing, stocked with AI's clothing line. The items on sale were produced by another NBA partner, Reebok, and included caps, T-shirts, sweatshirts, and baseball jerseys, all with an obvious hip-hop bent. A television in the middle of the display presented a black-and-white Reebok commercial of Iverson half-dancing and half-dribbling, displaying his outlaw crossover, as hip-hop artist Jadakiss raps about the otherworldliness of Iverson's game. To promote The Answer 5, the fifth installment of Iverson's signature Reebok shoe, Jadakiss composed an entire track about the impossibility of containing Iverson.

Once Iverson turned the previously miserable Sixers into playoff contenders, the NBA had a rousing up-and-coming team to feature on national broadcasts. After the strike-shortened 1998–99 season, during which Iverson led his team to the second round of the playoffs, the NBA put the Sixers on NBC eleven times for the uninterrupted 1999–2000 season. The following season Iverson, now working successfully with Coach Larry Brown, squared off against Kobe and Shaq's heavily favored Lakers for the NBA championship and made a series out of it, generating major television interest.

Less cautious than the NBA and with less to lose given the stagnation of its brand, in 1996 Reebok capitalized on Iverson's hip-hop credentials and undeniable talent by signing him to a $50 million ten-year contract—even before his first NBA training camp. The advertising theme for the first Iverson shoe was, as one *Village Voice* writer put it, "Allen's closeness to his roots and his loyalty to his boyz from the Newport News 'hood." Five years later, in 2001, Reebok reworked Iverson's contract into a lifetime endorsement and unveiled a new campaign that presented Iverson as the king of 'hoods nationwide. It released a two-page magazine ad highlighting Iverson's appearance and fashion taste. On one page Iverson is dressed hip-hop casual, sporting a bandana around his cornrows and diamond-studded earrings; his numerous tattoos are in clear view. On the adjacent page is the latest Iverson shoe, superimposed over a sea of diamond earrings. This was Iverson in all his decadent hip-hop glory—true "fabulosity," as Kimora Lee Simmons (who claims to have coined the phrase) would say, and a logical extension of how his followers already saw him: hip-hop royalty. Reebok proudly reported that Iverson had increased sales by 20 percent during the first half of 2001.

Through the Iverson campaign, Reebok saw the value in magnifying its association with hip-hop culture and ventured further in this marketing direction. In 2001, it launched a line of footwear and apparel called RBK, premised upon the marriage of sports and hip-hop; it used rap artists like Fabolous and Missy Elliot along with streetball icons in its advertisements.

The next step for Reebok was to give a sneaker line to a rapper, a nonathlete. Insisting that rap stars could generate even greater sales than star ballplayers, hip-hop marketing expert Steve Stoute (whom *Rolling Stone* once called "the bridge between Madison Avenue and the street") brokered a deal in 2003 in which Reebok gave Jay-Z his own sneaker line, the S. Carter. After the instant success of Jay-Z's shoe, 50 Cent, again with Stoute's involvement, scored an endorsement deal for a shoe named after his rap crew and label, G-Unit. Other rappers soon followed.

If the inordinately prolific Jay-Z could avoid being labeled a sellout after putting out eight solo albums in nine years (including an MTV Unplugged record), he had to know something about negotiating the mainstream while maintaining essential street legitimacy. As Reebok had done with Iverson, it followed Jay-Z's lead and sagely avoided any cheesy marketing of both the S. Carter and G-Unit lines. Reebok granted Jay and 50 atypical fashion freedom, signing them on to promote only their respective shoes and not the entire Reebok brand and leaving them free to wear whatever they wanted to in public.

With its label having grown dramatically, Reebok was now poised to position itself as central to popular culture—not just hip-hop and sports. It introduced its first TV spot for the "I Am What I Am" campaign during the February 2005 NBA All-Star Game. The spot was part of a massive push of TV, print, and movie advertisements designed by New York-based ad agency mcgarrybowen; the campaign gave Reebok its first slogan since "Planet Reebok" in the mid-1990s and touted it as relevant to sports, music, and movies. The slogan itself repeated "keepin' it real" in different words and mirrored the message and look of the Iverson advertisements. The ads matched a celebrity to a brief self-description related to the slogan. Using Iverson along with former drug pushers Jay-Z and 50 Cent, Chinese basketball standout Yao Ming, and Chinese American TV and film star Lucy Liu, Reebok showcased nonwhite icons who were, in their own words, imperfect, gritty, and—most important—real. Because of such traits, they were successful. The "I Am What I Am" campaign also celebrated the fresh, nonpreppy beauty personified by Iverson and Liu.

Reebok has cleverly allowed Iverson to steer its image. The ballplayer provided the company with brand credibility and an aura of freshness after years of creative and commercial paralysis. As the pulse of hip-hop, the entire way AI spontaneously carries himself both on and off the basketball court provokes precisely the sort of response from consumers that advertisers emphatically seek. Reebok has sold Iverson as he really looks and acts, even reproducing his "keepin' it real" message in the "I Am What I Am" campaign. Undoubtedly the success of the Iverson campaign and Reebok's sudden cultural relevance have impacted the NBA's attitude toward the company: Reebok is now the exclusive manufacturer of official NBA uniforms.

The skeptics in Philadelphia and fans nationwide who had previously been put off appeared to come around on Iverson after the 2001 postseason run that brought the Sixers painfully close to a world championship. Iverson's reputation morphed from thug to rebel, and with his all-out play, even while injured, Iverson, once labeled selfish, was now cast as a team guy who selflessly gave body and soul to the Sixers. *Philadelphia Daily News* writer William Bunch equated Iverson with other controversial local and national icons, including Frank Rizzo, Bill Clinton, and former two-term Philadelphia mayor Ed Rendell, whom many had ultimately come to love in spite of their shortcomings after perceiving their inner sincerity.

John Nash, the former GM of the Sixers who was on board during the team's 1983 title run, explained that "Iverson has achieved what [earlier franchise players] Charles Barkley, Dr. J and Wilt Chamberlain could not, and that is sell the building out consistently."

But this nearly universal acclaim for Iverson proved short-lived. His new fans seemed to assume that Iverson was suddenly doing things differently—doing things their way. After a disappointing 2001–02 season, in which the Sixers failed to advance past the first round of the playoffs, Iverson, who had overcome injury to lead the NBA in scoring, ranted during a thirty-five-minute press conference about all that had bothered him over the course of the season. With many digressions, a candid Iverson, revealing a vulnerability athletes rarely granted interviewers, stated that winning was the only thing he cared about ("Individual awards . . . don't mean nothing"); he admitted that trade rumors were devastating not only to him personally but also to his family, and he complained that criticism for his endemic absenteeism from practice was ridiculous and unfair given his performance in games: "Listen, we're talking about practice. Not a game. Not a game. Not a game. We're talking about practice. Not a game. Not the game that I go out there and die for and play every game like it's my last. Not the game. We're talking about practice, man. I mean how silly is that."

In July 2002, Iverson was involved in another legal scrape that devolved into a media maelstrom before ending up as a nonstory. After a domestic dispute, Iverson allegedly and most likely threw his wife out of the house. In the middle of the night, he went to a cousin's apartment, where he either thought she was or could get information about her location; he forced his way in, allegedly threatening the two men who were there. Authorities eventually issued fourteen felony and misdemeanor charges against him. A bizarre virtual house arrest scenario followed. After having pressed numerous criminal charges, a suddenly lenient Philadelphia police department allowed the ballplayer to stay within the gated confines of his estate rather than go to prison for the four days it would take for his lawyer, Richard Sprague, to return from a European vacation.

Upon Sprague's return, Iverson was required to turn himself in to the police, and he complied.

The wink-wink imprisonment became a public spectacle. The police, who chose not to post anyone in front of the house, relied on round-the-clock surveillance by the media horde that had immediately descended upon the property to capture film of Iverson, his wife (who had returned), and their kids, happily playing in the yard. All fourteen charges were eventually dropped as it became increasingly apparent to the prosecution that the episode in question was confusing and legally ambiguous and (hopefully) just a passing family crisis best left for the Iverson clan to work through privately.

Several news pieces exposed Iverson's preferential treatment by the police by juxtaposing his situation with that of black men of similar age and fashion sensibilities; several such interviewees complained that Iverson had received unusual clemency, which they surely would have been denied or actually had been denied. The media reveled in the irony: Iverson, king thug, had received the kind of star treatment denied to the common hooligan.

After the dual debacles of the "practice" press conference and Iverson's street justice approach to domestic discord, a new conceptualization of the player increasingly appeared in the press. As soon as Brown had taken over as the Sixers' head coach in 1997, he had regularly referred to his star player as a "kid." At the notorious "practice" press conference, the coach had felt like he was observing "a young kid reaching out for help." In a 2001 game against the Celtics, Brown, the proud father, crowed after Iverson's 47-point explosion that "the little kid was sensational." When his guy won the 2000–01 MVP award, Brown said, "He doesn't always do it the way I would expect or sometimes like. But I know where his heart is. This kid has great character." The media picked up on Brown's pet name and took issue with it.

The query *du jour* became whether Iverson had learned anything in the ten years between his first legal run-in as a seventeen-year-old high school sports prodigy and his most recent scrape as a twenty-seven-year-old NBA icon, multimillionaire, and family man. The consensus was that a gifted but troubled boy had never matured into a man. His story constituted a case of "arrested development," as indicated by William C. Rhoden, who articulated a new stance on Iverson in the *New York Times*. Some in sports viewed his purportedly stymied maturation as a personal failure: an indifference or denial of the responsibilities that accompany both adulthood and NBA stardom. Others saw it as the result of external forces—76er personnel, friends, and family—coddling their superstar. That Brown still called his best player, a father of two earning $12 million a year, a "kid" was "repellent" to the *Times*' Ira Berkow. For still others, it was a bit of both: a mixture of personal shortcomings and destructive outside influences. Yet in appraising the situation as a case of immaturity, the media again failed to see the bigger picture. Most sportswriters chose to evaluate Iverson by his ability or inability to conform to a set of white, middle-class values (precisely because these writers were almost always white and middle class). The most cogent and informative assessment of Iverson in the mainstream media came from black writer Gar Anthony Haywood:

> I and many other black Americans . . . understand that the matter of "keeping it real"—which is to say, following a code of behavior one's very life has literally depended on for years—is not so easily discarded. Or, at the very least, it should not be treated as a nonissue in the discussion of Iverson's inability (or reluctance) to straighten out his act.

Rather than conceptualize Iverson as an overgrown baby or someone too dense or stubborn to be rehabilitated, it is more useful to recognize that his attitude is often *influenced* by (not *determined* by) his connection to the value system of "keepin' it real." Iverson exposes himself to public relations nightmares because of that connection. His street-style way of resolving personal matters, just like his style of speech and dress, deviates from middle-class standards and sometimes legal acceptability.

More than a decade into his pro career, Iverson retains the basic look, attitude, and style of play with which he arrived. The "keepin' it real" mantra still resonates. On the court, nothing's changed. Today when Iverson is praised for how he plays it's because he's gotten better, more precise, and craftier at what he's always done. He hustles nonstop from tip-off to the clock's last tick, plays hurt, and plays basketball his way. He shoots all the time (always looking out for his shots and points), breaks down defenses with the dribble instead of the pass, and goes coast to coast with blinders on. Iverson has become the most impressive example of what Knicks announcer Walt "Clyde" Frazier sardonically calls "a good bad-shot shooter."

With Iverson playing his finest basketball this deep into his career and doing it on his terms, fans and media now mostly speak of him with a glowing but resigned praise that indicates he has proven them wrong. Even Iverson's mentor, John Thompson, realized long ago that the best way to co-exist with Iverson was to simply accept and embrace him rather than attempt to control or change him. When Iverson was a collegian at Georgetown, the no-nonsense Thompson required him to follow a dress code—suit and tie when traveling to games, no fancy jewelry—but on the court he turned his star loose, telling him right from the start that he would be given complete freedom when he was in the game.

Iverson's career and the way he has been handled by the NBA at different points provide a revealing case study for how the NBA, its partners, and the players themselves generally market the black athlete. Black players in the NBA generally present themselves and are presented by advertisers as superhuman (they have gravity-defying leaping abilities and colossal strength) but unthreatening (they help out in needy communities with programs like *Read to Achieve*, happily sign autographs for kids, etc.) In some instances, they are even aligned with cartoon stars in Disney films—for example, Michael Jordan in *Space Jam* and Shaquille O'Neal in *Shazam*. The association with Disney icons implies that like cartoon characters, these athletes are somewhat unreal and magical, but at the same time such a divergence from reality is safe for a child's consumption.

In Burger King's BK 2002 TV ad campaign for its new bacon cheeseburger, Shaq appeared as a mellow, present-day Shaft, the badass superhero from the Blaxploitation era. As the spot's theme music plays, Isaac Hayes, who wrote and performed the original score for the Shaft films, speaks of the delightful combo meal, replete with fries and dipping sauce, while Shaq, dressed in Shaft's trademark all-black leather, dribbles the length of a court and dunks, rendering the scrubby opposition inconsequential. Shaq then sits down with a small white child, and the two enjoy a BK lunch. Shaq may be big and bad on the court, but he's a gentle giant off the court. He is a good guy.

Players have a lot to do with advancing an image of themselves as child-safe giants, sound role models, and assimilated mainstream commodities. As a rookie, Iverson criticized the NBA for expecting him to dress like Michael Jordan, the consummate symbol of mainstream success and the most marketable and popular athlete in sports history. Although Jordan came from a vastly different home environment than Iverson (a middle-class, intact nuclear family), Jordan too had to carefully craft his image before he was able to transcend race and attract and inspire all segments of society.

When Jordan first entered the league, he did not wear Italian suits to publicity functions. Like Iverson, he wore casual gear, baseball caps, and lots of showy jewelry, and he was similarly hassled by the NBA for fashion deviance. MJ's first pair of Air Jordans, with their provocative, mostly black color scheme, was banned from the league in October 1985. Yet Jordan quickly realized that to achieve crossover success, he would have to tone down certain symbols of black youth culture. His fashion transformation also came gradually with age, and as he became a business executive, he naturally dressed the part. Jordan's evolution into pop culture icon was assisted by his decision to become affiliated with several of the world's largest mainstream companies—among them McDonald's, Gatorade, Nike, and Disney. By showing Jordan interacting with little kids of various ethnic backgrounds, as well as with cartoon characters, these companies marketed him as an ultra-friendly superhero with whom all young people could connect. They represented him as a superstar readily and proudly crossing racial and ethnic lines. This is not to say that Jordan disingenuously presented himself as something he was not. (In fact, I believe he has always wanted universal recognition and admiration.) However, it is important to realize that Jordan took active steps to redefine his image along mainstream lines.

While his extremely lucrative lifetime deal with Reebok has done wonders for Iverson's marketability and bank account, Iverson has vehemently rejected the steps necessary to cross over. He has managed to secure a loyal and growing following on his own terms. That AI hasn't changed to appease others is precisely what many find alluring. A piece in the *New York Times* pointed out that "to those who find that Michael Jordan and Tiger Woods have compromised their integrity by shilling for products like Gatorade and McDonald's while muting their own personal feelings on divisive issues, Iverson is refreshingly candid and independent."

In some instances, however, players bill themselves and are marketed as both superhuman and dangerous. Generally they're dangerous because they are inextricably bound to the perils of the inner city—they keep it too real. What follows is what sociologist John Hoberman (in *Darwin's Athletes: How Sport Has Damaged Black America and Preserved the Myth of Race*) calls "the merger of the athlete, the gangster rapper, and the criminal into a single black male persona that the sports industry, the music industry, and the advertising industry have made into the predominant image of black masculinity in the United States and around the world." The NBA's marketing of deviance and the duplicitous rationale behind reprimanding players for acts of aggression and indecency become jarringly obvious in videos and DVDs licensed by the NBA or produced by NBA Entertainment that show players committing punishable acts of indiscretion and embarrassing opponents with ankle-breaking crossovers and slams knocking a defender to the ground.

The NBA carefully manages any suggestions that connect basketball to a "street" game or culture. While NBA TV broadcasts a limited number of games from Rucker Park and the league has capitalized on the retro jersey fad popularized in ghettos and rap videos, today it rarely develops products with a street or hip-hop theme. Rather it's the businesses partnering with the league that usually create, produce, and market such products. If the products are deemed acceptable, the NBA licenses them, thus allowing them to include NBA marks (the NBA logo and team logos) and often NBA players. The NBA maintains its independence from such items because they are not technically NBA products. Video games perfectly exemplify how the NBA profits from hip-hop deviance while maintaining its distance. In April 2004, video game maker Midway debuted an NBA-licensed game, *NBA Ballers*; in it participants design their own streetballer, down to the color of his do-rag and the cut of his 'fro, and even replicate the tattoos of their favorite NBA stars.

At around the same time that the game was released, NBA legend Oscar Robertson ripped the NBA for its emphasis on style over substance—that is, highlight-reel flash over fundamentally sound team play. Robertson reminded gullible hoops fans that a dunk was still worth only two points. In *NBA Ballers*, however, a dunk was worth more than two points: flamboyant moves (along with cool clothes and cool friends) earned players bonus points and the chance to land a "bringin' down the house" dunk that put an immediate end to the game by ripping down the rim. When the game player pushed the right combination of buttons at the right times, an on-screen ballplayer could pull off "act-a-fool" moves like dribbling between an opponent's legs, flipping the ball behind his back and over his opponent, and throwing the ball off a defender's face.

In today's sports- and hip-hop-driven lexicon, a "baller" can refer to a talented ballplayer, a thriving entrepreneur, or a socialite (depending on context). The black nouveaux riches of the NBA are ballers in the truest sense because they integrate an off-court lifestyle with an on-court style of play such that looking good always counts. That's the idea celebrated in *NBA Ballers*, where wins earn gamers cash to spend on customized cars, cool dudes and sexy chicks for their posses, and extravagant homes (cribs). The game presents the NBA as a purveyor of the lavish hip-hop life.

Of course black ballplayers play an active role in creating a hypermasculine hip-hop persona for themselves because such an identity is simultaneously anti-establishment (in certain respects) and lucrative. On Iverson's unreleased CD, *Non-Fiction*, which was shelved in the wake of enormous pre-release controversy and major pressure from NBA commissioner Stern, Iverson advanced his "thug" image by rapping about the requisite, unoriginal themes of violence and misogyny.

Power forward Kenyon Martin built a reputation as a defensive enforcer whose explosive, sometimes thuggish play was learned not on the basketball court but on the streets. He would later parlay this image into a seven-year, $92.5 million deal with his current team, the Denver Nuggets, with a signature post-dunk ritual that he had patented while on the New Jersey Nets. In a familiar moment for Nets fans, in the fifth game of the 2002 Eastern Conference Semifinals between the Nets and the Charlotte Hornets, Martin, with his team holding a 3–1 series lead and less than a minute to play, caught an alley-oop from point guard Jason Kidd and, in one continuous action, emphatically threw the ball through the hoop, did a pull-up on the rim, and screamed in jubilation. New Jersey went up 8 points on Martin's dunk, and Charlotte no longer had a prayer as Martin's slam launched the Nets into the Eastern Conference finals for the first time in franchise history. Neither the significance of the play for the Nets nor its commercial value was lost on Martin. After finishing Kidd's pass with an undeniable display of athletic prowess, Martin pulled the side of his jersey across his body to reveal a message tattooed across his right pectoral: "Bad Ass Yellow Boy" ("yellow" referring to his comparatively light complexion, for which he was teased by other blacks as a youth). Martin's uncovering of his tattoo literally connected the act of dunking with its greater symbolic importance as a statement of on-court dominance and manhood.

Martin's often impressive play combined with his penchant for flagrant fouls and provocative gestures landed him on the April 22, 2002, cover of *Sports Illustrated* (SI). The "Bad Ass Yellow Boy" tattoo is in clear view, as a seemingly annoyed Martin tugs his jersey to the middle of his chest with his left hand and clenches his fist with his right. The caption on the cover reads "Bad Boy: Nets Flagrant Flyer Kenyon Martin Attacks the Playoffs." Martin isn't simply competing in the playoffs; he is "attacking" them, as his basketball game is subtly equated with an act of violence against the institution of the playoffs. The accompanying article describes Martin's rugged south Dallas upbringing and his turbulent career; in only his second season, he had been called for six flagrant fouls, which cost him $347,057 in fines and several suspensions. Here we again see the irony of Martin's being castigated by the media and the NBA. Both parties are reprimanding the very person that they are using to sell magazines and basketball tickets.

Is the notion of the "authentic" black man "keepin' it real" too difficult to accept? Or is it a farce? "How can 38 million people possibly have a single view of reality or authenticity?" asked writer and television producer Thad Mumford in 2004 in the *New York Times*. If there are elements—for example, the "cool pose"—with genuine roots in the American black experience, did they not exist in what Mumford calls "private burlesque," premised upon a "knowing wink [to fellow blacks] and satiric spine"? The self-mockery is removed when the swagger is on display for the masses and is laughed at by white sports commentators. In this context, post-dunk gestures and much about contemporary basketball (and other sports) today recall the vaudeville days, when blacks, out of desperation, cakewalked for whites. Mumford asks, "Is there a possible connection between the action of the white fan who cheers rabidly after sack dances on Sunday, then may be reluctant to grant bank loans for black businesses on Monday?" The timing for self-mockery is particularly poor: outside of athletes, there's a scarcity of role models for black kids to emulate. Are blacks selling themselves down the river? Are they mortgaging their youth?

The most destructive aspect of marketing a link between black athletes and violence—and, too often, lending evidence to substantiate such a link—is the suggestion that any black player who can be associated with the dominant notion of black authenticity, by way of dress or demeanor, is automatically a criminal.

Young black players, however, often consciously and actively dare America to make such a connection. Acting and dressing provocatively serve as a screening mechanism, a way of asking society if it can see a black man as anything more than simply a thug or an undesirable presence. For young black men, it's an effective means of determining who's with them and who's against them, who one's true supporters are. It is a problem that too often society—primarily white America—buys the idea that any large, tattooed black man or any athlete wearing a skullcap and gleaming crucifix to a press conference is *ipso facto* a criminal.

By marketing a connection between blackness and criminality or simply the possibility that the two are related, companies perpetuate ancient racial myths. According to Hoberman, "the 'violent black male' becomes the dangerous twin of the spectacular black athlete." This joining of black authenticity with felony also goes the other way: black wrongdoers are often assumed to have superior athletic powers. As an extreme example of this phenomenon, Hoberman cites the way in which police officer Stacey Koon described Rodney King, considered the victim of police brutality after he was stopped for speeding: a man with "Hulk-like super strength" and arms like "steel posts." The commercialization of the thug image leads, perhaps inevitably, to the problematic assumption that black men, not just athletes, are violent and dangerous. Moreover, too often the understanding that whites have of blacks is profoundly skewed by the simple fact that—as with the "Prep-School Gangsters"—whites interact with blacks only indirectly, through the consumption of a very limited number of representations. Listening to black music, watching black athletes on television, and seeing black criminals on the news function in lieu of direct communication. Since each of these forums is a space removed from everyday life—being famous or a criminal is to exist in the extreme—a transfiguration occurs in which blacks become characters, icons, symbols, or caricatures—that is, something other than human beings.

The "Prep-School Gangsters" idealized selected elements of blackness that commercial representations of black culture—primarily rap music and its videos—presented as genuine and central to the black experience. Young blacks also often buy into these frequently destructive representations of what being black is all about.

In certain respects, handling hip-hop has gotten easier for the NBA over the last five years. The influx of foreign players (who are mostly white and from Europe) has provided a balance in the look and style of play. Globalization has made the domestic marketing of hip-hop ballplayers less important for the NBA than attracting a fresh supply of consumers abroad, in the home countries of the new players.

Hip-hop has also changed in recent years. Although still very popular with white kids today, it's no longer the exclusive means to, or definition of, cool. The shift has come largely because hip-hop is no longer a singular force: it has integrated with rock music and frat culture (rap-rock mash-ups, for example); skate and surf culture (rapper Snoop Dogg and skateboarding legend Tony Hawk are equally likely to appear on television in baggy khaki shorts, a wifebeater, and canvas sneakers); hippie culture (socially conscious underground rap is popular with the L. L. Bean college set); Asian cool (there is an infatuation with Asian women in rap videos; Asian-themed hip-hop music videos and kung-fu/hip-hop action movies abound); Latino culture (reggaeton blends Latin American influences with hip-hop); and even the country music culture (country rockers have rhymed over hip-hop-tinged instrumentation). With time, hip-hop has mutated into an amalgam of different ideas and genres.

Iverson, however, hasn't changed: he still represents hip-hop in its grittier, more powerful and dangerous 1990s form.

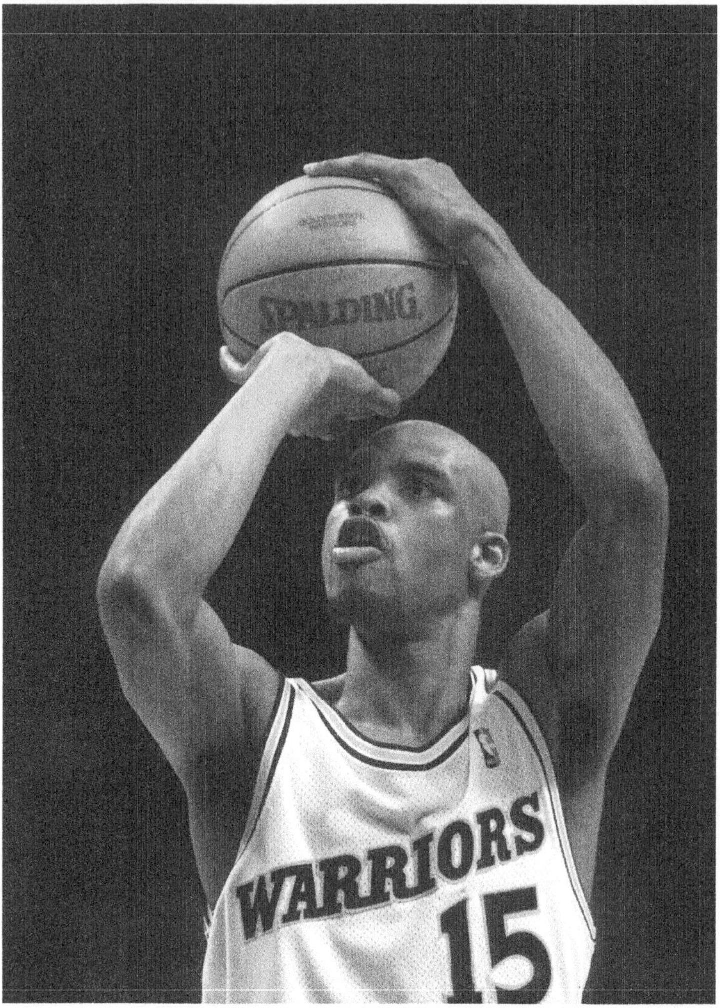

3. A bald-headed Latrell Sprewell takes a free throw for the Golden State Warriors in 1995. During a 1997 practice, Sprewell forever changed power relations and politics in the NBA when he assaulted his coach, P. J. Carlesimo. He resurrected his disgraced career in 1998 as the cornrowed star shooting guard of the New York Knicks. © imago/Claus Bergmann.

3 Power Game

Ron Artest, Latrell Sprewell, and Politics in the NBA

The disconcerting off-season leading up to the 2004–05 season levied extensive damage upon the NBA's image. In the summer of 2003 Kobe Bryant had been accused of raping a nineteen-year-old female hotel employee at a Colorado mountain resort, and his trial trudged along into its second summer to the detriment of the Los Angeles Lakers. Bryant's teammate—and nemesis—Shaquille O'Neal, the most dominant player in basketball, was fed up with Bryant and the Lakers. In conflict with Bryant, with whom he had clashed on countless occasions on and off the court, Shaq, a Florida homeowner, expedited his own trade to the Miami Heat in July 2004. Even after O'Neal's departure, the public bickering between him and Bryant continued. A detective's report in September 2004 indicated that Bryant had told Colorado police that the married O'Neal had "paid up to a million dollars already for situations like this [rape accusation]." Bryant followed this allegation with the twisted, boastful claim that while "Shaq would pay his women not to say anything," he "treat[ed] a woman with respect . . . [so] they shouldn't say anything." Before the start of the 2004–05 season, O'Neal went on ESPN and pretended never to have heard of Kobe Bryant while incessantly praising his new costar and Heat teammate, guard Dwayne Wade.

When Shaq split from Tinseltown, Coach Phil Jackson had already been fired roughly a month earlier (he later returned for the 2005–06 season). Most of what Jackson felt about Kobe Bryant and the Lakers amid the highly publicized trial and in-house wrangling came out in October 2004. Just before the new season, Jackson's book on coaching the 2003–04 Lakers, *The Last Season: A Team in Search of Its Soul*, hit stores. In a general sense, the best seller revealed just how little actual coaching takes place in today's NBA. Rather than diagramming Xs and Os and being the leader of a ball club, a coach in the pros is often reduced to managing talent, brokering tenuous peace settlements among star players, securing allies in the locker room and front office, and delaying or spinning information to keep the media at bay. In shedding light upon the irreparably fractured Lakers, the book showed that a helpless Jackson, one of the most respected and well-compensated coaches in the business and one of the few with genuine power, had failed to impose his will over this Lakers team mostly because he was unable to manage Bryant. Bryant came off as a prima donna who was more likely to answer his cell phone during a pregame locker room meeting than to answer to his coach.

The rape charges against Bryant, his trashing in Jackson's book, and the feuding with teammates O'Neal and Karl Malone (who, like O'Neal, was bound for the Hall of Fame) combined to effectively knock one of the league's brightest young stars from his pedestal. Bryant lost his standing as one of the faces of the NBA, millions in endorsement deals, and his privacy. The once clean-cut, champion golden boy looked hardened when the 2004–05 season opened: he had lost weight, gotten tattooed, and grown a beard.

For the NBA, the summer of 2004 included more embarrassment. The U.S. Basketball team underachieved miserably at the Olympic Games in Athens, leaving with the bronze medal after a shabby, medal-less showing two years earlier in the world championships. On June 1, HarperCollins released Jeff Benedict's controversial book, *Out of Bounds*, which, as noted in the introduction, pointed to the large percentage of U.S. basketball players who had criminal records. The buzz around the book culminated in a segment on ABC's *20/20* in which Benedict defended his findings during a debate with Billy Hunter, president of the NBA Players' Association. Commissioner David Stern, who had reportedly declined interview requests to appear on the show, told the *New York Times* that he was "disturbed" by the book's account but that the figure Benedict cited (40 percent) was "a fabrication" that disingenuously "lump[ed] . . . together" accusations with convictions.

With the airing of all sorts of dirty laundry, the NBA faced a mounting public relations nightmare; it was particularly crushing to a league that had managed its reputation with meticulous care and remarkable success since David Stern had taken over as commissioner in 1984. It would only get worse once the season started. Yet image is a cosmetic coverup that usually masks deeper, more substantial problems. For the NBA, much of the image crisis stemmed from entrenched racial, generational, and cultural gulfs within the league and between the players and fans. The gaps became even more apparent when one assessed the differing ways in which (1) Commissioner Stern's office, (2) team owners and team management, and (3) the players dealt with the issue of reputation. How these three groups responded to a string of public relations misfortunes in 2004 and 2005 and to related image problems speaks volumes about the nature and structure of power in professional basketball and reveals the real priorities and allegiances of the NBA brass, the franchises, and the players.

When the season opened on November 2, 2004, NBA executives had their fingers crossed. The past summer, however, proved to be a nasty harbinger of more problems. In the week before Thanksgiving, a brawl broke out between Pacers players and Pistons fans in Detroit during a live national broadcast on ESPN. Replayed repeatedly for weeks on every news outlet from every angle, the brawl humiliated the NBA and momentarily threatened pro basketball's uniquely intimate fan-player dynamic during games. The melee started when the Pacers' Ron Artest committed a hard foul on Detroit's Ben Wallace and Wallace answered by shoving Artest. Artest resisted retaliation and eventually relocated to the scorer's table, where—in what was surely a first—he simply lay down. The two teams approached one another as fans egged on the action. When a fan hurled a beer cup that hit the chest of Artest, who had appeared to have cooled down, the "social contract" (as Stern later called it) between the fans and the players disintegrated and chaos ensued. Artest and teammate Stephen Jackson, arms flailing, climbed into the stands in the general direction of the cup tosser and started taking on fans, exchanging blows with ticket-holding strangers. Just as the players, by entering the stands, had crossed an imaginary but once firm line between athlete and spectator, so the fans violated the same boundary by coming onto the court to take on the players. The Pacers' Jermaine O'Neal looped a roundhouse punch that floored one fan, Charlie Haddad, who O'Neal believed had knocked down his teammate Anthony Johnson. As children cried and fans frantically stormed the exits or rushed to find a safe place from which to either watch or participate, security and police struggled to restore order. Finally, the Pacers players who were involved, exchanging expletives and threats with the fans, were forcibly escorted by security and calmer teammates into the locker rooms, pelted on the way by food and drink from the concession stands, garbage, and the occasional collapsible chair. This incident was a low point in the history of the NBA and far and away the ugliest event in an unusually turbulent first half of the season.

A hideous showing of opportunism and greed followed. Immediately after his suspension, Artest hawked "FREE RON ARTEST" T-shirts on his Web site (for $15.99) and promoted an upcoming CD from a rhythm and blues group on his record label during a *Today Show* interview. (Only two weeks before the fracas, Artest had asked his coach, Rick Carlisle, for time off to pursue music projects.) John Green, a convicted felon who had thrown the cup at Artest and later struck the player from behind, went on *Good Morning America* and *Larry King Live* to demand justice and to parlay his infamy into self-importance. Several fans in attendance or claiming to have been in attendance during the brawl put all sorts of brawl-related "memorabilia" on eBay; reportedly one buyer paid $1,525 for a ticket stub and a cup that may or not have been thrown. According to *Sports Illustrated,* software and Web company CI Host offered $10,000 to the first brawl participant to brand his fist with a tattoo of the company's logo.

More trouble ensued for the NBA. Big-market teams like the New York Knicks and Los Angeles Lakers stank; star players like Bryant and the Rockets' Tracy McGrady appeared headed for off years; the year's rookies paled in comparison with the previous season's exceptional crop, led by Wade, LeBron James, and Carmelo Anthony. Latrell Sprewell, who had signed a five-year deal with the Knicks for $62.8 million in 1998 (after coming off of a year-long suspension), told his new team, the Minnesota Timberwolves, that their three-year, $21 million extension wouldn't cut it, claiming, "I've got a family to feed." Consequently Sprewell began the following season unemployed.

In domestic clothing sales, the NBA experienced a setback. After a 30 percent increase in the sales of its licensed apparel in each of the past three years, it floundered through its first down year. One of the potential culprits behind declining sales was a former ally, Jay-Z. A courtside regular at Madison Square Garden and a member of an investment group that had bought the New Jersey Nets (with plans to relocate the franchise to Jay's hometown of Brooklyn), Jay, a celebrated fashion icon for males, made jerseys instantly uncool for the fully grown hip-hop set: on his single "What More Can I Say?" Jay-Z told his followers that—now that he was "thirty plus"—his fashion sense had evolved so as to no longer include jerseys.

The February All-Star break couldn't have come sooner for the NBA. How would the league get its shaky fan base excited for the second half of the season and repair a damaged image? The NBA began "cleaning up" its look. In a move that foreshadowed the dress code implemented in the 2005–06 season and that would create a new merchandise base, it contracted with Headmaster, a California-based clothing company, to create a line of striped dress shirts with team logos printed on the undersides of the cuffs and vertically along the lapels. In retrospect, this collared company shirt, designed for players not in uniform to wear on the sidelines, looks like a first step in the dress code . The manufacturing of such dress clothing reflects a pattern in the league's shortsighted handling of its image. On the assumption that image was exclusively on the surface, the NBA has dealt with its image troubles on a purely physical level: it has simply adjusted the appearance of its players. If the players looked more respectable by middle-class conventions (the assumption went), then the fans would receive them with greater respect and—fingers crossed—maybe the athletes would even begin acting like "upstanding" young men.

The NBA introduced some comic distraction to lighten things up and steer attention away from the recent breakdowns in civility. It called upon quirky, aging (white) comedian Fred Willard, the star of offbeat Christopher Guest mockumentary films like *Best in Show*, to bring laughter. The NBA and Reebok, the exclusive maker of NBA uniforms and official NBA apparel since 2001, collaborated on a massive ad campaign for official NBA gear; the campaign featured television commercials set inside an imaginary NBA clothing factory where James Worthy and Kenyon Martin (among other past and present NBA stars) worked as goofy quality inspectors, misled further by Willard, their hopeless foreman. The brand of comedy in the commercials is telling. By using a brand articulated by a nearly seventy-year-old white man and not by someone like Chris Rock, who had done NBA spots before, the NBA slowed its hip-hop jets and redirected its focus. The campaign was aimed at two important, primarily white, constituencies: turned-off middle-aged or older middle-class fans and the affluent businessmen in the corporate seats. Because the bulk of the NBA's revenue comes from selling seats and these two groups could afford to buy seats, they were essential customers.

Then there was the issue of appeasing the corporations that partnered with the NBA—the businesses paying for (among other things) signage in the arena or a company brand in the name of the arena (for example, the Staples Center in Los Angeles). The NBA is a product sold to fans. But it's also an advertising venue sold to retail businesses that target the predominant demographic groups in NBA arenas.

A desire to simultaneously satisfy its customers, corporate interests, and an increasingly skeptical national television audience surely drove the NBA's decision to have Big & Rich perform at the halftime show of the particularly important 2005 All-Star game. Hiring Big & Rich, a popular, genre-blurring white country duo that performed hip-hop, was a logical attempt to appease everybody all at once: it would soften—but not eliminate—the league's hip-hop edge with a country drawl. When Big & Rich was accompanied by cohort Cowboy Troy, a large, black cowboy rapper, it was as if Karl Malone had gone hip-hop.

The NBA later hired Matthew Dowd, a campaign adviser for George Bush's 2004 reelection run, to help attract new customers and address declining television ratings and merchandise sales. Stern, a major contributor to the Democratic Party, demonstrated his impenetrable, nonpartisan commitment to the league by bringing in a strategist closely associated with the GOP who could connect with the Republican-leaning middle of the country. The NBA's allegiance to both its ticket buyers and its corporate sponsors—a loyalty that makes clear business sense—comes across in spectacular fashion in instances such as these. What better way to lighten the mood and galvanize dubious white fans than country music rappers, nonblack comedy, and Matthew Dowd?

Because they couldn't have gotten worse, things improved during the second half of the 2004–05 season, but this was still a tenuous time for the NBA. In another memorable postseason fans saw the San Antonio Spurs triumph over the defending champion Detroit Pistons in a grueling seven-game series. A lot had been happening under the boards—that is, the business side of professional basketball—and it was obvious that the coming summer would make or break the following NBA season.

The Collective Bargaining Agreement (CBA) between the NBA and its players' union was set to expire at the end of June 2005. A new deal was needed that would prevent a work stoppage and simultaneously appease the often conflicting interests of league brass, team ownership and management, and the players. Most important—at least to Commissioner Stern and the owners—a new contract would be a *de facto* means of improving the image of the NBA through specific, legally binding provisions on which all three estates of the professional basketball empire had signed off. Fortunately the three parties had a shared concern: their pockets.

Fearful of the financial implications of a labor stoppage and the hostility that would surely accompany a lockout, the owners and players, under the watchful eye of the NBA, rapidly ironed out a new agreement with nine days left on the old one. The new six-year deal granted several concessions to the owners: shorter player contracts (the maximum length of a contract for a veteran player staying with his current team dropped from seven years to six and went from six years to five for veterans coming from other teams and from three years to two for rookies drafted in the first round); a cap on annual raises during the course of a player's contract; random in-season drug testing; a minimum age requirement for American-born players, who had to turn nineteen at the end of the calendar year in which they were drafted and be one year beyond their high school graduation; and the limited conversion of the National Basketball Development League into a minor league system. In exchange, the players gained the following: a guarantee that they would receive no less than 57 percent of NBA revenues; a small salary cap increase; and sixty newly created jobs through the expansion of rosters from twelve to fourteen spots per team.

Commissioner Stern called the agreement "a 50-50 deal" for the owners and players. It surely pleased league brass as well by protecting the upcoming season and placing controls (such as shorter contracts and the age requirement) on a player population perceived as precarious. The owners, who would have preferred greater reductions in the duration of player contracts, nonetheless gained roster and payroll flexibility, which they had sought. At the same time, the players had maintained a soft salary cap and formalized their already unusually strong foothold in the salary department. (With a soft salary cap teams can exceed the amount set for salary spending in certain situations, such as when honoring the "Larry Bird Exemption," by which they re-sign their own free agents who have been with the team for at least three years.). The 57 percent of league revenues paid to players, the proportion that had been paid in the last two years, now became contractual. The fact that in the past two years the owners had paid the players such a giant chunk of total sales—categorized as Basketball Related Income (BRI) and including everything from regular season and playoff ticket sales to broadcast rights to beer sales at the arenas—without any written obligation speaks to the remarkable clout of the players and their union. While fans pay to see players and not owners or coaches, the players are still the employees in this business arrangement. It's exceedingly rare to find a business in this country that shares such a substantial cut of earnings with employees at the nonexecutive level. Imagine a strip club (where the audience also pays to see the performers) making sure that its dancers (who make most of their money from mandatory and voluntary tipping) walk away with the majority of the total profits—from the shows, bar, food buffet, cover charges, parking, etc.

To the NBA, however, the potential of these changes to effect other changes in the league is less important than the symbolism of the gestures. Dealing again on the cosmetic level, the CBA addressed the image problem primarily by creating a public impression of reform. Because the agreement focuses overwhelmingly on what's wrong with the players according to NBA executives and owners—too many young athletes looking and acting like thugs and buffered by too much power—rather than on what's wrong with the entire league, including its front offices and its teams, the CBA can achieve only cursory ends. Even revisions designed to modify the player population and transfer power to the owners at the players' expense, such as the new age limit and shorter player contracts, have more bark than bite. Their most substantial value is in the generation of positive media buzz.

The minimum-age stipulation is negated in large part by the increasingly prominent role of prep schools in readying prospects for the NBA. Already a popular option for high school stars with NBA aspirations, prep schools often buy young players a post–high school, pre-college transition year under the guise of preparing them more fully for higher education. They serve as one-stop markets for whatever will enable youngsters to play professionally—time to develop their games and profiles; initiate a relationship with a well-connected coach and program; or bolster their transcripts or SAT/ACT scores to meet freshman eligibility standards if the plan is to do a one-year stint in college before going pro. Now prep schools provide an additional service: a place to age for the NBA draft. To David Stern's credit, the commissioner lobbied to raise the requirement to the more meaningful age of twenty, but in vain. Meanwhile, the slashing of only one year off of player contracts gives teams only infinitesimally greater control when it comes to dropping problem players. There's barely a difference between a six-year and a seven-year arrangement. However, the more important part of contract guarantees was not addressed. Too often for their liking, owners are stuck with big-salaried troublemakers whom they can't shed because of the structure of their contracts.

The CBA item that created the most noise was not revealed until after the summer of 2005. In October, less than two weeks before the opening tip-off of the new season, the NBA announced a dress code effective at the start of the 2005–06 season. Perhaps surprisingly, the Players' Association acquiesced to the proposed plan in June. The dress code required that players wear business casual clothing for all team and league functions, including press conferences and all interviews, promotional events, and the arrival and departure from games. "Business casual" in this instance meant a collared dress shirt, turtleneck, or sweater, accompanied by khakis, slacks, or dress jeans. Approved footwear included dress shoes, dress boots, or "other presentable" shoes. Players attending games but not in uniform had to add a sports coat to the outfit. More significant than what players must wear were items that were no longer permissible: jerseys, all headgear (i.e., baseball caps, do-rags, bandanas, and headbands), sunglasses indoors, sneakers, construction or casual boots, and chains and pendants—bling). In essence, these were all the trendy staples of hip-hop clothing that black players in their twenties wore abundantly. The NBA's line of thinking was that by bettering its outward appearance, the league could improve its reputation in the quickest, most obvious way. After all, people first responded to others visually, and while one's opinion of another is subjective, certain commonly accepted markers of professionalism imply that one also has certain traits associated with professionalism—namely, civility and sophistication. By dealing with image when there were deeper problems, the NBA was fixing the exterior in hopes of reaching the interior in the process: if fashion deviance reflected and possibly encouraged behavioral deviance, then fashion conformity would precipitate general conformity. And if that never transpired, at least the NBA had given the impression of handling its problems.

From the off-season leading up to the 2004–05 season through the one leading up to the 2005–06 season—from the Lakers' dismantling in June 2004 through the brawl-plagued, messy 2004–05 season—the NBA's image had sustained extensive injury. The new CBA in June 2005 ostensibly served as a cooperative attempt to institute reforms and rehabilitate professional basketball—a sort of community cleanup. However, what really took place from June 2004 to June 2005, culminating in the CBA and the dress code, was an aggressive yet not always obvious power struggle within the NBA, whereby Commissioner Stern and league management, owners and team management, and the players fought to protect and advance their respective interests during uncertain times. What each party wanted and generally got out of the CBA offers a telling look at who has the power in the NBA, who does not, and how the power is expressed and contested by the different groups in the league.

All of the events during this period can be seen as either wounds inflicted upon the NBA's image or Band-Aids that covered over the injuries to that image. Benedict writes about rampant criminality in the NBA, and then a brawl takes place in Detroit to confirm his contention. To remedy the problem, the NBA creates a smoke screen of harmless, Fred Willard comedy and then makes the players remove their do-rags and flat-brimmed hats and put on "business casual" clothing. But let us first look at whether the NBA had suddenly become a more violent and dangerous place since players started dressing as though they were from the streets.

Two of the most serious acts of violence in American sports in recent memory have taken place in the NBA and have solidified the league's "thug" image: Latrell Sprewell's assault on Coach P. J. Carlesimo during a 1997 Golden State Warriors practice and the 2004 brawl between the Indiana Pacers and Detroit Pistons fans. But, although it may be hard to believe, the game on the whole is less violent today than it was in the 1980s and early 1990s.

In the 1980s, players used to shove, claw, elbow, knock opponents to the floor, and even throw punches during the course of a game—and then cool off and play some more. Larry Bird, a legend of the period, reflected in a recent interview about what it was like in his heyday: "The game was different then. You could take somebody out. You could make a harder foul. You could shove a guy in the face and not get kicked out of the game. Now everybody takes it personally." Ejections were hardly automatic for particular offenses, and Stu Jackson wasn't around every corner, ready to levy fines and take disciplinary action. Before the introduction of the half-circle, painted four feet from the basket and defining the area in which defensive players could not hold their positions, there was more formidable contact, much of it mid-air, when offensive players went to the hole. Such contact resulted in countless tumbles and an entire category of charging calls that no longer exist today; now defensive players in this space, instead of bracing for impact and forcefully falling backward as an offensive player flies into them, either get out of the way or attempt to block a shot. Greater leniency in the allowance of contact and hand-checking on the perimeter throughout the 1980s and 1990s also contributed to the more physical style of the game.

After Stern took over in 1984—the same year Chicago drafted Michael Jordan and the Celtics-Lakers rivalry was tied at two championships apiece—the NBA grew dramatically in stature, and an expanded bureaucracy began to more tightly monitor what was happening on the floor. Today every minute of NBA play is recorded, reviewed, and cataloged by the league. But the reins of control were tightened only gradually. The Pistons of the late 1980s and early 1990s, known as the Bad Boys, defined Eastern Conference basketball as far more physical than the soft stuff played out west; they matched the personality of the city with that of the local basketball franchise: gritty and sometimes violent. That the NBA brass allowed the Pistons to beat up on Michael Jordan and to ride their brand of tough-guy basketball all the way to consecutive championships is probably the best example of the previously rougher nature of the game. The Bad Boys could not exist today: a team could not use players as goons and get away with it; bullies like Bill Laimbeer and Rick Mahorn would not enjoy the same career longevity; and the Pistons' strategy—what came to be known as the "Jordan rules," for example—wouldn't fly with Basketball Operations. To a lesser degree, the Pistons applied the "Jordan rules" philosophy to all the teams they faced. The plan was simple: consciously and consistently foul Jordan hard when he entered the lane in order to make him think twice about driving the ball, prevent and-one baskets, and impel him to shoot jump shots. The scheme's success varied depending on Jordan's ability to adjust, how closely the refs called the game, and how well the defense carried out its initiative. When it worked, the plan wore Jordan out physically with charley horses, bumps, and bruises; more important, it wore him out mentally by instilling if not fear, at least hesitancy in his game. The "Jordan rules" can be understood as a perverse extension of the old defensive adage espoused by coaches for generations: No layups! With time, Jordan got top-notch star treatment from the refs but not before a lengthy period of paying his dues. When Pat Riley took over as head coach of the Knicks in 1991, he surprised many by borrowing the Pistons' approach and departing from the fast-breaking offense he had coached with the Lakers. Power forward Charles Oakley, who used to protect Jordan when he was his teammate on the Bulls, served as the team's enforcer/bully and as the prototypical 1990s Knick: earthbound but tough as nails.

The notion that players today are more dangerous than before is both right and wrong. On the court, players are better behaved and less physical, but off the court, they're worse than ever. Today a team would not be permitted to knock down LeBron James, now the league's biggest star, every time he took it to the basket because, as Bird said, "now everybody takes it personally." At the same time, while the 1980s and early 1990s game was physical and smash-mouth, it was absolutely harmless because it wasn't charged by energies outside of the game. The game had a smaller following and lower profile and far fewer corporate connections; moreover, with television highlights years away from becoming a major force, things happened without the world seeing them over and over again. Things also happened without a player's "boys" in the audience. Today's entourage culture is a major force in the lives of new-money celebrities. In contemporary sports, many athletes travel around the clock with a team of friends from the old neighborhood who weigh in on every matter with a mix of envy and outsider knowledge. As a consequence, the players often act as though they're trying to impress their high school cliques.

Add to the entourage culture the enormous financial incentive of being "the man," as well as the legal and social problems that Benedict discusses, and the result is a league with an undercurrent of aggressive impulsivity. Violence is likely to break out amid the racial, generational, cultural, and financial differences of those who make the NBA go. The Sprewell incident in 1997, which I'll discuss at length below, and the Pacers-Pistons brawl in 2004 were emblems of a power struggle and were, to a certain degree, inevitable.

From the moment a coach or scout calls a young player a future star while that player is still of a tender young age, a lengthy socialization begins that fosters a sense of both entitlement and nonaccountability. It creates an understanding that the player is an individual in a cutthroat sport and business who must operate independently of any allegiance to a coach or team in order to excel. In the NBA, the coddling from authority figures continues on a larger scale; now the money is really big, and the cameras are watching. Simultaneously wiser and more thoroughly spoiled than they were as naïve kids and empowered by the cash in their pockets and a clear conception of what they're worth to other people, NBA players often locate themselves on one side of the fence and place the NBA, the team owners and management, and often the coaches on the other.

This division is cemented through such situations as the discipline charade, by which players receive candy-coated punishments in a token flexing of team or league authority. Disenchanted fans may complain to one another and to equally displeased sports radio hosts about greedy, thuggish players, but owners, general managers, and coaches have a financial and personal stake in the behavior and reputation of their players. What players do and the implications of their actions on a team's image impact the profitability of an owner's business. The level of control that GMs and coaches are perceived to have over their players may determine their employment status. But, counterintuitively, it often seems that those with ostensibly the most power and a vested interest in their teams are the ones who soften or look the other way when their players get in trouble. Indeed, players routinely get away with atrocious behavior because they are protected by a culture of tolerance in the NBA, a powerful union, influential agents, and the terms of their contracts.

Discipline in the NBA is mostly a farce. A punishment can come from the team or the league. Each group establishes flat rates for transgressions. If a player kicks a ball into the stands, for example, the NBA will bill him $5,000. But unless a player serves out a suspension, which looks worse to fans and to the media than a fine and can cost a star player upwards of $80,000 a game, the cost of committing an infraction fails to act as a deterrent. The $5,000 kicking fine, for example, is mere chump change for a player—it represents no more than a night at the clubs for him and his boys and is probably a good story to laugh about. Sometimes punishments are so light that even the coaches and general managers don't take them seriously. The Mavericks' general manager, Don Nelson, allows players to reduce fines by making shots from different points on the court during practice.

The *Wall Street Journal* recently traced several fines that had been handed down in various sports, and it uncovered a notable trend: players don't even pony up. Fines in all major sports leagues, not just the NBA, are consistently reduced or forgiven completely; the act of disciplining an athlete is a publicity move rather than a legitimate exercise of authority. During a film session in February 2005, Darius Miles of the Portland Trail Blazers repeatedly insulted his head coach, Maurice Cheeks, prompting the Trail Blazers' brass to suspend Miles for two games without pay. Miles, who makes $75,000 a game, filed a grievance with the NBA Players' Association on the urging of his agent, Jeff Wechsler. Using the grievance as negotiating leverage, Wechsler then lobbied the Trail Blazers to rescind the punishment and pay back the sum with interest. A side deal was cut specifying that Miles would serve his suspension but get back the money in exchange for doing what should be givens: listening to his coach and working harder in practice. Portland president Steve Patterson's response: "I don't think anybody is interested in seeing athletes who are making millions of dollars turn over money to owners who are worth billions of dollars." (Microsoft cofounder Paul Allen, the seventh richest person on the planet with a net worth of over $22 billion according to *Forbes*, owns the Blazers.) Thus the only point of a punishment seems to be to create a public impression that an organization is in control of its players. When the media ask why Miles is not playing, the Blazers can explain that Miles mistreated his coach and that the matter has been dealt with internally by a reprimand and a fine.

The NBA is all about the players. Just like those behind the scenes who deal with Broadway entertainers or musicians on tour, the bureaucrats of the NBA placate the league's celebrities to keep them on the stage of the hardwood. Consequently, discipline must be administered with kid gloves to protect inflated and fragile egos and to avoid upsetting shaky relationships in the locker room and between players and management or players and owners.

Jeff Wechsler and the NBA Players' Association served as key allies in the Miles incident, providing council, effective strategy, and influence. Agents and the union are the tools by which players can exercise their power in a coherent, official way. They offer the legal expertise and authority to actualize the wishes, rights, and financial interests of the players. At the same time, the players are already a brotherhood infused with political strength; they often stand by one another with unbending resolve when one of them is in trouble. This unity manifested itself in the aftermath of the 2004 Pacers-Pistons brawl, when nearly all NBA players highlighted the role of the fans in provoking and participating in the fracas. Seemingly concerned that the media would place the blame squarely on the players' shoulders, many players reminded their interviewers that buying a ticket did not entitle fans to taunt the athletes or throw things at them. Jermaine O'Neal, who received a twenty-five-game suspension after punching out a fan, expressed regret but explained his response as self-defense: "There's 15 of us with Pacers jerseys on against thousands. If you listen to some of the 911 calls, people were afraid. What about us? If people can come onto the court, there's no way in hell you can get off the court." Deflecting the responsibility of the players, Quentin Richardson of the Phoenix Suns shifted the focus onto the caprice of the fans, commenting to ESPN, "Man, there are going to be some lawsuits. You don't think some of those fans aren't going to want some NBA money?"

After watching a tape of the brawl, the Lakers' Lamar Odom said, "Just think about what it takes for NBA players to go into a crowd. . . . Fans get kind of out of hand, but it must have taken a lot for NBA players to go into a crowd and start a fight." Odom implies that the usually restrained players must have been pushed past their breaking point by unusually provocative spectators.

While some former players like Bill Walton, who called the infamous 2004 Pacers-Pistons game for ESPN, ripped the players for violating a cardinal rule of never entering the stands, many retired players now working as TV commentators attributed a disproportional amount of the blame on brutish fans. Former NBA players Tim Legler and Greg Anthony did not criticize the players for going into the stands. Legler asserted: "The blame should be put on the Detroit fans."

On the night of the brawl, John Saunders, the host of ESPN's NBA *Shootaround*, a recap show, called the fans "a bunch of punks" and stated, "I don't blame the players for going into the stands." ESPN's executive vice president, Mark Shapiro, later articulated a new stance on the brawl that held the players liable and admitted that the analysis on the show had been swayed by emotion. Responding to ESPN's revision of its own coverage, the Pistons' president Joe Dumars, a Hall of Fame player before moving into the front office, alleged to the *Detroit News* that the NBA, a partner with ESPN, had read "the riot act" to the cable network. Player unity is so strong that it often carries over into retirement. By rallying together while deflecting blame, players save face and manage their images.

Billy Hunter apologized for the players immediately following the brawl: "The Players' Association deeply regrets the events that took place in Detroit on Friday night. . . . On behalf of all of our members we want to offer our sincerest apology to NBA fans everywhere." Then Hunter quickly mobilized when Commissioner Stern began to hand down suspensions. Stern, who has unilateral power in the area of player discipline for on-the-court infringements, levied a seventy-three-game, season-long ban on Ron Artest and thirty- and twenty-five-game bans respectively on Stephen Jackson and Jermaine O'Neal. Hunter, hoping to have these punishments reviewed by an impartial third party, explained to the press, "I'm going to challenge the authority to do what he [Stern] did," and he filed appeals.

The brotherhood among players became unequivocally clear the last time a player had to sit out for the balance of a season. Latrell Sprewell, the poster boy for violence in the NBA before Artest, missed the final sixty-eight games of the 1997–98 season for choking his coach, P. J. Carlesimo. The numerous and significant parallels between Sprewell and Artest speak to the power retained by the players. Like when the players rallied behind Artest in the Pacers-Pistons brawl by keeping the focus on the spectators, a similar, even more tenacious solidarity among the players emerged after Stern handed down Sprewell's suspension.

Before a quickly souring run with the Minnesota Timberwolves, Sprewell had made a phenomenal comeback from a suspension as a member of the New York Knicks. Winning over the local media and boosting his popularity with a sneaker deal with AND 1, Sprewell successfully recast himself in New York as both a winner and a fierce, team-oriented competitor with a surprisingly mellow side. He would play ferocious, high-energy basketball on both offense and defense, and then he would put on a Bill Cosby–style sweater and nonprescription glasses to meet the press and softly answer all of their mundane questions with detailed eloquence. Knicks coach Jeff Van Gundy supported Sprewell during their concurrent tenure with the club, emphasizing Sprewell's quality of character, passing, and intensity of play (but not his personality).

The Pacers' general manager Larry Bird repeatedly went to bat for Artest by praising his on-the-floor fire tempered by a gentle, generous side—the same duality that Sprewell espoused during his Knicks years. Bird appeared with his fallen star on the cover of *Sports Illustrated* for the 2005–06 NBA season preview issue; he extolled Artest's virtues and refuted the charges against a misunderstood athlete. Like Sprewell, Artest played very well in his much anticipated return to the court at the start of the 2005–06 season. But his auspicious comeback proved short-lived: he bailed on the Pacers less than one month into the season, demanding to be traded; then he was indefinitely suspended and sat it out while the team shopped him around for several weeks. (It finally made a trade with the Sacramento Kings for Peja Stojakovic.) Lacking the same calculated image management as Sprewell, a comparatively uncouth Artest appeared in the company of barely dressed women on the cover of *Penthouse* for the magazine's NBA preview; the issue was released during the same week as the *Sports Illustrated* issue that was intended to repair his reputation.

A shrewd Sprewell manipulated his image in two different ways to achieve two different ends. His first goal was to earn the approval of the NBA higher-ups, the media, and at least a few team owners. By proving himself a reformed athlete and a relatively safe investment—with the props of the fake glasses and overstated tenderness—he could reclaim his still burgeoning career and sign a few lucrative contracts. However, Sprewell couldn't keep up the exaggerated good guy act for long, and he eventually fell out of favor with Knicks management and ownership. But with Madison Square Garden and the almighty New York media as his platform, Sprewell moved right on to the then title-contending Timberwolves.

After procuring a contract with the Knicks and validating his signing with quality play and exaggerated sensitivity, the business-savvy Sprewell took his downfall-and-resurrection script in another direction through his sneaker deal. In the shoe campaign with AND 1 Sprewell contradicted the image that he had presented to appease the NBA. His message to potential sneaker consumers was, "I beat the system; I got over." "Getting over" is AND 1's hip-hop-driven marketing theme; an irreverent, smaller-budget shoe company, it is challenging the big boys (such as Nike and Adidas) through street buzz and partnerships with renegade NBA players and streetballers. To spread its ideology and sell footwear, AND 1 created faux political campaign posters on which Sprewell's face was superimposed over the American flag; the caption read, "The American Dream." The posters were given out at Knicks games, and AND 1 ran TV spots tying Sprewell's persona to Jimi Hendrix's electric guitar rendition of the national anthem. Hendrix's iconoclastic performance recaptured Americana and patriotism for the upstarts, reminding the nation of its rebel sprit and history of subversion.

Later during his time with the Knicks, Sprewell, in a bizarre coincidence, was involved in another fan-player boundary breakdown when an inebriated Calvin Klein got out of his front row seat and walked over to Sprewell, who was in-bounding the ball from the sideline. Security pulled Klein away while he exchanged what seemed to be pleasantries with the smiling Sprewell. New York State subsequently implemented the "Calvin Klein Law," which specified maximum fines for criminal trespassing at a sporting event and making physical contact with an athlete.

During a Warriors' practice in December 1997, in the midst of a losing season, Coach P. J. Carlesimo, a disciplinarian and sideline screamer better suited for university field houses than the player-centered NBA, clashed violently with his star perimeter player, Latrell Sprewell. According to witness reports that appeared in *Sports Illustrated*, Carlesimo had instructed Sprewell to "put a little mustard on those passes" while he was working on a drill. Sprewell responded, "I don't want to hear it today." Carlesimo then started moving toward Sprewell, and Sprewell warned him not to approach. Carlesimo continued walking in Sprewell's direction, and Sprewell threatened to kill him while the two came nose to nose. Sprewell wrapped his hands around Carlesimo's neck, dragged him to the ground, and choked him for ten to fifteen seconds before being restrained by teammates. Roughly twenty minutes later Sprewell came after his coach again and hit him in the neck before players intervened for a second time. Prior to the incident, Carlesimo had been unpopular with some players, many of whom took issue with his yelling and confrontational behavior when they made mistakes.

On San Francisco TV, Sprewell issued the following statement about the assault: "I couldn't take a lot of the verbal abuse he gives. . . . I couldn't just walk away. . . . I don't condone the behavior. It's something that happened. I can't change it. I have to move forward." The player later apologized to his coach personally (over the phone) and publicly. The Warriors fired Sprewell and voided his four-year, multimillion dollar contract, and the NBA suspended him for a full year.

The mainstream press hardly touched on two particular points that were relevant to the analysis of the confrontation. First, the authoritarian college-style coach typified by Carlesimo was less likely to thrive in today's NBA. Second, players would stick curiously close together in specific instances. Ten to fifteen seconds is an inordinately long time to choke someone if there are other people in the immediate vicinity. Choking is not like a fistfight, whereby two people on an equal footing exchange punches, most of which do not land squarely; it's the life-threatening endpoint of a confrontation in which one man is unequivocally at the mercy of another. When Sprewell choked his coach, his teammates did not rush to separate the two men. They looked on and allowed the choking to continue. These same teammates then flanked Sprewell during Sprewell's press conference. While Sprewell was not the victim but the perpetrator, he was the man accorded a public showing of post-assault support. Some teammates later played with Sprewell's number written in marker on their sneakers.

When describing the incident, one of Sprewell's teammates, who elected to remain anonymous, told the *Sun Reporter*, a black newspaper in San Francisco, that "P. J. . . . provoked it. He could have stopped or walked the other way. But he didn't. He kept going." It is unclear in this context precisely what Carlesimo kept doing. Did he persistently ride Sprewell verbally? Did he continue to walk toward Sprewell even after he was told to keep his distance? Was Sprewell any more or less accountable for his actions if Carlesimo approached in spite of having been forewarned? What is clear from this player's account is that Carlesimo played an important role in his own attack: he knew Sprewell had reached his limits and consciously chose not to back off, be it verbally or physically.

Several prominent black players not on Sprewell's team spoke out against the severity of Sprewell's penalty, and there was even substantial talk, led by Charles Barkley, about boycotting the All-Star Game (although it never materialized). The Players' Association stepped in to file grievances. Sprewell filed a lawsuit against the NBA, claiming a lack of due process in the league's decision to punish him, and he hired Johnnie Cochran as his lawyer. Indeed, the turn of events was startling after the announcement of Sprewell's suspension.

On March 4, 1998, John Feerick, the dean of Fordham University Law School, acting as arbitrator, reduced Latrell Sprewell's punishment by reinstating the final two years of his contract. (The contract was worth $17.3 million. Feerick's judgment meant that Sprewell would lose $6.4 million.) Feerick also abridged the suspension that the NBA had imposed from one year to seven months. While Feerick decided (contrary to Sprewell's assertions) that the NBA had given him due process and that the coupling of his NBA suspension with the termination of the Golden State contract was not a case of double jeopardy, he ruled ultimately in Sprewell's favor. He not only determined that Sprewell's act had shown no premeditation but he also affirmed that the assault was not in violation of the "moral turpitude" clause in the standard NBA contract, in part because the Warriors had helped create the volatile environment that had precipitated the altercation. Feerick also maintained that there was no precedent for the severity of the original punishment, as previous acts of player violence had been met with comparatively inconsequential punishments.

Sprewell, the teammates and fellow NBA players who had stood behind him, and the Players' Association thus accomplished what proved far more difficult nearly seven years later in the Pacers' debacle: they successfully challenged Commissioner Stern's authority. As in the aftermath of the Pacers' brawl, the Sprewell-Carlesimo debacle made it evident that the NBA was facing a power showdown, with the players, who are black, on one side and the overwhelmingly white team and league brass on the other.

Many in both the mainstream (mostly white) media and the black media took issue with what they considered an inappropriate showing of solidarity based upon race. When Johnnie Cochran agreed to represent Sprewell, many griped that race was not only totally irrelevant in this situation in the first place but also that it was being used shamelessly to make Sprewell look like a victim and to give an opportunistic group of black leaders some air time. According to an editorial in the *New Republic*, "When a black professional basketball player physically assaults his white coach, it is merely an act of violence, not an act of politics. But there are those whose celebrity hinges on turning every emotionally charged encounter between whites and blacks into national psychodrama." The editorial claimed that the "Free Spre campaign" had been set in motion by parasitic black rabble-rousers looking to stir up trouble for personal gain. A writer for the *Sporting News* sarcastically wondered why "Al Sharpton hasn't signed on yet."

In a black paper, the *Michigan Chronicle*, an editorial expressed that Sprewell's action had been detrimental to his race and warned that color alone should not serve as sufficient grounds for calling a fellow black man "brother." The editor's message: blacks must select carefully whom they decide to support and defend. Even Sprewell's own allegiance to the black community should be questioned because prior to the altercation with Carlesimo, he had retained a white lawyer and agent. The editorial used the case of O. J. Simpson as a parallel. Simpson was a black man who had married a white woman, lived a suburban ("white") lifestyle, and took clownish acting roles, such as that of a bumbling detective in *The Naked Gun* series. Only after his arrest did this one-time "sellout" become black in the eyes of the black public, who cheered him on to legal victory. By hiring Johnnie Cochran and highlighting race as a factor in the case, Simpson "became a brother" retroactively; he repositioned himself as a black victim in the hands of white justice. Disturbed that blacks had rallied around Simpson, the editor asked: why should blacks rush to Sprewell's defense simply on the basis of Sprewell's physical appearance?

For the most part, the mainstream press offered an uncomplicated understanding of both the attack and Sprewell. Sprewell, a thug-athlete, had violently erupted when criticized for his shabby effort in practice. The black press, on the other hand—as if engaged in a dialogue with the mainstream outlets—emphasized that Sprewell's attack on Carlesimo had its roots long before the two ever hooked up. Carlesimo hadn't been able to get along with certain players before Sprewell, and his inherently antagonistic brand of player-coach diplomacy was bound to push one of his athletes over the edge. The black media, who unapologetically take as a given that we live in a society divided and charged by differences in race and class, went deeper: they considered the overarching racial and social tensions that had precipitated the altercation—for example, the racial divide between players and owners/managers and the race- and labor-based solidarity of the players.

After the Players' Association had filed formal grievances against the NBA and the Warriors and after black leaders like San Francisco mayor Willie Brown had become involved, a piece in *Forbes* by black neo-conservative Thomas Sowell condemned the mobilization as "blind and amoral" tribalism reminiscent of that practiced by whites decades earlier. Aside from the absurdity of comparing highly racist past traditions of white tribalism with black support for Sprewell, Sowell's charge implied that race had been retroactively interjected into the Sprewell-Carlesimo conflict, gratuitously transforming an altercation that wasn't racially motivated into one about race.

Was race really irrelevant in the Sprewell incident? If so, why did a show of solidarity follow? Did the black players who stood behind Sprewell elect to do so because Sprewell was black or because he was a co-worker? On the one hand, the solidarity on the part of the players was less about race and more about economic rationalism. Sprewell had been thrown out of the NBA for one year and had had his entire contract nullified, leaving his professional career uncertain. If the players didn't fight back, it could set a potentially dangerous precedent: if something like this happened again, they could be out of work, out of their "guaranteed" money, and Commissioner Stern would have unilateral control over their basketball destinies. In this light, the parallel conflicts between Carlesimo and Sprewell and the players and the league did not come down to a matter of black and white but simply to one of green.

The social separation between Sprewell and Carlesimo that may have precipitated hostility was also a generational and cultural rift. The nearly fifty-year-old coach subscribed to a disciplinarian model of coaching that no longer readily worked in the NBA, and the player, in his twenties, had been raised in the individualistic, super-corporate era of professional hoops. In other words, both Sprewell's and Carlesimo's understanding of coaching and professional basketball corresponded to the predominant player-coach model during the time of their basketball upbringing. The showdown could be reduced even further to a conflict without any sociological foundations: two frustrated people on a losing team got into one another's face, and one of the two completely lost control.

No matter how you slice it, however, without a consideration of race, only part of the story is told. The significance of race is revealed through the gravity of Sprewell's punishment, the coverage of the event, black player unity, and Sprewell's relationship to Carlesimo.

A few weeks before Sprewell choked Carlesimo, Tom Chambers, a white forward on the Phoenix Suns, punched his assistant coach. In response, the Suns shipped Chambers off to the Philadelphia 76ers as the NBA looked the other way. No suspensions were handed down. In a reversal of roles, Indiana University coach Bob Knight, who is white, was caught on tape choking one of his white players, Neil Reed, during a practice in 1997. (The tape did not become public until 2000.) Even in light of Knight's abusive past, Indiana decided to let the coach keep his job. Knight was merely given a three-game suspension, a $30,000 fine, and an embarrassingly obvious "zero-tolerance" policy warning regarding physical contact with anyone at the school; Knight later again violated the policy. Furthermore, in an incident in the NFL that appeared on national television, Kevin Steele, the linebacker coach of the Carolina Panthers, confronted linebacker Kevin Greene after the player had botched a play. Greene, who is white, first told his superior to get lost and then grabbed the coach by the collar and threatened him before teammates intervened. Greene's punishment was a one-game suspension (costing him $118,000).

When Sprewell's punishment is compared to the responses to similar acts of violence perpetrated by white offenders (Sprewell's choking was the most brutal, but it had also occurred in the semiprivate environment of practice), the existence of a double standard premised upon race is difficult to dispute. One can also safely assume that Stern and the NBA wanted to make an example of Sprewell that would deter future transgressions and make plain the league's authority. The players who backed Sprewell reacted as fellow black men perceiving racial injustice: a white institution gratuitously exercising its power over a black man in order to keep other black men from getting out of control.

The mainstream media's handling of the Sprewell episode also suggests why race was relevant. Most in the media insisted that race played no part in the attack and that the black men supporting Sprewell were disingenuously making a nonracial issue into a racial issue for personal ends. However, while muting the issue of race, they drew conclusions about the incident and about Sprewell based squarely on racial assumptions. After the attack, Sprewell's status as villain was all too apparent; his name, in many articles, was replaced by negative pseudonyms—"the choker," "the strangler," "the choke artist." One writer dubbed him "a hard shadowy figure." Sprewell was called a "street thug" who had "gone full gangster." Sprewell's identity had been supplanted by aliases generally given to bad guys in comic books, whose actions are guided by a smoldering inner evil. Howie Evans of the *Amsterdam News*, a black newspaper out of Harlem, remarked, "Around the nation, columns continue to be written about Sprewell as if he's a member of the Charles Manson crew."

Even in mainstream articles that were supposedly more sympathetic, the conception of Sprewell as inherently and consistently violent often swayed the writing. In a *People Magazine* piece on December 22, 1997, the authors visited the suspended star at his home in Hayward, California. Sprewell, dressed casually in shorts and without shoes, explained that he was "doing all right . . . can't complain about anything." From the interview and description of Sprewell, one gathers that Sprewell was polite and relaxed, sufficiently comfortable with his company. Yet the writers seem to want readers to believe that Sprewell was putting up a facade; they had been fortunate enough to have caught the volatile and very large Sprewell in a mellow state. That Sprewell was "doing all right" at the moment was "just as well, since the 6'5," 190-lb. Sprewell is not a man you would choose to antagonize." The goal of the article appears to have been to humanize Sprewell—he too lounges around his house barefoot like the rest of us—but the authors come back to the idea of Sprewell as unstable, poised to lash out at any moment. The implication that Sprewell would attack company who had joined him at his home to write a supposedly positive piece about him is ridiculous.

Meanwhile on the radio, disc jockey Don Imus remarked that the black men standing behind Sprewell at his press conference (mostly his teammates) "looked like the Bloods and the Crips." In television, less than three weeks after the assault on Carlesimo, Kevin Cosgrove, a senior producer at *Good Morning America*, explained to talent bookers that he needed "spades" to serve as black interviewees for a segment on Sprewell.

To deny that race played a part in the Sprewell-Carlesimo conflict is to deny the reality that on some level, race shapes everything. To assume that the clash had no racial significance is to additionally assume far too much: that Sprewell's cornrows occupy the same space in the imagination of black people like the teammates who joined Sprewell at his press conference and the white people like Don Imus who saw these men as gangbangers; that Sprewell's perception that Carlesimo had disrespected him wasn't partially driven by the dominant expectations of black manhood; that the unprecedented severity of Sprewell's suspension wasn't influenced by racial stereotypes of his character; that the media didn't infer traits about

Sprewell's character (or lack thereof) and call him names based on his race; and that the Warriors were in no rush to separate Sprewell and Carlesimo simply because they were too shocked to act.

A look at a typical NBA player contract tells us much about why owners' hands are often tied when dealing with problem players. The contract contains an entire "termination" section that gives teams the right to terminate a player's contract if the athlete has committed numerous transgressions. Theoretically, a player can have his contract voided for attacking a team or NBA employee; failing to conform to standards of good citizenship, character, or sportsmanship; not staying in top physical shape; or even failing to play with adequate skill or competitiveness as defined by the player's team. However, while owners have numerous "outs" on paper, it's extremely difficult to terminate a player because there is limited precedent—the players in the Sprewell case fought precisely to avoid such precedent—and because the athletes retain strong representation. Essentially, players are major cash investments, and owners must continue to contribute to the investments—almost no matter what happens—over long periods of time. Contracts seem unmercifully long to the owners paying a player who is performing below expectations. In addition, after January 10 all players' contracts are guaranteed, an arrangement by which players often receive their full salaries regardless of performance, injury, fitness level, or even insubordination.

By guaranteeing salaries, the NBA provides a major safety net for its players. And because no more than 25 percent of a salary can come from bonuses—money given to a player for either signing a contract or reaching a particular performance quota—NBA players collect a secure, very large base salary. In contrast, the incentive structure of NFL contracts offers players in a more dangerous sport only a very limited guaranteed base salary. A football player's performance, which depends largely on his health, determines the majority of his earnings. Not only are NBA players well paid—so well, in fact, that the Players' Association can terminate the CBA if the average NBA salary (which comes in at just under $5 million per season) falls below that of salaries in the NFL, Major League Baseball, or NHL—but they are also contractually safeguarded.

Because owners frequently have to disburse millions of dollars of guaranteed cash to players they no longer want but whose contracts have yet to expire, often the most practical solution is to trade a player for one with a similar salary structure or for a less talented player with a more desirable contract situation. In a generally fruitless exercise, general managers routinely exchange underachieving, overpaid players in a circle of misery, justified only when one of these players thrives in his new environment. If a player cannot be moved via a trade or other measures, such as placing him on waivers (cutting him but paying most of his salary if he isn't picked up by another team during an either two- or ten-day period) or reaching an agreement with him about a contract buyout, the team keeps him and deals with the ramifications. If the player who stays is a star or at least has star potential, the team often caters to him entirely in the hopes of keeping him happy and being able to extract the best out of him. (Teams trade star players all the time because of their inflexible contracts, fears that they may have health problems down the road, a perception that they're overvalued in the marketplace, a belief that the team can get someone even better, etc.) In catering to a star player, a team may fire a coach of whom he doesn't approve or for whom he doesn't play hard, trade away disliked teammates with less financial clout, or turn a blind eye to any of his indiscretions.

Coaches theoretically occupy a higher rung on the power ladder than players; their jobs were once predicated upon demanding excellence and administering discipline from a position of superiority. But in today's NBA, because star players are generally far better compensated and enjoy higher profiles than their coaches, the top players frequently call the shots. When Darius Miles, overpaid to the tune of $48 million over six years, clashed with Coach Cheeks, the team unambiguously sided with the player. When, unbeknownst to Cheeks, Miles's agent negotiated a deal with the front office that would repay Miles his lost salary in exchange for doing what he was already paid to do—listen to his coach and work hard in practice—Cheeks rightly knew his days with the organization were numbered.

As New Yorkers know all too well from following the Knicks and Mets, large payrolls don't always translate into similarly large win totals. The long-term guaranteed money of NBA contracts can be doubly detrimental for NBA owners: players aren't just making a lot of money; they are also often overpaid. *Sports Illustrated*'s Ian Thompson noted that on a given week in February during the dreadful 2004–05 season fifty-seven players were each making $8 million or more per year, but twenty-five of them had failed to be among the top fifty in either points, rebounds, or assists. When a player underperforms like these twenty-five guys did, an owner faces a potential financial disaster. When a supposedly top-level player (who is being paid top dollar) struggles, his team usually does too. Fewer wins than expected means lower attendance and, in turn, less revenue. A team with poor attendance and a high payroll risks spending more than it takes in; hence the potential double jeopardy for owners that comes from overblown NBA contracts.

The design of contracts; the tolerance that coaches, management, and owners are forced to show when players act out; and the strength of player representation, both formally through the Players' Association and informally through demonstrations of player solidarity—all suggest that the power balance tips in favor of the athletes. The NBA, after all, is a players' league. But if the players truly have such a good gig, why did Rasheed Wallace explode about the status of NBA players in December 2003 when he was interviewed by his local paper, *The Oregonian*? (*The Oregonian* also broke the story about the Miles side deal.) Wallace's message: the NBA exploits its black talent. The younger and more clueless the player, the more he is prey, Wallace maintained, as the huge contracts are only a smoke screen for the fact that the athletes are divorced from positions of power. Wallace laced his statements with profanity, unflinchingly used the N-word, and spoke so freely that his unscripted statements were not always coherent. Here was a college dropout making millions of guaranteed NBA salary dollars to play a game he'd been enjoying since his youth, and he was blasting the league that had made him rich and famous. Why? As in the case of the Sprewell debacle, the answer lies in the reaction to Wallace's eruption and a closer look at what was going on in the league at the time of his comments.

David Stern wasted no time in responding to Wallace's interview. The commissioner blasted Wallace right back, dismissing both his credibility and his understanding of his peers. Wallace's comments were "ignorant" and "an insult to all NBA players." End of discussion. And yet Stern, who is the commissioner and not a player, never asked a single player what he thought of Wallace's comments. How could he honestly say that *all* NBA players were insulted by what Wallace had said? Stern later reacted to the Pacers' brawl with the same snap judgment. As commissioner, Stern single-handedly both determines punishments for on-court behavior and evaluates the appeals of his punishments. After having handed down his suspensions in the Pacers-Pistons case, Stern made light of his unilateral powers, remarking that the vote on penalties was "unanimous: 1–0," and then promptly rejected the idea of a third-party review or any sort of arbitration. (At the behest of the Players' Union, however, an arbitrator, Roger Kaplan, later became involved, even as the NBA refused to participate in arbitration. A federal judge upheld Kaplan's decision to reduce O'Neal's twenty-five-game suspension to fifteen games just before Christmas of 2004 on the grounds that fighting between players and fans during a riot did not constitute on-court conduct and therefore fell beyond the scope of the commissioner's powers. According to Kaplan, O'Neal's punishment was shortened because he had been a solid NBA citizen prior to the event—"his one punch of a spectator, while excessive, was clearly out of character"—and his role in the brawl was motivated in significant part by an attempt to protect his teammates during a chaotic situation.)

Most of the sports media told Wallace to shut his mouth. NBA fans burned up their keyboards blasting Wallace on message boards on fan Web sites. Even John Thompson felt that Wallace was barking up the wrong tree with his references to the NBA as an exploiter of black labor.

Mike Wise (sports columnist with the *New York Times*) was one of the few in the media who did not rush to silence Wallace. Wise pointed out that with the killing of the messenger—a player with a history of temperamental behavior and technical fouls who cursed and ranted through his interview—the message was killed too. While Wallace was not a trained sociologist or even the elected voice of the players, he was a veteran black player who was popular with his teammates and around the NBA. At the very least, he had a better sense of the pulse of the players than Stern, a nonplayer.

Stern's knee-jerk reaction to quiet Wallace, restore the status-quo, and not talk about race relations in professional basketball is exactly what isolates the commissioner from the players and is probably what led Wallace to feel like an overpaid puppet. The players will take the money because they'd be fools not to, but it confirms the point: part of that cash is hush money.

And what point exactly did Wallace intend to make? That black players were at the mercy of a white management and ownership that may choose to abuse its power? Was that totally ridiculous? When Wallace made his comments in 2003, the NBA had only one black majority owner, BET founder Robert Johnson of the expansion Charlotte Bobcats, and twenty-nine white majority owners. Of all of the executives with the power to make player and personnel decisions, only four were black: Billy Knight (the Atlanta Hawks' director of basketball operations); Joe Dumars (president of basketball operations for the Detroit Pistons); Elgin Baylor (vice president of basketball operations with the Los Angeles Clippers); and Billy King (president and general manager of the Philadelphia 76ers).

The first half of the 2003–04 season, during which Wallace had made his feelings known, was a particularly brutal period for black coaches in the NBA. Of an astounding seven coaches who lost their jobs before the All-Star break, six were black. Most distressingly, these firings came at a time when positive change seemed to have taken hold in the coaching business. While the athletes in the NBA are mostly black, blacks are severely underrepresented in ownership and management—that is, in positions having to do with the structure and direction of the league. Such a lack of power is particularly jarring when we consider that blacks possess only a very limited amount of control over a decisively black sport and vehicle of culture.

For decades a sports joke had been all too shamefully applicable to the NBA:

> Q: What do you call a white guy with twelve black guys around him?
> A: Coach.

Even as recently as the last years of the 1990s, coaching in the NBA has been an overwhelmingly white occupation. In the strike-shortened 1998–99 season, management made seven head coaching changes during the extended off-season, and all seven of the replacements were white. The 1999–2000 season opened with only four black coaches on the sidelines, not one of whom coached in the Western Conference.

Things seemed to have changed when the 2003–04 season opened. Eleven black men—all retired pro players (with the exception of Sixers coach Randy Ayers, who had been drafted in 1978 but never played in an NBA game)—held head coaching positions. The always glaring racial, generational, and cultural chasm between the league's players and coaches suddenly appeared to narrow. However, by the All-Star game seven head coaches had lost their jobs—a record-breaking number. One coach, Jim O'Brien, stepped down as the Boston Celtics floundered; the other six coaches were fired. All six were black. Virtually no one in the sports media addressed the devastation of what had looked to be a promising year for black coaches.

In recent years, the spawning of a new class of coaches—younger black coaches, often fresh from distinguished playing careers—has opened up the coaching business. Taking over coaching duties in the new millennium, former backcourt top guns Byron Scott, Maurice Cheeks, and Nate McMillan promptly made a name for themselves as head coaches.

This tenuous shift in the kind of coaches increasingly entering the NBA made sense. As has been noted, the NBA is a players' league in many respects, and the Sprewell-Carlesimo eruption made it clear that the yelling, college-style coach was outdated. With the player-coach experiment similarly a thing of the past, the next best option for bridging the gap between players and coaches was the employment of coaches who were *almost* players—in other words, recently retired black players who were both able to lead from the sideline and were often still capable of suiting up in practice, teaching by example and schooling rookies with finger rolls rather than simply finger pointing.

With a greater number of black head coaches, black employees are now more likely to have black supervisors and black male mentors. If there's an inherent paternalism in the player-coach relationship, the terms of this dynamic immediately change if the paternalism contains a racial element: a white figure in the role of superior for blacks is different from a black man directing other blacks.

Some saw the eleven black head coaches at the beginning of the 2003–04 season as evidence that the racial division between players and coaches had been bridged and that while coaching in the NFL was still a nearly all-white profession, the NBA had become an increasingly progressive league. The opening night of 2003 was a promising moment for black coaches. But that was all it proved to be: a moment, a flash that quickly passed. In the transient NBA coaching business, the tides had shifted midway through the season with the loss of six black head coaches.

The question of race in the NBA, to which we keep returning, and its role in the power play between players and coaches and players and management is significant but rarely discussed and often difficult to quantify. How can one measure or prove that race played a part in the decision to fire six black coaches? For example, at a certain point in Byron Scott's fourth season as head coach of the New Jersey Nets, Scott lost the respect of his team and, shortly thereafter, his control. What did this have to do with Scott's being black? In other instances where black coaches had been fired, the teams had simply been struggling because of a paucity of talent, effort, or both. Coaches in the NBA, as in all of sports, have always been the fall guys.

The issue of race in the NBA is thus best understood by an analysis of the big picture, a consideration of the trends and the context for these trends. Right after black coaches Bill Cartwright, Doc Rivers, and Frank Johnson got off to poor starts and were promptly dropped within the season's first few weeks, Wallace ripped the NBA. "They [the NBA] just want to draft niggers who are dumb and dumber—straight out of high school . . . because they come into the league and they don't know no better," Wallace claimed.

That these deposed black coaches were all accomplished pro players highlights another reality of coaching in the NBA: only blacks who have first excelled as professional players generally have a shot at head coach. This is not the case for white coaches, for whom professional playing experience is not a prerequisite. This observation calls to mind the worst of racial mythology, which stipulates that blacks are better equipped in the physical domain while whites are better in the mental. A casual observer of the game can easily guess which man has lived out his hoop dreams and which has lived them vicariously by noting the physical difference between a coach like Paul Silas, an enormous black man who competed in the NBA for sixteen seasons, and a coach like Lawrence Frank, a five-foot-eight white man who played neither in college nor in the pros.

For many fans and sportswriters, a comparison of Frank's very gradual ascendancy to NBA head coach with Scott's immediate rise to the position verified several racialized assumptions about coaching in the NBA. Frank pulled himself up by his bootstraps through the business. Lacking the ability and size to first excel as a player,

Frank began his coaching career in the consummate role of tag-along: he was a manager for a college team at Indiana University, shagging errant three-point attempts and keeping tabs on the towels, while learning from a supreme strategist, Bob Knight. From there, Frank moved on to assistant coaching positions at the college level; he entered the professional level as an assistant under Brian Hill for the Memphis Grizzlies and later joined the Nets' assistant staff. Frank represents the quintessential student of the game, who learned his craft in small increments and by trailing the masters.

Byron Scott had more of a job switch than a lengthy period of paying dues from the sidelines. Scott enjoyed a distinguished playing career; he parlayed his fame as a standout on Magic Johnson's Lakers and his reputation as a savvy veteran on the Pacers into a head coaching job with New Jersey. His only coaching stop along the way to the Nets' job, which began in 2000, was with the Sacramento Kings, where he served as an assistant for two seasons.

Thus the stereotypical assumption is often that blacks don't have to work as hard to get into coaching and that they can simply use their cachet as players to avail themselves of coaching opportunities. Such an assumption eschews several truths. First, playing experience is in fact an invaluable coaching credential. Second, playing experience has become a necessary qualification for black coaches looking for work in the NBA (one that does not apply to white candidates). Finally, finding an NBA head coaching position is extremely difficult for all candidates, white or black. Silas, for example, waited sixteen years—the entire duration of his playing career—for his second chance at head coaching in the NBA after his first stint with Houston ended in 1982.

The NFL officially recognizes race as a force that impacts management's decision to hire and fire coaches. Under NFL policy, any team that has a coaching vacancy is required to interview at least one minority candidate for the job. The NBA has neither taken any action to increase the number of blacks hired (or at least interviewed) as head coaches nor addressed the issue of black coaches in the NBA in any capacity. This does not mean that race isn't hugely relevant in NBA coaching. Race was a major part of the story in the firing of the six black coaches midway through the 2003–04 season, and the firings raised suspicions about the expendability of, and assumptions about, black coaches, as well as about the politics of power in the NBA. Because, as is evident time and again, the NBA and the media do not want to talk about it, the race issue in the NBA must be interpreted through trends, symbols (like Sprewell's violent showdown with Carlesimo), and stories (like Frank's and Scott's). With the notable exception of Rasheed Wallace's quickly hushed comments, rarely is anything spoken.

Coaches, particularly younger black coaches, often find themselves vulnerable and impotent. They have neither the validity that comes with being better paid than those they are coaching nor the authority to establish themselves as a political force in the league. Coaches like Phil Jackson and Larry Brown, who command respect and prime dollar, are rare, and they enjoy an individual power rather than a collective, organized power akin to that of the players. Even Jackson and Brown must play their cards carefully in order to navigate through a high-pressure, unstable profession. Jackson always makes sure his roster includes a couple of "character guys" who will vouch for him should the team struggle and who will loyally serve as insiders and allies in the locker room. Veteran Ron Harper, for example, whom Jackson first coached in Chicago and who rejoined Jackson in Los Angeles, acted as peacemaker and informant in the Bryant-O'Neal saga with the Lakers. Knicks coach Larry Brown is a cunning tactician—a true hustler in hip-hop parlance—when it comes to the business side of coaching. Brown moves stealthily from one underachieving team to the next, building each up and then leaving when there's nowhere to go but down. Though not without critics, Brown conducts business on his own terms and coaches with firm resolve but maintains a reputation as both a dependable coach who is worth the big bucks and a players' guy. In addition to Jackson and Brown, San Antonio Spurs coach Gregg Popovich, who has led his team to three championships in seven years, has earned similar respect, monetary compensation, and influence in the front office. No black coaches have ever reached this elite plane.

That the group of well-respected and influential coaches is as small as it is is a reflection of the general status of coaches in the NBA. As noted above, in pro sports, coaches and managers are the designated fall guys when things go awry; it's easier to dump one guy than it is to remake an entire team. In the hierarchy of professional basketball, one can argue about exactly where the players fit in the pecking order—their brand of power is the most difficult to quantify—but it's indisputable that the coaches occupy the lowest position. Black coaches fall even a notch below coaches in general: they are the weakest parties in the NBA.

The players have a unique kind of power At the bargaining table for a contract extension, for example, a player shamelessly practices invincible individualism to achieve his full-market value. Steered by the "Me against the World" message of street life and hip-hop, he's willing to skip out on his coach, his teammates, and the organization that drafted him for a better payday elsewhere. At the next moment, this same player will be a vulnerable teammate's die-hard ally, a comrade locked arm in arm with a fellow athlete in peril. While one could argue that by supporting someone like Sprewell or Artest, a player is simply protecting his own financial interests, such an argument ignores the racial element of player solidarity. This solidarity is infused with racial pride and defiance because of the fact that the power ladder has a racial caste: it gets lighter up the chain of command and darker on the way down.

For all the tolerance and pussyfooting when it comes to allowing overpaid athletes to misbehave both on and off the court, the owners and the NBA higher-ups still maintain the upper hand in many respects. The NBA exercises its authority by intimately monitoring the players and editing how they present themselves; the monitoring was taken to new heights with the dress code banning do-rags and heavy jewelry. Commissioner Stern has two bureaucratic bodies to manage the actions and appearance of the players: Basketball Operations (headed by Stu Jackson) handles all on-court affairs—it makes the schedule, watches over the referees, and administers discipline for the players; the recently formed Community and Players Programs organizes public relations opportunities (i.e., community outreach) and monitors players off the court, keeping close tabs on what players wear, say, and do during public appearances.

Team Marketing and Business Operations runs the Business of Basketball Program, an educational series designed to socialize players, impart etiquette, and explain the business side of the sport. During the preseason, players are required to participate, as specified in the new CBA. The program recently included a video of retired basketball legends talking about how NBA players should comport themselves both on the court and in their daily lives. The program's primary goal is to teach players how to successfully manage their individual "brands." The league wants players to see that sound individual management benefits the collective NBA brand and improves team business, which further bolsters the players' financial interests, including—most important—their salaries.

Rookies receive more thorough tutelage. During the Rookie Transition Program, first-year players learn how to appropriately present themselves as role models through a series of role-play exercises, discussion groups, and video sessions. They are coached on dressing in accordance with the dress code and thinking in terms of the public consequences of their actions. Media training is an integral part of the program: players are urged to deflect controversy by speaking in clichés and refraining from comments that may be misconstrued out of context. Basketball players recycle the painfully trite sports sayings about "giving 110 percent" and "leaving it all on the field" partly because they are groomed to do so.

In a bit from *Never Scared,* his Washington DC stand-up show on DVD, Chris Rock goofs about the difference between being rich and being wealthy. His example: Shaquille O'Neal is rich, but the man who signs his check is wealthy. The difference between the players' brand of power and that of the owners comes down to the money question to which Rock alludes. The players are rich because their money is new money; their cash and much of their power is determined by their current contract. They must do right or they may be in major trouble because they don't have the safety net of accumulated old money—i.e., the security of wealth.

The players are given ample cash, and ample space to muck up but it's still new money that hasn't been tucked away for long or had time to diversify and grow through generations of investment. Players, especially those with large networks of family and friends to support, must manage their new money wisely while having no experience for doing so. Being rich is a younger, riskier, more exciting financial situation and state of being, but compared to wealth, it offers only a limited amount of true power. The owners, for the most part, are wealthy. They have the authority and confidence that comes with old, inherited, bedrock money. Wealth carries institutional, time-tested power. Because of this power difference between players and owners, the players are still at the mercy of the owners, still have trust issues with owners and managers, and will at one moment watch a fellow player's back and at the next moment run over his brother for personal gain. From this angle, the players' brand of power is clearly less potent.

The three factions of the NBA community—NBA brass, team owners and managers, and players—come together on one issue: moneymaking. That's what brought everyone together over the 2005 summer to quickly put together a new CBA and prevent a lockout. All three parties benefit from the NBA's centrality in popular culture in the United States and abroad and the perception of it as a site of athletic prominence; an international marker of cool; and a lucrative but safe business investment for partnering corporations. However, they are not all on the same page when it comes to the issue of image.

The players are positioned as the sole source of the league's image problem. But as ESPN's Chris Broussard asked rhetorically after the announcement of the dress code, what American institution doesn't have image troubles? The White House, Major League Baseball, the Catholic Church, the health care industry, Hollywood, you name it—all routinely confront scandal and disparagement. For NBA players to confess to an image problem would be a collective admission that *they* had failed morally, that they had the problem—not the NBA as a whole or as a system—and that they will be the fall guys. Such a confession would be an enormous act of courage, as well as generosity, given that NBA executives and teams are also responsible. A communal shouldering of the blame by the players is also extremely unlikely given that players are conditioned to think and act as individuals looking out for their self-interest. The NBA, on the other hand, is concerned with its collective, general reputation. Some players push the envelope in terms of behavior, attitude, and fashion (in large part to the commercial benefit and cultural relevance of pro basketball). Meanwhile, the NBA strives for an overall sense of control, conformity, and safety and can always cite the old proverb "A few bad apples shouldn't spoil the bunch" in times of trouble.

Pro basketball's three estates have handled the recent string of image-tarnishing events in the manner that advances their particular interests and corresponds to their specific type of power. As suggested above, Stern and his fellow NBA executives possess the broadest powers as they dictate all elements of operations. While the league has addressed fan behavior at games by increasing arena security and prohibiting fourth-quarter beer sales, the biggest problem to the higher-ups has been the players, and that's where they have focused their reform initiatives. To avoid implicating itself and to handle what's considered an image problem at the surface level, the NBA has placed more controls on the players—both those already in the league and those entering the league in the future. The controls affect how the players look, how old rookies must be, the sorts of contracts players can sign, and the substances they can put into their bodies. However, ticket prices are not being changed so as to broaden the current racially and socioeconomically uniform fan base and to bridge the racial divide between the players and the spectators. Nor are changes foreseen in the hiring policy for team management and coaching positions, and the moratorium on speaking about race remains. Indeed, race is sadly taboo in conversations within the league, between players and the league, and between both the media and the league and the media and the players.

Team owners—sitting pretty in the knowledge that they're forever wealthy and ever-cautious of undermining sensitive, upstart players—fought for greater roster flexibility and new controls on the players in the CBA negotiations, but ultimately they defer their authority to league management. Because their interests are basically the same—that is, an increase in revenues through corporate partnerships and overseas markets—team owners bank on the NBA to look out for them, petitioning it when they feel that they need stronger support.

The players often assume that the general image of the NBA player population is out of their hands. They can manipulate their individual images, and by adjusting how they present themselves—as Sprewell did so masterfully during his comeback—they can cash in on financial opportunities. Indeed, the attitude celebrated by Sprewell's "American Dream" campaign speaks to a shared feeling among players: get over in an imbalanced system by beating the hustlers at their own game. However, the power of the players derives only in part from their guaranteed NBA salaries. To their advantage the players can use their own celebrity status, which accords them tremendous privilege—exceptional tolerance from those supposedly in positions of authority, adoration from fans and corporations who want a piece of them, and a union that realistically makes bold demands.

4. The Celtics' Larry Bird, one of professional basketball's all-time greatest players, driving hard to the hoop in 1986. As the NBA's last American-born white superstar, Bird is beloved by nostalgic white hoops fans nationwide and particularly fans in Boston. © Icon Sports Media.

4 The Last White Superstar

Larry Legend and White Nostalgia

On a summer night in 1979 a midnight telephone call jarred Jeff Cohen, the Celtics' vice president, from his sleep. An unidentified caller informed Cohen that Larry Bird, the future of his franchise, may have already gotten himself into serious trouble. Bird, the Celtics' first pick in the 1978 NBA draft, had just arrived in Boston and had been spotted at Burke's Tavern. No ordinary watering hole, Burke's was a notoriously rough bar in a dubious part of town and no place for an oversized, gawky out-of-towner with celebrity credentials. Fearful, Cohen raced over to the bar, where he found his future superstar, dressed in overalls and a John Deere baseball cap, bellied up to the bar and chumming it up with the regulars. The locals instantly adored him; "They were loving him and half of them didn't know who he was," recalled Cohen in an interview. Bird was among his people, entirely at home. That night the joke was on Cohen. "They take one look at me, in a jacket and tie, and I thought I was going to get killed," said Cohen, who left the bar immediately.

That Bird was drawn to Burke's Tavern for what likely was his first night out in Boston is no coincidence. Located in Jamaica Plain, Burke's Tavern in 1979 was one of the last relics of a white, working-class presence in the area. Boston's growing black population, situated primarily in Roxbury, had expanded into neighboring Jamaica Plain, and the bar's days as a white, blue-collar hangout were numbered. Bird, in overalls and cap, with his slow, country drawl and small-town humility, was a natural fit. Just as he had integrated seamlessly into the scene at Burke's that night, he would mesh perfectly with Boston and its sports culture. In a city that had changed abruptly from an industrial town to a center of technological and intellectual development, the blue-collar way of life remained close to the Bostonian heart, and it was often revisited and cherished in the city's sports heroes. Larry Bird would become Larry Legend.

Ethnically and racially too Boston had changed rapidly and dramatically from a city almost exclusively inhabited by European immigrants from Ireland, Italy, and England to a multiethnic metropolis with a depleted white population. While the relocation of white families to the suburbs during the 1970s was reconfiguring the social structure of Boston (and American cities nationwide), a similar flight of whites in basketball was already well under way. By the mid-1960s, the recruitment of black players at top college programs was normal practice. Such a shift in recruitment practices undermined basketball's Jim Crowism—practices like the "three-fifths" rule (three starters must be white) and "the two blacks at home–three on the road–four when behind" rule—and facilitated a boom in the number of black players at the professional level in the 1970s. By 1979, Bird's rookie season, the NBA was 70 percent black.

Whether they admitted it or not, white basketball fans began to wonder where all the white guys had gone. That night in 1979 at Burke's Tavern the last white superstar surfaced in Boston. In Larry Bird, Boston fans, like white sports buffs nationwide, reveled in the union of two vanishing icons in one sports hero: the blue-collar factory man and the white athlete.

Comedian Chris Rock, in one of his stand-up routines, jokes about the fear of many whites that increased immigration and the advancement of minority groups will spell the devastating loss of ground for white society. Playing the part of a frantic white guy, Rock yells in horror, "We're losing everything, we're fucking losing!" Mocking this hysteria, Rock then asks rhetorically, "If y'all losing, who's winning?" In this moment of satire Rock explodes the essence of white nostalgia: a rampant paranoia that white society has relinquished too much. This anxiety, which influences anything from a family's decision on where to buy a home to public policy, produces a mournful longing for a romanticized, racially homogeneous past ("the good ol' days") and a desire to safeguard white visibility and authority.

White nostalgia in basketball (and in sports in general) manifests itself both as a sentimental sense of bewildered deprivation ("What happened to the white guys?") and an impassioned devotion to the fair-skinned few who hold the key to white inclusion and the preservation of control. There may be something natural and essentially innocuous about mulling over the disappearance of white athletes and desiring to still belong, but an unfortunate, destructive element of white nostalgia posits whiteness as the antidote to blackness. In sports, whiteness is synonymous with the forces of good—hard work, tradition, sound fundamentals, morality. Fans and sportswriters often portray white athletes as sport's saviors—those capable of recouping its purity and original purpose, which have been corrupted by the hot-dogging swagger, reckless behavior, and iconoclasm of black athletes like Charles Barkley and Allen Iverson.

Bird is arguably basketball's last American-born true white superstar. The few nonblack megastars in the game today come from other countries—players like Dirk Nowitzki of Germany and 2004–05 MVP Steve Nash of Canada. For many white basketball junkies in Boston and in all parts of the country, Bird offered splendid proof that the white athlete hadn't disappeared and that a white ballplayer could still shine (and even outshine his African American peers) in the NBA. Most important, white folks had a hero, someone with whom to identify: the really tall guy next door, drinking a can of Pabst on his stoop. But Bird, whether or not he realized it or cared to realize it, had a burden: the race-driven responsibility of saving the Celtics and professional basketball. Bird purportedly possessed the throwback values, moral character, and true American spirit necessary to repair both a team and an entire league racked by undisciplined black underachievers.

Bird neither asked for nor embraced the part of white savior. Jackie MacMullan, sports columnist at the *Boston Globe* and former pro basketball specialist for *Sports Illustrated*, explained during an interview that Bird "really detested" the savior role and never understood it. "As far as he was concerned, he and Magic Johnson were the same; he really never made a distinction between race, and I think most of his teammates would tell you the same thing," said MacMullan. Summarizing Bird's legacy exclusively as that of a character filling a void undermines his greatness as a ballplayer and scoffs at the innocence of sports that Bird internalized at least as well as anybody else.

Some might argue that sports at its best rises above race; when we love our athletes for what they do on the court or on the field, we are all color-blind for an instant. However, when viewed through the lenses of race and class, the popularity and marketing of Larry Bird set in sharp relief Boston's relationship to its sports teams and heroes, the malleable relationship between fan and athlete, and the power of white nostalgia.

Discussing Bird's appeal to Boston fans, Jeff Cohen stressed that "for whatever sophistication Boston sports fans think they have, what they really like is to see a guy working hard. They really like blue collar." The hard worker who gives his body and soul to the team goes a long way in Boston. The Boston Bruins, even during the lousy years, have always been loved by the home crowd for their effort and down-and-dirty style. Before Bird's arrival, the Celtics of the 1970s featured redheaded Dave Cowens, an undersized, six-foot-eight-and-a-half center who battled bigger men at the pivot almost nightly. Cowens regularly played one of the game's all-time best, seven-foot-two Kareem Abdul-Jabbar, to a standstill by tirelessly forcing himself between Jabbar and the ball. Boston fell in love with Cowens because of his toughness and intensity.

During our conversation, Cohen pointed out a counterexample to demonstrate Beantown's love affair with the blue-collar athlete. According to Cohen, the sensational Ted Williams was booed throughout his career because he made it look too easy; the game seemed to come to him effortlessly. Consequently, when Williams failed to deliver the winning hit, fans often saw it as a lack of exertion or concentration. His stature as local hero and baseball icon came only in retrospect, in the years following his retirement.

The same spirit of self-sacrifice and hard-nosed perseverance that Cowens had embodied drew Celtics fans to Larry Bird in the following decade. Said Jackie MacMullan of Bird: "He was a workingman's guy . . . a lunch pail [type], and the people in this town loved that . . . the kind of success story people around here just eat up." Jeff Twiss, the Celtics' current vice president of media relations who has been with the organization since 1981, noted that "When Boston drafted Larry . . . [Boston fans] kinda said, gee, he's one of our own. . . . New England's a very stubborn, cynical, hard-working, tough [place]. . . . Larry's that way." As Bird continuously confirmed his reputation as a scrapper willing to bleed for his ball club, the adoration of Boston fans only grew. Bird "started recording triple-doubles, diving on the floor . . . playing forty-eight minutes a night . . . [coming out] to play again . . . after he got whacked . . . and nearly lost his eye; people hear that and they're going, 'Man, they're not paying this guy enough money to play here.' That's a throwback player."

By now, the Larry Bird story of a "small-town boy who made good in the image of Horatio Alger"—to borrow biographer Mark Shaw's description—is well known to hoops aficionados. Growing up in Indiana's tiny West Baden Springs and neighboring French Lick, Bird triumphed over poverty to achieve basketball immortality by working harder than others. An interesting part of Bird's blue-collar image is its sheer authenticity: his workingman credentials are as much literal as symbolic. As a youngster, Bird supplemented his family's limited income by picking up odd jobs and menial employment. Bird's first go-round at college basketball didn't work out at Indiana University. For one thing, money was a factor, and Bird was broke. For another, he was overwhelmed by the size of Indiana University: "Thirty-three thousand students was not my idea of a school—it was more like a whole country," wrote Bird in his autobiography, *Drive*. He hitchhiked home after only twenty-four days at IU and joined French Lick's Street Department. Instead of playing college ball, he picked up trash, repaired streets, and shoveled snow; he claims to have "loved every minute of it."

In his autobiography, Bird portrays himself as a blue-collar man by nature: "If I hadn't been a basketball player, I'd probably be a construction worker or in some other profession, using my hands, and I would have enjoyed that too." At the factories in and around French Lick, like in the Kimball Piano and Organ Company, where his father had worked, Bird learned from his neighbors: "The people . . . put in a hard day's work and then they just enjoyed themselves. I think that is the way it should be: the American Way. . . . I was brought up to work real hard every day and I do believe that's why I try to give 110 percent in every game I play—my workday."

Throughout his Celtics career, Bird demonstrated unwavering allegiance to his humble beginnings. Put off by the often obscene spending tendencies of athletes with new money, he used the cash from his first pro contract to buy an unassuming house and furnish it one room at a time. Said Bird: "The way I live, I'd be happy making ten or twelve thousand a year." Bob Woolf, Larry Bird's first agent, explained that the only financial goal Larry had for his first contract "was a garage full of six-packs and some way that a six-pack could automatically be replaced each time he took one out." Biographer Mark Shaw speculates that Bird's notoriously frugal ways may have contributed to his physical demise as a basketball player. On numerous occasions, Bird's insistence upon doing his own home maintenance probably aggravated chronic back problems. Identifying with Larry Bird was always natural for working-class fans largely because Bird never assimilated into the celebrity lifestyle.

Bird consistently reminded fans of his small-town origins. After winning his first championship in 1981, he told onlookers at the Celtics' championship celebration in Boston: "There's only one place I'd rather be . . . French Lick." The self-proclaimed "Hick from French Lick" returned home for the summer after the last game of the season to be with his mom and take it easy. In 1984, after beating Magic's Lakers for the title, Bird revealed his loyalty to another small town. He dedicated the win to Terre Haute, the home of his alma mater, Indiana State, runner-up to Magic's Michigan State Spartans in the 1979 NCAA championship game.

In more recent years, Bird has polished his speech and purchased nice suits to properly recast himself as a coach and front office executive; however, as a Celtics player, he never strayed far from his roots. He showed up to press conferences in a T-shirt and jeans; he softened his speech with "Jeez" or "I suppose"; he drank cheap beer. He was an apathetic celebrity, a millionaire by default, and he vehemently rejected the clothes, mores, and status markers of those in the same income bracket. Because Bird was such a regular guy, ordinary people felt genuinely connected to him.

Why is it that the "blue collar" tag—the endearing notion of the selfless athlete who labors tirelessly for his team and who has presumably so labored throughout his life—sticks best with white athletes in Boston (and in all parts of the country)? Perhaps this racial coding reflects the enduring belief that white athletes have to work harder than their more "naturally" gifted black peers do. Paul Silas, a black forward playing a stereotypically white brand of earthbound basketball for the Celtics, saw to the essentials that allowed Cowens to gamble on defense and flourish offensively; yet Silas never received the acclaim that he deserved. Cowens, superior to Silas only as a scorer, struggled miserably after Silas left. In the 1950s and 1960s, Bill Russell revolutionized grunge work and ruled the paint like no other player had previously done, but Boston fans could not have cared less. Wrote Harvey Araton and Filip Bondy in *The Selling of the Green: The Financial Rise and Moral Decline of the Boston Celtics*, "Russell was always an underdog against such a physical marvel as Chamberlain. . . . A less discriminatory society would have embraced Russell for the same reasons in the sixties as it did Cowens in the seventies."

Regardless of the racial implications, the notion of a Boston sports culture rooted in a blue-collar tradition requires clarification. Today's Boston is hardly just a working-class, industrial hub trapped behind the times; quite the contrary, as noted above, Boston is generally associated with cutting-edge technology and the intellectual buzz of major universities like Harvard and MIT. Over the last twenty-plus years, the Boston area has emerged as a leader of the new economy, the East Coast's answer to Silicon Valley. Yet Boston is an interesting American city precisely because of this duality: it is a bustling, high-tech epicenter, on the one hand, and, on the other, an inflated small town still married to its industrial past. This tension—often evident between those who come to Boston to work or study and those who are from the area—intersects with the city's sports establishment. True Bostonians love throwback players—those who offer a glimpse of an earlier time—precisely because of this romance with the past.

In 1973, Harvard's own Daniel Bell released a groundbreaking work of sociological prophecy, *The Coming of Post-Industrial Society*. The book rightly anticipated the reconfiguration of the nation's economy from manufacturing to a service-based system driven by the generation of ideas and the development of new technologies. According to Bell, America's budding intellectual economy, dependent upon highly educated service workers, would push the blue-collar labor force to near extinction.

Although Bell's forecast for change has played out in cities across the country, nowhere has this economic, as well as social and cultural, conversion occurred more rapidly or completely than in Boston. In 1950, one out of five people employed in the Greater Boston area worked in textiles or the nondurables industry; by 1990, that proportion had fallen to one out of twenty. Bird's factory-worker buddies from Burke's were swiftly becoming obsolete. In 1990, the percentage of employees in Boston working in the service sector significantly exceeded the national average, while the percentage working in manufacturing was notably below the mean. By 1999, according to the New Economy Index, Massachusetts ranked first in the U.S. "digital economy," ahead even of California, the home of Silicon Valley. Boston is home to many of the country's brightest engineers and scientists, routinely churns out government patents, and serves as a prime destination for venture capitalism.

Yet for all its growth and new economic importance, Boston still often feels like a small town. After opening night of the 2002–03 Celtics' season, I waited for the "T," Boston's metro system, with a platform full of fellow attendees; I grimaced when I saw that the trains coming and going at this hour (around 10:30 p.m.) carried only two cars. Not much past midnight, all public transportation shuts down. "Blue laws," a vestige of Boston's Puritan past, restrict the sale of alcohol on Sundays and keep the bars from operating late. The insularity of Boston's various ethnic enclaves, while destabilized partially by gentrification, remains prominent. Today, police still have trouble probing a crime that occurred in (say) the heavily Irish section of Charleston because a curtain of silence keeps local affairs in the neighborhood. Each of the various suburbs—whether working class or affluent—that form Greater Boston tends toward a sort of self-containment and independence. Often residents of one suburb are knowledgeable about their immediate surroundings yet comparatively uninformed about other areas, including, in many cases, urban Boston.

This small-town quality of Boston, which eased Bird's adjustment to city living, is a double-edged sword, making Boston feel sublimely homey and quaint but painfully cliquish and rigidly segregated all at once. Over the last half decade, in tune with a tumultuous three-century history of social upheaval, rapid racial and ethnic changes have exploded Boston's small town mentality and nostalgic desire for its whiter, "simpler" past.

As quickly as Boston had morphed economically, racially, and ethnically, its demographics had probably transformed even faster. In 1950, Boston's white population totaled 759,000. Forty years later, the white population had declined by more than half, to roughly 361,000. During this same period the proportion of Boston's minority population rose dramatically, from 5.3 percent in 1950 to 40.8 percent in 1990. A massive exodus of the white population from urban Boston led to an enormous population growth in middle- and upper-class suburbs. White people raced north, west, and south, relocating farther and farther away from the metropolis. White flight from urban centers into the suburbs was a national phenomenon; it coincided, not by accident, with the liberalization of U.S. immigration policy after 1965 and another wave of black migration north from the U.S. south. By 1990, urban Boston, as well as the working-class suburbs of Chelsea, Lawrence, and Cambridge (all of which declined in overall population with the evaporation of blue-collar labor), now contained a minority population of over 25 percent. Boston, over the course of forty years, had changed completely. The new economy no longer opened its arms to the third-generation textile worker whose family had settled from Ireland. A population redistribution and the extensive immigration and migration of nonwhites had rendered Boston a hotbed for white nostalgia.

On numerous occasions racial and ethnic tensions have boiled over. In the pre-Bird 1970s, anti-busing riots tore the city apart. Beginning in the fall of 1974, poor white schoolchildren, whose parents couldn't afford to put them in private or parochial schools or move to suburban school districts, were bused to schools in depressed black areas. Simultaneously, poor black children were bused to poor, all-white neighborhoods. Inexplicably, the busing plan was restricted to the low-income sections of town. From 1974 through 1976, a steady stream of violence shook the neighborhoods of Roxbury, South Boston, Charlestown, and Hyde Park. Blacks were attacked in white neighborhoods and retaliated by attacking whites in black areas. Jeff Cohen commented, "I don't think that anyone who lived through Boston in the seventies could say to you with a straight face that this was not a racist town."

In 1989 (toward the end of Bird's playing career), the Charles Stuart debacle again exposed the racial tensions in Boston. As part of a life insurance scam to cash in on his spouse's policy, Stuart murdered his wife and then shot himself before calling the cops. Stuart, who was white, told police that a bearded black man in a jogging suit had entered the couple's Toyota while they were stopped at a red light and had attempted to rob them. When Stuart told the assailant that he didn't have his wallet, the man killed his pregnant wife and then shot Stuart in the stomach before making his getaway into the Mission Hill projects, a black housing development. A massive, highly publicized manhunt ensued. The police aggressively combed the Mission Hill area, strip-searching black men for several days. Finally, under much public pressure, the police apprehended a black man with previous criminal offenses. The case finally broke and the suspect was released after Stuart's brother came forward with details of the scam. Once he was exposed, Charles Stuart jumped to his death off the Tobin Bridge. The Stuart ordeal revealed two racial realities in Boston. First, the city was ready to accept Stuart's story (whites had relocated to the suburbs to protect themselves and their families from this sort of urban crime), and second, police investigated the murders of black residents with relative laxity.

Boston's racial heat burned black players on the Celtics in different ways at different times. In the 1950s and 1960s, Bill Russell anchored the greatest championship run in the history of the sport; between 1957 and 1969 the Boston Celtics captured eleven titles in thirteen years. Through what should have been the most blissful time in an athlete's life, Russell remained remote, irritated, and lonely. He considered Boston the most exclusionary and segregated city that he had ever seen, its biggest problem being its sense of complacency and denial of its tensions. Russell must have seen the explosion of violence in the mid-1970s coming years earlier.

Even given Boston's preference for hockey and the overt racism of the time, Boston's indifference to the Celts and its coldness toward Russell are still astonishing. During an era of unparalleled dominance the Celtics nonetheless struggled to sell enough seats to keep the Boston Garden half full throughout the 1960s. Always a far bigger attraction on the road, they literally had to skip town to feel appreciated. When the phenomenal white playmaker Bob Cousy retired in 1963, the Celtics' home attendance fell significantly—by roughly 1,300 fans per game—even as the Celtics continued raising championship banners. Bill Russell revolutionized the game with his defense and rebounding, bringing the Celtics immortality as the greatest franchise in NBA history. Yet the city rejected him. In many cases it went beyond apathy. Russell was the target of all sorts of hate mail and name calling. Even his house in the suburb of Reading was burglarized on numerous occasions. One time a person entered his home, defecated on his bed, spread feces on the walls, and left, taking nothing from the house.

Russell's style and demeanor clashed with the local white culture. Russell was standoffish in public; he seemed angry much of the time. He didn't talk about the kinds of things that most Bostonians discussed, he didn't hang out in the same places, and he didn't dress the same way. Said Jeff Cohen, "The town just couldn't identify with this big, black activist . . . and Russell, with his aloof personality, made it very difficult to identify with him, anyway. . . . Russell wore frilly shorts and Nehru jackets and was the height of fashion." In the 1960s, Russell was already talking and writing about race, the repressive nature of society, and the hostility and elitism specific to Boston. Moreover, the local media kept Russell on the outside by focusing primarily on Cousy's contributions to the success of the Celtics' dynasty.

In *Shut Out: A Story of Race and Baseball in Boston*, Howard Bryant explores the kind of black players who have a chance in Boston and those who are doomed to a tortured existence. The wrong kind of black man for Boston sports was the serious type, the black man with "shit on his mind." Fans resented center fielder Reggie Smith, who from 1967 to 1973 compiled consistently solid seasons with the Red Sox, because he was a thinker, a black man who pondered his status as a minority member on the team and in Boston and who voiced his discontent to others. Jim Rice, who played his entire spectacular career in Beantown in the 1970s and 1980s, was also too cold, too matter of fact, for the city's taste. When he quarreled with a reporter one day, that was all the confirmation that was needed: this was a hostile black man. The black players seen as laid back and funny fared far better and were received with greater warmth. The eccentric big-game pitcher Luis Tiant, a black Cuban who smoked cigars in the shower and left interviewers in stitches with his sharp humor and thick accent, was a fan favorite in the 1970s.

Today Russell and Boston seem to have made their peace. His accomplishments and centrality to the Celtics' legacy finally have become apparent to Boston fans, who welcome him with a standing ovation when he joins them for home games. Russell can even be seen smiling at courtside. But his time with the organization as a player was never remotely as pleasant.

In the 1980s, the Celtics' next great black center, Robert Parish, felt uneasy in Boston. While it was no longer the 1950s or 1960s, Jackie MacMullan recalls that Parish did not enjoy walking through the North End, a mostly white Boston neighborhood. "He didn't feel welcome there or comfortable there. . . . The North End was five minutes from Boston Garden." One-third of the greatest front line in pro hoops history, a Celtic who lived in Boston in the off-season and contributed charitable work to the community, Parish felt apprehensive in his own backyard.

In September 1990—one year after the Charles Stuart saga and the same year the Boston Red Sox, who resisted integration in Major League Baseball with bitter resolve, started the season with one African American player, outfielder Ellis Burks—the Celtics top draft pick, Dee Brown, experienced a hostile run-in with the police. Brown, a black point guard who rose to fame after he had captured a slam-dunk title by pumping up his Reeboks, was house shopping with his white fiancée, Jill Edmondson, in the one percent black suburb of Wellesley Hills when he was mistaken for a bank robbery suspect. When an employee of a bank that had been robbed by a black male a few days before saw Brown sitting in his car, the manager called the police. Seven police officers surrounded Brown's vehicle, detained him at gunpoint, and searched him while he lay on the ground.

Brown played down the whole incident, attributing the aggressive manner of his detainment to the way the dispatcher had phrased the alert call, and he decided to go ahead with the purchase of a house in Wellesley Hills. The police department apologized, and the town gave him $5,000. Ironically, after Brown had been drafted by the Celtics, his friends had teased him that he was heading "up South" to play ball. Going on even less information than the police had had when they went searching for an anonymous black man in a jogging suit somewhere in Mission Hill, the police sent seven officers to check out Brown, a future millionaire resident of the area.

The overlap of the racial climate in Boston in general and among the Celtics in particular became clear during two ugly seasons right before Bird's rookie year. With the talented likes of John Havlicek, Dave Cowens, JoJo White, and Paul Silas, the 1970s were mostly a good time for the Green. From the 1970–71 season through the 1976–77 campaign, Coach Tom Heinsohn's boys enjoyed impressive winning seasons, finishing at the top of the Eastern Conference five consecutive times and winning two NBA championships. Things came crashing down in the 1977–78 season. Injuries and time had slowed the core players who were still left from the teams that had won two championships earlier in the decade. John Havlicek, the Celtics' top scorer during the 1970s, retired at the end of the year, and an older, disenchanted Cowens was on the way out. Plagued by instability on and off the court, the 1977–78 Celtics not only failed to make the playoffs but they also finished a dismal 32-50. The following year was even worse: amid a second coaching switch in two years and a change in ownership, the Celtics ended the 1978–79 season 29-53. Their brilliant point guard JoJo White, hampered by injured heels, was shipped to the Golden State Warriors for a draft pick. New co-owner John Y. Brown blasphemously went over GM Red Auerbach's head in his business dealings, only to lead the franchise into deeper disarray.

There is another layer to the story of the Celtics' demise at the end of the 1970s. When the Celtics captured a title in 1976, amid the city's anti-busing maelstrom, the Boston Garden emerged as a safe zone and perhaps even a reason for hope. Jackie MacMullan believes the Celts "became sort of the example of how it [racial integration] could work. . . . They really probably galvanized the city to some degree." But would Boston continue to see the Celtics in this encouraging light if the team's tenuous racial balance shifted and the Celtics started losing? During most of the decade, the team maintained a racial equilibrium—roughly half white and half black. JoJo White believed that Red Auerbach "was always smart enough to understand racism is there" and consciously kept this balance to provide a desirable product for the town's fickle fans. But during the horrendous 1977–78 and 1978–79 campaigns, the Celtics had become a mostly black team. The fact that the lowly Celts now had mainly black players would alone have challenged Boston's stubborn fans, but the *type* of black guys who were leading the Celts down the tubes infuriated them.

In 1976, the Celts brought in former UCLA standout Sidney Wicks from the Trail Blazers and then swapped Paul Silas for Curtis Rowe, Wicks's college teammate, in a three-way deal. Both Wicks and Rowe were already tagged as underachieving professionals whose best days had come and gone with their college glory. Before the start of the 1977–78 season, the Celtics traded for Don Chaney and Kermit Washington. At the time of the trade, Washington, a burly power forward, was still serving a sixty-day suspension for striking Rudy Tomjanovich with a punch that nearly ended his life. In other words, the Celtics had traded for the most despised black player in the league, the poster boy for violence in sports. (The Celtics promptly shipped Washington off to the San Diego Clippers before the start of the 1978–79 season.) During the 1978–79 season, John Brown swapped three first-round picks for Bob McAdoo, a high-scoring African American forward who had been labeled a black hole on offense.

This was not the group of guys to bring in to play before the fans at the Boston Garden. The now defunct Garden featured an upper-level section dubbed "Nigger Heaven" by the hysterical racist regulars who occupied the deck. Jeff Cohen cannot recall a single black season-ticket holder during the 1960s and 1970s. This was an all-white club. *Boston Globe* columnist Dan Shaughnessy shared with me that even in 2002 at the Fleet Center, which replaced the Boston

Garden (and now named the TD Banknorth Garden), "it feels like the only black people you see . . . are with the players."

Fans loathed these new Celtics, not just for their losing, but also for the way they carried themselves. Wicks and Rowe promptly landed in Boston's doghouse. Wicks was the sort of player that Boston fans had been programmed to despise: the selfish and lazy contemporary athlete. Jeff Cohen recalls Wicks's very first play as a member of the team: he failed to get to a pass, and the fans "booed him and . . . never stopped booing him from that moment on." While Cohen believes that the booing had nothing to with Wicks's being black—he just "wasn't a Celtic"—Cohen also adds that whatever racist attitudes some fans had tucked away when the Celtics were winning reared their "ugly head" when the team faltered.

Rowe sealed his fate in Boston when he stated, "There's no Ws and Ls [wins and losses] on the paycheck." While many players may think this way, to actually come out and say so is a big step toward career suicide in any town. In Boston, such a statement represents the boldest of insults, the ultimate slap in the face to the Celtics and their fans. For a player to say that he was only out for the money in an organization that stood for all things team, the club that had invented and institutionalized the sixth-man position, was nothing short of sacrilege.

During the painful 1978–79 campaign, Bob McAdoo put up lofty individual numbers while the Celtics won only twenty-nine games. As McAdoo gunned his way to a scoring average of 24.8 points per game, the unimpressed Garden fans chanted, "McAdoo, McAdon't, McAwill, McAwon't." McAdoo became a prime scapegoat, yet he played in only twenty games for the Celts that year and his biggest crime was trying to do too much himself. McAdoo, who believed his image was irreparably damaged in his short time with the Celtics, told Araton and Bondy in *The Selling of the Green* that "black talent in Boston fits in. White talent runs the show." Not coincidentally, when the Celtics opened training camp for the 1979–80 season, Bird's first year, the roster featured eight white players out of the fifteen invitees.

In addition to McAdoo, black former Celtics Wicks, Rowe, White, Charlie Scott, Tom Boswell, and Cedric Maxwell, who each played for the Green in the 1970s, all have voiced discontent with either the organization, the city of Boston, or both.

Even in recent years, the mostly black Celtics have been the targets of nostalgia-driven outrage for behavior deemed un-Celtic. Sportswriters and fans blasted Antoine Walker right out of town for behavior deemed cancerous to the Celtics' long-standing concept of "team." They overlooked that Walker, who was a showboat who sometimes sulked when he played poorly, was also the most consistent and dedicated passer and rebounder on the team during the seven years he spent with the club. While fans used to love seeing Red Auerbach light up a victory cigar while games were still in progress, Walker's giddy behavior and flamboyance were considered utterly unacceptable.

When I asked several longtime Boston fans to reflect upon this late 1970s stretch—referred to contemptuously as the Wicks-Rowe Era—many of them directed the conversation toward a general discussion of the NBA. They recalled that the league's image had been seriously damaged by severe drug problems, and virtually all teams were floundering in financial trouble. A testing policy had yet to be established, so players were using drugs freely. The drugs were also easy to get because owing to limited security, drug dealers were able to slip into the locker rooms. Regardless, the place of the Wicks-Rowe Era in the imagination of some fans is interesting for two reasons. First, it shows that Wicks, Rowe, and other players of that day were associated (for some at least) with drug use and criminality. Second, it illuminates the circumstances surrounding Bird's arrival. When Bird entered the NBA, his task was not simply to revive a troubled franchise, but also to resuscitate an entire league severely racked by a racially coded image nightmare. The Celtics were not the only ones desperately awaiting white rescue.

To grasp Bird's full importance to fans and to the NBA, one must consider the racial politics and state of professional basketball prior to his arrival in 1979. From a business perspective, the 1970s were, to say the least, trying times for professional basketball. By merging in 1976 with the ABA, its upstart rival, the NBA had taken a huge gamble. In the ABA, the NBA acquired a chaotic, small-potatoes operation that had notoriously conducted business under the table, and neither sports fans nor newspaper writers nor television executives seemed to care about it. Yet despite the fact that fans were not buying at the time, the NBA scored a brilliant black product that would later be sold to the world.

Though the ABA featured several phenomenal white players, the league celebrated basketball as a black sport and subculture in the late 1960s and 1970s. With the advent of the three-point line and a shortage of effective big men, ABA teams spread the floor, relying on one-on-one play and fast breaking for their offense. Showmanship and innovation took center stage. According to the legendary Julius "Dr. J" Erving, players in the ABA, clad in vibrant, multicolored uniforms and sporting heaping Afros, would simply "open up and let . . . [their] creative juices flow." This freewheeling, full-court style of play looked a lot like playground basketball, and when the ABA, hoping to snatch the newest talent away from the NBA, allowed teams to draft players directly out of high school or before they had completed college, the league gained even more of an edge.

A look at pro basketball's first dunk contest offers both a sense of the ABA's cutting-edge black style and its blatantly low-budget atmosphere. In 1976, some of basketball's all-time finest aerial performers gathered at Denver's McNichols Arena. Contest winner Julius Erving, who leaped from the foul line for probably the most famous dunk in history, and runner-up David Thompson, who executed a breathtaking 360-degree slam, flashed their stuff for $1,000 and a new stereo before a panel of judges that featured an elderly lady with season tickets and a local concert promoter.

Today's NBA, with its flamboyance, one-on-one play, three-point shooting, thunderous dunking, and cradle-robbing tendencies on draft day is built upon many of the innovations introduced by the ABA. Nike recently reminded us of this connection with sneaker commercials set in 1975; they feature current NBA players/playas superimposed onto ABA games, dicing opponents to the music of 1970s funk icons Bootsy Collins and George Clinton, along with new school incarnate Snoop Dogg.

But in its day the ABA constantly struggled to stay above water. Its pro-black intensity, playground demeanor, tricolored basketball, and halftime entertainment turned off traditionalists. Many team names were too hokey to be taken seriously. Consider such questionable calls as the Anaheim Amigos, the Miami Floridians, the Minnesota Muskies, and the Pipers of Pittsburgh and Minnesota. During the ABA's first season in 1967, the average attendance per game failed to break three thousand. Players had to take flights with three stopovers and get by on food budgets of $7 a day, only to play before a few hundred spectators in a nontelevised game in an obscure, often makeshift gymnasium. Over time, interest increased slightly as more talent joined this hodgepodge federation, but it was clear from the onset that the ABA was incapable of unassisted survival.

By absorbing its struggling rival, the NBA saved some franchises and several careers at the expense of its own reputation. The image of professional basketball in the pre-Bird 1970s was that of a sport that had failed morally and socially. As noted above, drug use was extensive, and there was criticism that players who left school early or skipped college altogether were hurting themselves and the league. With a 70 percent black NBA by 1979, much of this grumbling was racially coded. No one raises an eyebrow when athletes who play baseball, tennis, or golf skip college or leave early. Yet suddenly basketball players were doing something awful. Too often fans and sportswriters conceived of the NBA as a rotting sports league trapped under a big, black cloud of general delinquency.

The talent of the 1970s also changed. The departed stars of the previous decade left fans with a sense of loss. George Gervin, Kareem Abdul-Jabbar, and John Havlicek, though undeniably great, were a notch or two below Elgin Baylor, Wilt Chamberlain, and Oscar Robertson. Some of the decade's most accomplished players—guys like rebound specialist Truck Robinson or passing whiz Kevin Porter—are unrecognizable to today's younger fans. No dynasties emerged in this disjointed era; there was not a single flagship team. A far bigger dilemma for the league—and what was keeping the fans away—was the disappearance of the white superstar. By the 1978–79 season, none of the top-tier white players was still in his prime. Major draws like Jerry West, Billy Cunningham, Rick Barry, Dave Cowens, John Havlicek, Bill Walton, Dave DeBusschere, Bill Bradley, and Jerry Lucas had all retired or slowed down significantly.

Given the troubled state of the NBA and America's love affair with football, the NBA struggled miserably in the television market throughout the 1970s and even into the next decade. Baseball and football were prime-time sports; basketball, rarely shown live, could be flipped on while a commercial was showing during a rerun. CBS elected to tape the 1980 NBA finals between the L.A. Lakers and the Philadelphia 76ers rather than air the series live. The tape-delayed games did not come on until 11:30 at night, when fans in major television cities could finally witness Magic Johnson's heroic 42-point masterpiece while he was playing the pivot for the injured Abdul-Jabbar. In 2002, the NBA signed a six-year, $4.6 billion television contract with several networks, but in 1979, it could get only $400,000 for national broadcast rights from a second-rate cable station that later became USA.

Attendance was abysmal as well. By the end of the 1980–81 season, sixteen out of twenty-three teams had reported financial losses, some of which were so severe that the smaller franchises were nearly forced to fold. Forty-two percent of all arena seats were empty that season.

The NBA was a sports league in dire straits. Unbeknownst to Bird, who never paid much attention to the NBA before turning pro, the timing of his entrance was impeccable. Larry Bird's arrival signaled a fresh start for the NBA, sparking a return to prominence for the league's greatest franchise and fostering an era of white inclusion and rehabilitation in professional basketball.

While Bird was still in college, long before he had set foot on the parquet of the Garden, Boston fans and the Celtics organization invested heavily—financially and emotionally—in their Great White Hope. Ignoring apparently inconsequential league memos explicitly instructing teams not to draft Larry Bird because he was headed back to school, the defiant Celtics front office selected him anyway. One summer later, the notoriously tightfisted franchise, after aggressive contract talks with Bird's agent, made Larry Legend the highest-paid player on the Celtics and the highest-paid rookie in the history of professional sports: $650,000 a season for five years. Bird had yet to play one minute of professional hoops.

As the national sports media debated Bird's potential as a pro, the usual caveats that accompanied white players that looked really good in college circulated: "He's too slow"; "He can't defend"; "He can't jump"; "He can't move that well"; "He's not athletic enough." These warnings fell upon deaf ears in the Boston area; desperate Celts fans wanted so badly for Bird to work out that they refused to listen. Rewarding the organization's faith in Bird, the fans also believed in the young player, purchasing a record six thousand season tickets before the start of the season. As Bird began to prove himself every bit worthy of all the hype, Celtics fans flocked to the Garden in unprecedented numbers. An arena that had been filled only to half capacity while the team had won eleven championships in the 1950s and 1960s was now consistently full. Less than halfway through Bird's rookie season, the Celtics sold out the Garden, and it stayed that way through Bird's twilight years of the early 1990s. In the words of one long-time Celtics fan perched at the bar at O'Reilly's Restaurant and Pub outside the Fleet Center on opening night of the 2002–03 season, from the very beginning, Bird was "holier than God" to Boston fans.

The Larry Bird epidemic quickly swept across the nation. Jeff Twiss recalls the cross-coastal popularity the Celtics enjoyed: "[It was] like the Beatles' following. . . . Everywhere you turn, it's green and white shirts; this is people in L.A., Golden State, out in Oakland, in Denver. . . . And the media flocked to them. . . . Suddenly we have more press than we can handle." Even today, this fervor endures on a national scale. White collegiate culture—a slice of society predisposed toward the celebration of white folk heroes, musicians in particular—immortalizes Bird's legacy. Like Grateful Dead windshield decals and bumper stickers, photos of Larry Legend and Celtics paraphernalia adorn the rooms of white college kids and those who identify with this culture or time in one's life. This is not simply a Boston thing; it's a white thing. I visited a friend at Georgetown University in 2001 and stayed with him and his buddies in an off-campus house in suburban Washington DC. As my friend showed me around the place, I noticed a common theme in the bedroom decor of his housemates: American flags and Bird posters were on the walls, often even side by side. These kids weren't from Massachusetts either; they weren't even New Englanders; they were simply young white guys. Throughout my time in college, during visits to friends at several colleges and universities across the country, I always noticed that wherever there existed centers of white collegiate culture—fraternity houses and preppy college bars—one could find Larry Bird memorabilia.

Many white fans old enough to have followed professional basketball in the 1950s and 1960s lost interest in the game in the 1970s and didn't get back into the sport until Bird's arrival in 1979. As if their membership card had suddenly expired, these fans again stopped caring after Bird's departure in the early 1990s. Even younger white fans, turned off by the showboating, individualism, and jumbo contracts of today's NBA players, date the start of their disillusionment to Bird's retirement.

As indicated above, it's hard to ignore the roles of racial identification and nostalgia in fueling the country's infatuation with Larry Legend. Whiteness has been critical to Bird's lasting iconography and his ability to garner a following as far west as California, home of the more dominant Lakers of the 1980s. Dan Shaughnessy, ever wary of reducing Bird's appeal or contribution to the game to a matter of racial preference, conceded that "having a white superstar definitely aided and abetted the explosion in popularity of the Celtics." He mused further: "Around the country, there was a perception [that] the game had been taken over by black athletes. Here's a guy who could not only compete [but also] he's one of the best players in the league. . . . The white population probably gets some sort of extra thrill out of that."

In the 1980s, the Celts often started three white players—Bird, Kevin McHale, and Danny Ainge—and they fielded a mostly white bench. Riding the pine and contributing to varying degrees were Jerry Sichting, Rick Carlisle, Greg Kite, Scott Wedman, Mark Acre, Jim Paxson, Fred Roberts, and Bill Walton. Most remarkable, however—and precisely what Shaughnessy believes charged some white fans—was that the Celtics assembled primarily white teams that blew away the competition. The 1985–86 Celtics, featuring eight white and four black players, rank as one of the best teams in NBA history. While eight of ten players in the league were black, almost seven out of ten players on the Celtics were white. Led by a black coach, K. C. Jones, the Celts compiled a 40-1 home record, won twenty-nine straight games at the Boston Garden, and beat the Rockets for the championship, finishing with a 15-3 playoff record. Bird captured the MVP and Walton, "Sixth Man of the Year" honors.

As the *Boston Globe*'s beat reporter for the Celtics from 1982 to 1986, Shaughnessy sat courtside each night:

> You would regularly see five white guys on the court and that got people's attention. I can recall guys coming down from the other side of the press table [the visiting team's reporters], saying there were five white guys out there on the Celtics. . . . Of course, we [the Boston reporters] stopped noticing. You stop noticing the same way you stop noticing how many black players there are.

The fans and reporters regularly watching the Celtics literally became desensitized to the sight of an entirely white group in action. In reviewing Celtics games from the 1980s, I sometimes felt that I had entered a sort of basketball twilight zone. During a first-round game against the Bulls in the 1986 playoffs, the Celtics put a team of five white guys on the floor, and the TV commentator announced that the Celtics had just inserted their "fast unit."

The belief that the Celtics deliberately pursued white players and consciously wanted a whiter team than the rest of the NBA circulated extensively in the national media. According to Shaughnessy, "It was good that K. C. [Jones] was the coach because it certainly helped to diffuse [these sorts of theories]." Any time the Celtics' record on race was called into question or a reporter accused Auerbach of playing to the town, the GM and his supporters reflexively reminded critics to brush up on their history. The Celtics were the first team to draft a black player (Duquesne star Chuck Cooper in 1950), the first club to put five black players on the floor at the same time (Bill Russell, Willie Naulls, K. C. Jones, Sam Jones, and Tom "Satch" Sanders during the 1963–64 season), and the first NBA franchise to hire a black head coach (Bill Russell in 1966). While these precedents undoubtedly denote a progressive outlook, too often they are employed blindly to entertain and then promptly quash any discussion of the Celtics and race.

The unusually high number of white players that landed in Boston prompted different responses from whites and blacks. Many black basketball fans in Boston identified more closely with the Lakers, the preeminent team of the 1980s that featured an almost entirely black group. The Philadelphia 76ers also attracted a large black following with a nucleus of gifted, flamboyant black players like Dr. J, Moses Malone, Darryl Dawkins, World B. Free, and later Charles Barkley, who reveled in a sense of black bravado.

For many white fans, in Boston and in all parts of the country, the Celtics were fulfilling a privately and not so privately held fantasy that white ballplayers could still outplay black guys. At the Boston Garden, this "dirty little secret" never stayed under wraps for very long. Whenever Kevin McHale blocked the shot of an opposing black player, the crowd would erupt in a brand of raucous applause reserved especially for these moments. Jackie MacMullan remembers some of the Celtics letting her in on the fact that for Robert Parish, a perennial All-Star and arguably the second most important player on the 1980s Celtics, it was "stinging" to hear the overwhelming ovation whenever he was replaced by his backup, Bill Walton. MacMullan attributes this response to Walton's magnetic personality and fan excitement that the oft-injured center was healthy enough to play. Nonetheless, that Boston devotees went gaga for Bill Walton, who only joined the team for a short stay, suggests a readiness to take him in as one of their own.

By "outplaying" the league's black guys, Bird's Celtics helped to enact the drama of white dominance and fulfill the (implicit or explicit) desire of putting black people in their place. This, then, raises a question: Was it the Celtics-Lakers rivalry that resurrected the NBA in the 1980s, or was it simply the rise of the Celtics? Could the Celtics have had an equally compelling rivalry against any "black" team or against an array of elite black teams? After all, it was Bird and the Celtics that galvanized white fans and revived interest in the NBA; it was not Julius Erving's NBA debut or Magic Johnson's arrival.

Of course, the Celtics-Lakers showdown did make for brilliant theater. Just as the Celtics energized white fans, so the Lakers empowered black fans. In addition to the black-white dynamic, geographical, historical, and cultural factors contributed significantly to this dazzling rivalry.

When Magic Johnson, Bird's college adversary, landed in L.A. the same year Bird made it to Boston, the league scored the perfect foil for its blue-collar everyman. Magic Johnson embodied black cool: he wore sunglasses, his smile melted hearts, and on the basketball court, he saw without looking. After real estate mogul Jerry Buss bought the L.A. franchise in the late 1970s, the Lakers went Hollywood. The "Lake Show" presented the prettiest dancers, the coolest kids in the stands, and (as Magic dubbed their offense) "Showtime" on the court—the sort of Tinseltown pretentiousness that New Englanders loathed almost as much as they loved their Celtics. The bright, gaudy, and comparatively high-tech L.A. Forum contrasted astoundingly with the musty, non-air-conditioned, and somewhat dilapidated Boston Garden.

Film and pop culture critic Todd Boyd likens the full-court attack of the 1980s Lakers to jazz music in its improvisational form, while he compares the more methodical, half-court approach of the Celtics to classical music, "wherein performance is centered on the replication of a supposedly superior style." While the quality of play and the intensity of the competition in and of themselves made the Celtics-Lakers rivalry breathtaking, the style differences further stimulated the fans. The battle between the hip, freewheeling black Lakers and the blue-collar, formulaic white Celtics embodied whatever sort of clash or contrast a fan could imagine. (That the Celts' success also hinged upon the team's first-rate black talent was edited out of the story.) It could be jazz musicians versus classical composers, celebrities versus the common man, the scene in L.A. against the serenity of New England, Kareem's shaved dome versus Larry's floppy mullet, doing it with pizzazz or simply getting the job done. The strength of this rivalry, coupled with its inherent racial and cultural elements, resurrected interest in professional hoops and even extended the league's popularity overseas. When Magic's Lakers and Larry's Celtics met for the last time in the finals in 1987, the games were aired in twenty-seven countries.

Although the Celtics may have been the team of choice for whites—specifically the older, more conservative audience—plenty of white fans jumped on the Lakers' bandwagon. The mainstreaming of blackness in the 1980s helped to facilitate this leap. Arguably the biggest star of each major wing of the entertainment industry was a black man: Michael Jackson in music, Bill Cosby in television, and Eddie Murphy in film. Each of these artists parlayed a nonthreatening brand of blackness particularly well suited for mainstream acceptance. The pulp genre of blaxploitation of the 1970s gave way to Eddie Murphy's Axel Foley character, a funnier, softer badass, and in the 1980s everyone went to the *Beverly Hills Cop* movies. Magic Johnson, with his happy-go-lucky smile and warm personality, fit the mold of the nonconfrontational and endearing black superstar.

Ironically, although Bird's game was stereotypically white—his craftiness and outside shot compensated for unexceptional athleticism—his approach to hoops mirrored a style of basketball associated with blackness. Bird was both a showman and a ruthless competitor, committed to dominating and humbling his opponents. His arrogance could be dazzling: when he launched a jump shot that he knew was money, he sometimes just walked away while the ball was still in mid-flight, no confirmation needed. Bird is one of the game's all-time biggest trash-talkers. At the first-ever All-Star weekend three-point contest, Bird walked over to the other contestants and asked who would be finishing second—before going on to capture the crown.

The ultimate talkers always call victories ahead of time. Against Atlanta, with the series tied 3–3 in the second round of the 1988 playoffs, Bird guaranteed a game 7 victory; he then proceeded to hit nine of ten from the field in the fourth quarter to best a red-hot Dominique Wilkins and the Hawks. Bird even talked trash to the local reporters covering the Celts. (Of course, he made good on it.) After injuring a finger in a bar fight during the 1985 conference finals against the Sixers, Bird was practicing with his fingers heavily taped. When Shaughnessy asked doubtfully if he was going to play like that in the game, Bird informed the reporter that he could tape up his entire hand and still outshoot him. He then had the trainer tape his shooting hand into a fist and challenged Shaughnessy to a shooting competition: one hundred free throws at $5 a shot. The two took turns shooting in rounds of ten. Bird, resting the ball on the palm of his bound right fist and guiding it with his left hand, made eighty-six shots, and Shaughnessy owed him $160. After the reporter paid up the next day before the Sixers game, Bird, like a cruel older brother, placed the eight twenty-dollar bills in his sock and played the whole game with the money in his shoe.

Being dissed is the ultimate violation of one's manhood in the eyes of many young black men; Bird too internalized this value. During his amateur and professional playing career Bird beat people up. He rumbled in taverns, he fought at Indiana State, and when he entered the NBA, he mixed it up with anyone from no-names like the Sixers' Mark Iavaroni to resident tough guy Bill Laimbeer to NBA legends like Kareem Abdul-Jabbar and Julius Erving. During the 1985 conference finals against the Philadelphia 76ers Bird damaged his always tender shooting hand while slugging it out in a Boston bar a few nights after game 2. Dan Shaughnessy believes that the re-injury to his already mangled right index finger, sustained during this fight, hampered his shooting ability for the rest of his career.

Regardless of what was real and what was imagined about the Celtics, the NBA happily pushed the same plotline for the team: the Celts were the guardians of old-school team basketball. In an NBA-produced segment summarizing the Celtics' 1986 first-round playoff series with the Bulls, which aired during game 5 of the Celts' 1987 playoff matchup with the Pistons, the NBA highlighted the (implied) racial difference between a legitimate team—the Celtics—and a one-man show—the Bulls. The narrator of the segment billed the series "a classic battle: the athlete against the team," in which the athlete (Michael Jordan), through spectacular individual play, managed to leave his mark on "the fabled parquet floor" of the Boston Garden but failed to oust the hometown Celts. Ultimately, the "Celtic tradition . . . and . . . old Celtic magic" proved too much for one person to overcome, and "while the athlete got his record [scoring an unprecedented 63 points in a single playoff game], the team got its win."

The racially driven marketing of the Celtics and Larry Bird coincided with technological change and the visionary direction of David Stern, who took over as league commissioner in 1984. If video killed the radio star, it made the NBA superhero. By the time the NBA had moved into prime time, networks had already mastered the technologies that would bring out the best in televised sports. With the refinement of instant replay and slow motion, basketball fans were given the tools necessary to fully digest the milliseconds of athletic brilliance that passed before them all too quickly. Highlight shows—a television trend gaining steam in the 1980s—converted lopsided games into thrilling spectacles by simply piecing together the finest moments of play. The NBA under Stern's leadership followed the highlight show model and began releasing all sorts of pseudo-documentaries on teams, superstars, up-and-comers, trends, and the like that were basically highlight reels set to music and sometimes accompanied by narration. The *NBA Superstars* series presented four- or five-minute MTV-like music videos of a star player's most exciting moments, set to a particular song that fit thematically with the athlete's "persona." In one piece, Charles Barkley dunks and struts provocatively to George Thorogood's "Bad to the Bone," while in another, Larry Bird swooshes jumpers straight from the heartland to the tune of John Mellencamp's "Small Town." NBA athletes were now literally video stars, plugged as character types.

In NBA Entertainment's documentary, *Larry Bird: A Basketball Legend,* Bird is presented as the little white guy who could. Listening to narrator Daniel Stern, the voice of innocence inside the head of Kevin Arnold, played by Fred Savage on the *The Wonder Years,* one could almost believe that Larry Bird and Kevin could have a thing or two in common. Insecurity, social awkwardness, and small-town naiveté made both of their lives difficult at times. While shyness complicated Bird's adjustment to the spotlight, nerves seemed to do in Kevin any time he tried to tell a girl how he really felt. The similarities may not go much further; after all, Bird was a six-foot-nine basketball superman and Arnold, a love-struck teenager who looked about four-foot-ten on camera. Yet the video makes us root for Bird for the same reason we pull for Kevin Arnold: both are cast as major underdogs. Bird, an average Joe with limited natural athletic abilities and raised in humble surroundings, toiled doggedly to overcome adversity and make it big as a ballplayer.

The subplot of the triumphant underdog/everyman in *Larry Bird: A Basketball Legend* mixes with another story line: Bird as basketball's equivalent of apple pie. The film's imagery and narration, mostly a collection of analogies and clichés, align Bird with all things sacred and tradition-based in sports and America. Larry Bird, "a gangly country boy . . . resembling a twentieth-century

Huckleberry Finn . . . would play with the passion of the underdog, the purity of tradition, [and, after a stellar career with the Celtics as] the savior of their proud tradition, he would . . . leave behind . . . a legacy."

A television piece entitled *History of the NBA*, which aired on HBO in 1990, opens with a montage that matches images of basketball hoops in different environments with shots of the NBA's all-time best in action. Produced by HBO Sports and NBA Entertainment, the documentary's voiceover informs us that while the game has grown and changed over time, it retains a "simple purity." With these words, the film cuts to a shot of two horses passing a basket mounted on a grass field (presumably on a farm) and then goes to a slow-motion sequence of Larry Bird pulling up for a three on Charles Barkley. Like horses and farmland, Larry Bird represents what is still untainted in America.

After the Boston Celtics beat the Detroit Pistons in the 1987 Eastern Conference finals, Detroit's Dennis Rodman, a rookie who had just been torched by Bird's hot shooting, told reporters that Bird was overrated because of his race. Rodman's teammate, Isiah Thomas, agreed. Much was made of Rodman's statement and Thomas's agreement; the two, who were labeled racists by the media, later called a press conference to rescind their statement and apologize to Bird (who didn't seem to care either way). If Bird were black, he would still have been a phenomenal basketball player; his gifts were undeniable. However, he would not have meant the same thing to white hoops fans nationwide, to a desperate NBA, and to the legacy of the Celtics organization.

In large part, Bird's national popularity and lasting legacy were propelled by an impulse that is probably inside of all white fans. It is simultaneously a frantic desire to be included and a patronizing belief that the white athlete can restore the sanctity that has been traditional to sports and reverse the damage caused by black irreverence. This is the motivation behind the long-lasting phenomenon in sports of rooting for the white guy; it combines a nostalgic remembrance of how sports used to be with anger over what's become of them. The NBA Entertainment videos tapped into this very theme of the white underdog/throwback—and made Celtics fans all the more bitter about the Wicks-Rowe Era.

In the music video for the 1992 hit single "Jump Around," Everlast, lead lyricist of the white rap group House of Pain, donned a Larry Bird jersey. That year, House of Pain's debut album was one of the top five in hip-hop. Just as white hoops fans have positioned Bird as the white savior in basketball, so white hip-hoppers use him as a symbol of white inclusion and substance in the black-dominated realm of rap music. House of Pain and its alignment with Bird, the Celtics, and all things Irish (the group routinely wore Notre Dame gear as well) offered white kids a point of entry into a black space, as well as a sense of credibility. This accessibility and hip-hop cachet is a generous offering—one that is eagerly and gratefully accepted when whites are entering a world into which they have been looking from the outside.

That hip-hop is not, by design at least, a white language always becomes painfully obvious when black and white guys are singing along to a rap song and reach a part with the word "nigga." While the black guys recite the word at the same volume and with the same intensity as they used for the other words, the white guys fumble uncomfortably, lowering their voices, mumbling the word, omitting it all together, pausing for a bit and joining in again later, or going for it (albeit often with a wince). Although white folks have been an integral part of hip-hop since the genre's birth, both on the business and consumer ends, hip-hop constitutes a black art form that allows black artists to communicate for and about the black community. White fans have, for the most part, simply been listening in on the dialogue, enjoying it, and living the rap lifestyle vicariously.

Just as Larry Bird made basketball accessible to white hoops buffs, white rappers (who know better than to use the N-word) have made hip-hop more personal for white music fans. But while House of Pain and Eminem have brought hip-hop closer to home for many whites (appropriating a black genre in the process), Larry Bird not only brought basketball closer to home but he also brought it *back* home, reclaiming occupancy and preeminence in an area whites had originated and once dominated. This is the element of white nostalgia that helps drive "Bird Mania" and why whites in pro basketball and whites in hip-hop are not part of the same phenomenon. Whereas rap music descends from reverberations of black resistance in the South Bronx and Harlem, as well as from earlier forms of black music, basketball started in 1891 as a tool for socializing European immigrants at the YMCAS.

That said, the same desire for white relevance and underdog enthusiasm that sparked many Bird fans has helped facilitate Eminem's rise to the top of rap music. Eminem isn't simply white marketing fluff; he, like Bird, is an incredible talent who at times embodies certain traits associated with blackness. His lyrics are original, biting, and poetically sophisticated, and when mixed with producer Dr. Dre's beats, his music can consume the listener.

Eminem got so big that he is now considered one of the most consistent and influential stars in the genre's history. The best-selling album in hip-hop music history belongs to Eminem (*The Slim Shady LP*). *Rolling Stone*'s 2002 readers' poll of the greatest one hundred albums of all time, based on the responses of twenty-three thousand music fans, featured only two rap albums: Eminem's eight-times platinum *The Marshall Mathers LP* and his 2002 follow-up, *The Eminem Show*. For a while, the voice of the black experience—rap music—was the voice of a white guy. Eminem's hip-hop ascendancy suggests the latest occurrence of a long-running trend in the music business, well-documented by Nelson George in *The Death of Rhythm and Blues*: black culture creates a genre and ultimately relinquishes control as white culture takes the genre over, exploiting and expanding it. The Great White Hope phenomenon appears even in areas of culture that originally never were white.

While Eminem's work is highly original, his authenticity and his acceptance in the rap game are predicated on his mastery of an African American vernacular—the accent, slang, tonality, and persona of a black rapper. Herein lies the irony in Eminem's whitening of hip-hop: white fans love him largely for how "black" he appears. Similarly, Bird fans reveled in the fact that Larry Bird, whose "throwback" ways supposedly functioned to offset black flamboyance, had internalized the sort of trash-talking and badass swagger generally associated with black basketball.

Larry Bird holds the extraordinary distinction of being the only man Magic Johnson ever feared on the basketball court. As a hoops marvel who played his best when it mattered most, Bird's brilliance lay precisely in what he could do on the court (everything). However, his enormity in Boston, his value to the NBA, and the mystical space he occupies in the imagination of fans speak to the sociology of Boston, the NBA, and popular culture. While Larry Bird meant many things to his fans—a "throwback" ballplayer, an everyman (only taller), a fantasy fulfilled, a moral savior for a debauched team and league—the only thing Bird ever seemed to notice (unlike Eminem, who self-consciously parlays his whiteness into celebrity) was the scoreboard. Still, as Eminem today gives white rap fans a similar face with which to identify among all the black faces in the crowd, Bird's legacy offers fans the same munificent gift—belonging, visibility, the image of a triumphant underdog—and a nostalgic link to basketball's "purer" past.

5. Legendary college coach Bob Knight, then at Indiana University, directs Hoosier star Steve Alford in 1987. In 2000 Knight was fired after his abuses of power came under media scrutiny and the Hoosiers were no longer a force in the NCAA tournament. Knight, who ruled the Bloomington campus for twenty-nine years and symbolized control in a sport many believed to be irreparably damaged by undisciplined, showboating athletes, moved to Texas Tech. © Tom Hirschfeld, Arbutus Yearbook, Indiana University.

5 My Dad Was a Military Man

Bob Knight, Paternalism, and Hoosier History

My Degree Is From Knight School

Sign appearing at a campus rally for Bob Knight after he was fired as head coach of Indiana University

Second-year coach Mike Davis finally earned some short-lived respect by taking his Indiana University team to the 2002 NCAA title game (against the University of Maryland). That respect was not easy to come by in a state that derives much of its enormous pride from its local history and traditions, particularly in basketball. Any break from the past is met with hardy skepticism, if not downright contempt, from the conservative core of Indiana. By attempting to forge a fresh identity for the beloved Hoosiers, Davis, the first black head coach of any sport at IU and the successor to coaching legend Bob Knight, had embarked on the boldest of challenges.

Knight, who had ruled with absolute authority over the Bloomington campus for twenty-nine years, had been banished from the sidelines almost two years before the 2002 championship matchup, but his presence loomed everywhere. Knight had recruited many of the Indiana players competing for the 2002 crown, and several of them retained a loyalty and sense of indebtedness to "the General." After Knight's firing in September 2000, several of the Hoosiers who competed unsuccessfully for Davis's first title threatened to transfer and lobbied teammates to join them.

Davis's team even retained the old-school look typical of Knight's boys. The Indiana Hoosiers of 2002 were whiter, ganglier, and more military looking than the players on the other tournament teams, and they dressed far more simply. While the Maryland Terrapins donned fancy jerseys with red, black, and yellow checkered trim and baggy shorts with giant school logos, the Hoosiers sported their classic red and whites; the back of the Indiana jersey listed only the player's number. Not an attempt at hip-hop chic, the "retro" appearance of the Hoosier uniforms didn't reclaim the past but simply continued it: the uniforms just hadn't changed much over the years. The omission of names on the jerseys—a literal and intentional rejection of individuality within a team sport—also communicated this same extension of tradition.

Constant collisions with the force of the past made Davis's brief career as head coach of Indiana University tumultuous and onerous. After IU dismissed the beloved, oft-forgiven Knight for the last of many physical altercations with a member of the school community, the university erupted in violent protest. Knight's adversaries on campus were forced into hiding, while disgruntled alumni sought legal action to undo the unthinkable firing. When Davis was named interim head coach, many Knight diehards saw Davis as an unacceptable replacement for a local icon. Nostalgic Knight supporters held "We Miss Knight" signs during games, while the hostile ones called for Davis's head, flooding his e-mail account with hundreds of hate-filled, often racist letters and threats. Davis eventually stopped opening his e-mail altogether. Even the 2002 NCAA tournament proved bittersweet for the young coach, as many Hoosiers fans maintained that a scheming Davis, Knight's assistant coach, had treacherously advanced to the championship round with the General's men.

What, then, was so threatening, so upsetting and unacceptable, about Knight's departure and Davis's appointment that it prompted such hostility? Knight's leaving represented what hadn't taken place in the Indiana University basketball program in almost thirty years: change. While the world of basketball (mirroring transformations in the broader society) had changed all around Bob Knight over the course of three decades, Bob Knight—his philosophy, coaching style, and recruiting strategy—stayed the same. Bob Knight's Indiana University held strong as the last mainstay of half-court, rural white basketball in a game completely redefined by black players, artistry, and style. By remaining in place, Knight preserved the mores, ethics, and vibrations of an earlier time, the era in which he had come of age. The time is perhaps best summarized by a picture on the back cover of the 1970 media guide for the Army basketball team: the head coach of Army at the time, Bob Knight, an austere young man coming into his thirties, and team captain Doug Clevenger, wearing an officer's hat and coat, stand in front of a statue of General Patton. The caption reads, "Leadership Determination Courage." Fifteen years after this picture was published, former Marquette University coach Al McGuire, a friend and coaching colleague of Knight, identified the strata of the United States who steadfastly loved and admired Bobby Knight and what he symbolized as those who "believe in discipline . . . crew hair cuts . . . the 40s and the 50s, [and] General Patton." These are the elements of the past that Indiana fans believe Knight protected during his time in Bloomington, and this is precisely why many basketball fans believe that the game desperately needs him. Where many see basketball as a sport wrecked by individualism and rebellious, undisciplined black youth from fatherless homes, at IU Bob Knight represented the consummate father figure and an unrelenting symbol of control. On a local level, the way Knight coached, the style of basketball he taught, and his entire approach to the coaching profession and to the sport preserved a racially entangled part of both basketball and state history in Indiana, an era of containment for which many people still long.

In college and pro basketball, ball clubs often take on specific racial identities. Though the influx of foreign players over the last decade has complicated and enriched the racial mix of basketball, at the professional level race is and has always been a binary category. We talk about basketball—its players, teams, and coaches—literally in black and white. By 1970, basketball was fast becoming a game dominated by black athletes, and by now the notion of black hoops supremacy has indelibly imprinted itself in the psyche of sports fans. Today, the NBA is roughly 80 percent black, and Division I men's college basketball is roughly 60 percent so (and is even higher among the top-tier programs). At the televised level, basketball is a black sport and cultural institution. Thus when a team fields a notable number of white ballplayers—and this number can be as small as five or six on a fourteen-man professional roster—fans and sportswriters immediately take notice. These "white" teams, of course, still have black members—perhaps even a black majority—yet the blackness of the ball club is often negated by the conspicuous white presence. The Celtics of the 1980s are considered a white team, and, indeed, they were whiter than the rest of the NBA. This racial designation, however, masked the importance of several essential black members on the Celtics' roster—stars like Robert Parish, Cedric Maxwell, and Dennis Johnson and their magnificent African American coach, K. C. Jones.

The racialization of certain clubs often stems from perception as much as from fact. Identities are drawn from both the literal racial composition of the athletes and coaches and the team's personality—its playing style, attitude, dress, rituals, and interactions among teammates and with the opposition. Whether a team is liked or disliked or is considered smart or stupid, consistent or inconsistent, boring or fun, or dirty or scrappy has a lot to do with its racial identity. This identity has an impact on how fans and reporters alike talk, think, and write about a team and its players. It is often said, for example, that "Bird's Celtics were a throwback bunch, a pure team, a smart ball club." Indeed they were, but what made them any purer or sharper a team than Magic's Lakers?

Though blackness is the norm in basketball, the loaded meaning of "blackness" in the everyday ensures that it leads to all sorts of assumptions and stereotypes about black players and "black" teams. Whereas whiteness in everyday life is treated as normal because whites are the majority (Sylvester Stallone, for example, is an action star, while Wesley Snipes is a *black* action star), the same criteria do not apply in basketball, where blacks make up the majority and whites the minority. In hoops, blackness carries one set of meanings and expectations and whiteness carries another.

In the minds of fans and sportswriters, then, there are "black" teams and "white" teams. Clubs like Larry Bird's Boston Celtics and the Princeton Tigers exist in the imagination of fans as "white" teams. In heavily Mormon Utah, where white players are always dramatically overrepresented on the collegiate and professional levels, the home teams are often described using a loaded array of "white" adjectives: heady, disciplined, team-spirited, old school, less athletic, slower, and earthbound. For more conservative, nostalgic hoops fans put off by changes in court fashion during the mid- and late 1990s—specifically the loosening and lengthening of shorts—the phenomenal all-white backcourt of John Stockton and Jeff Hornacek, who piloted the Utah Jazz for the better part of the 1990s, also preserved a fading element of respectability in the game. As the rest of the league flopped around in parachute pants, Stockton and Hornacek ordered their shorts cut snugger and hemmed well above the knee. From their fashion sensibility and appearance, fans, sportswriters, and officials inferred greater meaning. Stockton, one of the most accomplished guards in NBA history, enjoyed an immaculate image as a clean and fair competitor; the image was informed largely by his race, boyish looks, and comparatively conservative style. This squeaky clean reputation infuriated rivals, who dubbed Stockton an elbowing cheap-shot artist in hip-huggers who escaped under the radar of officials because of his presumed sainthood.

Retired black power forward Karl Malone, a member of the same Jazz teams as Stockton, has always been treated as royalty in and around Salt Lake City, as much for his off-court persona as a neoconservative country boy as for his mastery of the sport and almost incomprehensible on-court longevity. While Malone was statistically the greatest NBA player ever at his position, hoops fans outside the state and rival players often loathed him because his self-celebration as a rancher/cowboy/trucker appeared to be a grossly overdone attempt to assimilate into a "white" team and white community. This feeling came to a head when Malone feuded publicly with East Coast rival forward Derrick Coleman and Coleman called Malone an "Uncle Tom."

Although most teams are primarily black, some are conceived of and deemed more authentically or particularly "black" than others. Teams like Nolan Richardson's University of Arkansas Razorbacks in the mid-1990s, with their "forty minutes of hell" pressing defense; the Philadelphia 76ers of the early 1980s, with spectacular, funky showmen like Julius "Dr. J" Erving, Darryl "Chocolate Thunder" Dawkins, World B. Free, and an up-and-coming Charles Barkley; Magic Johnson's Lakers; and the Detroit Pistons' Bad Boys teams of the late 1980s and early 1990s—all are veritable institutions of black popular culture. As Nelson George points out, on the college level the official "black" team of the 1980s was John Thompson's Georgetown Hoyas, especially during the Patrick Ewing years. Like their coach, the all-black Hoyas from DC were big and tough. They played physical, aggressive defense that bullied their opponents—"bullied" was the word often selected to describe their style of play—forcing turnovers, sending shots into the stands, and owning the boards. Thompson recruited gritty, talented, and often troubled black kids, and while shielding them from media scrutiny (freshmen didn't do interviews, veteran players were available only for fifteen minutes at a time), he pushed them as ballplayers and individuals. Since he was protective of the black athletes he seemed to systematically recruit, a mostly white media conceived of the private, enigmatic Thompson as something of a black nationalist. Different parties read all sorts of racial meanings into the nearly all-black basketball program in a primarily white Jesuit university. Suspicious fans and sportswriters believed that Georgetown had a separationist agenda and marked John Thompson as the Marcus Garvey of NCAA basketball, leading a "Back to Africa" movement within the Big East Conference. Although, as noted, it was the coach's long-standing policy to bar freshmen from interviews, when Thompson prevented reporters from talking to his dominant but shy seven-foot freshman Patrick Ewing (who spoke with a Jamaican accent and occasional stutter), the media took this as proof that Thompson was up to no good. Those distrustful of Thompson and jealous of Georgetown made Ewing their scapegoat and the target of vicious, racist baiting and slander. During games fans of opposing teams held up signs like "Ewing Kan't Read Dis," as well as bunches of bananas. However, if Georgetown's blackness meant stupidity, primitiveness, and fraud to some, it was synonymous with cool and cutting-edge style to others. For minorities and "down" white kids, Hoya gear was the height of ghetto fashion through the 1980s and into the next decade. The team's trademark blue and gray Nike high-tops (Thompson was one of the first coaches Nike paid to have his team wear its shoes); hooded jackets, with a scowling bulldog on the back; and G-town baseball caps and basketball jerseys became must-have urban wear.

The University of Michigan's Fab Five teams—named after the five brash, sublimely talented African American freshman starters—succeeded Georgetown as college basketball's "official" black team and the coolest campus program in the early 1990s. In their two years together, coached by Steve Fisher, the Fab Five gave collegiate hoops an enduring hip-hop makeover. Led by future NBA stars Chris Webber and Jalen Rose, the squad tirelessly talked trash and played breathtaking, flamboyant basketball that was either revolting or brilliant or both. That the sportswriting community consistently compared Michigan with the Harlem Globetrotters—an all-black traveling troupe of basketball entertainers playing staged basketball games—was emblematic of the equation of Fab Five basketball with black playground basketball. Clad in enormous, shiny maize shorts (ordered a full four inches longer than in the previous year by a fashion-savvy, eager-to-please assistant coach), black low-cut socks, and black Nike Air Max sneakers or the latest Air Jordans, the proud players would huddle at the start of each game for their trademark chant. Locked arm in arm in a circle, what did they remind one another before each contest? Words to live by from the Geto Boys, a legendary Houston-based rap group: "Let Your Nuts Hang." The Fab Five's pregame chant, fashion sense, style of play, and general vibe communicated two pieces of essential information: the players, not the coaching staff or the university, were in charge, and, in the words of Sidney Dean, Wesley Snipes's character in *White Men Can't Jump*, "This here [referring to the game of basketball] is a black thing."

A difference in the racial composition and character of two opposing teams tends to both heighten the drama of a rivalry and magnify other contrasts. During the Fab Five era, whenever Michigan and Big Ten Conference rival Indiana got together, the juxtaposition made for irresistible sports theater. Sportswriters and the announcers calling the games pumped up the various narratives: individuals versus a team; the freewheeling versus the disciplined; the "athletes" versus the "players"; talent versus coaching. And yet some of the differences were real.

Mitch Albom, author of the national best seller *Fab Five: Basketball, Trash Talk, the American Dream*, explains precisely what separates Indiana from Michigan and all other college programs and provides a starting point for the story of race relations and white nostalgia at Indiana University and within the state:

> There are 301 Division I college basketball teams in America. And then there's Bobby Knight and the Indiana Hoosiers.
>
> While most coaches scour the country sniffing for prospects in the Great Recruiting Chase, Knight walks out his back door and hustles up a barracks' worth of in-state soldiers. And while most big schools can't help but let their players become stars, Knight remains the marquee name on the roster; his players [are] simply cast members lucky enough to work for him. Fab Five? Long shorts? Ha! Hoosiers don't even have names on the back of their uniforms! . . . As a result, Knight's teams always

feature good role players, kids who follow orders, and—considering the makeup of topflight programs today—a large number of whites. The 1992–93 squad had seven white players, and six of them were raised in Indiana—including Knight's son Pat. Most of them looked similar, brush cuts, square jaws, good teeth. . . . Knight's staff was entirely white as well, no black assistant coaches . . . no black trainers or doctors, and only one black student manager. . . .

And they win.

The reputation of Bob Knight's Indiana University Hoosiers as a white basketball program is, to a significant degree, rooted in fact. Of the twenty-nine teams Knight coached, twenty-five were primarily white. Of the remaining four, two had an equal number of whites and blacks, and on two squads seven of the thirteen roster spots were occupied by African American players. On average, 62 percent of Knight's roster spots belonged to white players. Throughout the 1970s, just over two-thirds of Hoosier teams were white. The 1972–73 team was 85 percent Caucasian. In the 1980s and 1990s, the lineups hovered around 60 percent white and 40 percent black. Indiana stands alone as the last truly dominant Division I program to field a primarily white team year in and year out.

During the 1983–84 campaign, Knight often started an all-white lineup led by Steve Alford, Uwe Blab, and Marty Simmons. The following year, twelve white players and only four black players suited up for the team. While the 1985–86 team, featuring ten whites and six blacks, may have seemed more balanced by IU standards, three of the six black players eventually left the team. Only four of the thirteen roster spots on the 1993–94 squad were given to black players. The 1996–97 team fielded three black members. That's three black players on a Big Ten team in the late 1990s! Although collegiate teams in this part of the country—in tune with the racial breakdown of these geographic areas—have generally featured more white players than teams in places with larger urban centers and black populations, Indiana represents the extreme: it has consistently had the best and whitest program around. Even team photos from the 1990s look like they could have been snapped in the 1950s.

A telling example of IU's unfamiliarity with black players can be found in an old media guide in a section called "Pronouncing the Hoosiers." The section provides phonetic spellings for tricky names generally belonging to individuals of foreign descent. Guard Jeff Oliphant's name is written out as "ALL-a-funt," forward Steve Eyl's as "ISLE," and Mike D'Aloisio's as "Da-LEW-see-oh." Along with the Oliphants and D'Aloisios, the first name of an African American guard, Jamal Meeks, is broken down as "Ja-MALL." Mystery solved.

The old-boy network at Indiana University was tempered by the fact that black players were consistently overrepresented in both the starting lineup and the scoring column. Although twenty-five of Knight's IU teams were primarily white, eighteen of his twenty-nine squads featured a black leading scorer. The 1985–86 and 1986–87 teams each dressed six black players, and four of these usually started. Leading scorer Steve Alford was the lone regular white starter on both teams. Many of Indiana's greatest players during the Knight era were African American, including Quinn Buckner, Scott May, and Mike Woodson in the 1970s; Isiah Thomas (whose freshman season began in the fall of 1979) and Jay Edwards (who, like Thomas, bolted early for the pros) in the 1980s; and Alan Henderson, A. J. Guyton, and all-time leading scorer Calbert Cheaney in the 1990s.

Suggestive of a conscious effort to maintain a whiter team and particular reputation, IU's bench during Knight's tenure was consistently stocked with white role players. A similar phenomenon notoriously took place in Boston, where the Celtics, until recently, always made room on the pine for mediocre white journeymen and career backups.

Undeniably, Bob Knight and his Hoosier empire signify one of the last and most visible representations of basketball as a white man's game. For sports fans around the country, Indiana serves as basketball's heartland; it is a timeless sanctuary to white basketball, commemorated in the film *Hoosiers* and in countless images of baskets attached to barnyards, and it is immortalized in Knight's coaching legacy. Author Lee Daniel Levine explains the meaning of Indiana basketball and the success of the film *Hoosiers* in broadcasting this meaning:

> The word "Hoosiers" has become better known . . . with the film of the same name, which has helped bring about a nationwide awareness of the Indiana basketball tradition. . . . The film's popularity derived to a great extent from nostalgia for the heartland and its traditional values that are perceived as purely American. Basketball in Indiana hearkens back to a bygone era, when values were simple, the work ethic pure, the family central, and the community close-knit. In many ways, that bygone era still exists in Indiana, preserved and strengthened with the help of the basketball culture.

For Levine, the film captures the nostalgic connection between Indiana basketball and the state's agricultural past. As he shows, basketball became a beloved pastime in early twentieth-century Indiana largely because the game meshed perfectly with the logistics of small-town rural life. With roughly 30 percent of the state's population living on farms in the 1920s and an even greater proportion involved in agriculture, the hoops season—between the harvesting and planting periods—came right when Hoosiers had the most time on their hands. And since basketball is an inexpensive sport that requires only one person to play and five people to field a legitimate team, it was an ideal sport for tiny high schools with limitations in both funds and enrollment.

In describing the connection between Indiana basketball and the proud history of the heartland, Levine implies that the state's nostalgia for a "bygone era" is more than just nostalgia for a presumed simplicity of life. The era has been described as easier, purer, and somehow more authentically American. In Indiana, more so than in any other state in the north of this country, such references to earlier, more natural times carry a decisive racial connotation. As basketball was becoming popular in 1920s Indiana, so too was the Ku Klux Klan (KKK). Under the leadership of D. C. Stephenson, a salesman who became the Imperial Wizard, the Klan achieved its strongest level of political power in any state, northern or southern, and it dominated Indiana's government and school board. The Klan was not merely an extremist group at this juncture: between one-quarter and one-third of all American-born white males in Indiana were members during this decade. In rural communities, over half of all the men and women are estimated to have been either Klansmen or Ladies of the Golden Mask.

The movie *Hoosiers* captures both the enormous pride Indiana takes in its basketball tradition and the throwback aestheticism routinely attached to this pride. Two former IU students, director David Anspaugh and writer Angelo Pizzo, collaborated to recreate an immortal slice of Indiana folklore, the "Milan Miracle," which is considered by many the greatest Cinderella story in all of hoops history. In the film, the undersized but resilient boys of Hickory High overcome the odds and a minuscule enrollment (only 161 students) to capture the state title. (Hickory High is modeled after Milan High School in Milan, Indiana, which was the source of the real "Milan Miracle" in 1954.) The accuracy of the film is close enough for a Hollywood production; more important, what basketball means to the people of Indiana comes across in spectacular fashion. The sport is infused with monumental significance and powers: it represents the fabric of rural life and the glue that holds fathers and sons together, and it is a means of personal salvation for both a town drunk and a disgraced coach who assaulted a player (sound familiar?).

Hoosiers is the quintessential David and Goliath sports flick. (It was nominated for an Academy Award in 1987, but both Anspaugh and Pizzo proudly missed the Oscars ceremony because Indiana was playing Syracuse for the NCAA title on Oscars night.) In the movie underdog Hickory High triumphs over the big-school favorite, and a farm town bests a "big" city. It is also the true story of little, all-white Milan High School, in a town without a single black resident, which outplays both integrated and all-black schools on its way to a state championship. Although the year is changed in the film, the basketball season of the real "Milan Miracle"—1953–54—was the last before the U.S. Supreme Court handed down its decision banning racial segregation in the schools in *Brown vs. the Board of Education.*

To locate the significance of Bob Knight's coaching style and philosophy within the grander scheme of race and basketball in Indiana, one must start by looking at the state's high school basketball legacy and its accompanying racial dynamics. Although the Milan High title run was nothing short of remarkable, the Milan High Indians were by no means a bunch of scrubs. The team had made it to the semifinals of the state tournament the year before, and all of its top players returned for the 1953–54 campaign. Before its championship march through the tournament, the team had compiled an impressive 19-2 regular season record. Contrary to the six-deep Hickory High Tigers in *Hoosiers*, the real Milan team had ten players (enough to practice five on five and to weather the injuries and fatigue of a season). In Bobby Plump, (who in the film is represented by the character of Jimmy Chitwood), the Indians had an unstoppable shooter and scorer. Most important, at this point in history, high school basketball in Indiana was dominated by small-town programs—literally the boys who grew up shooting on a basket nailed to the side of the family barn—rather than teams from more populous urban centers. While no school that had previously captured the state title was as minuscule as Milan, high schools from Indianapolis (the state's capital) hadn't fared any better than smaller rural schools. It was a favorite razzing point for those from the country that the city boys from the capital had never won a state title.

Although the real Milan High team was considerably better than the film leads us to believe, it was still an enormous underdog. The Indians were intrinsically flawed: short on height and hops. The Indians' center stood all of five-foot-eleven. Thus what Milan needed to compensate for its limitations and to neutralize the size and athletic advantage of the competition was an effective strategy. The strategy Plump and his teammates would masterfully use in their title run would forever change the way the sport was played in the state. Milan's coach, Marvin Wood, a twenty-six-year-old up-and-comer, was nothing like Norman Dale, his counterpart in the film (played by Gene Hackman), an aging mentor with skeletons in the closet. Wood brought an offense to Milan that he had learned from Tony Hinkle at Butler University. The scheme was a very deliberate half-court set designed to retain the ball, eat the clock, and carefully pick and choose the shots to take on offense. This style is the antithesis of fast-break, full-court ball, and it is precisely the sort used to slow down and frustrate freewheeling teams that play a quicker game. This often yawn-inducing strategy made basketball games less a contest based on the speed, talent, and size of its players and more of a chess game between two coaches. Since most Indiana high schools played up-tempo basketball at the time, this game plan was also new and often baffling. This style can be infuriating for the more aggressive, fast-playing teams in the same way that it is infuriating for an attacking tennis player to compete against a "pusher," someone who consistently keeps the ball in play and waits for his opponent to make a mistake.

Milan's offense looked like the now well-known four corners offense, in which a guard stands with the ball at the top of the key and the remaining four players spread out in the half-court to occupy the four points of a box, one side running parallel to the baseline and the other running parallel to an extended free-throw line. The action ensues when a second guard comes to get the ball from the guard at the top of the key and the first guard takes the spot of the player to whom he has just passed. Meanwhile, the other players cut to the basket and end up in one of the four corners if they don't receive the ball during or immediately after cutting. Unless a cutter is wide open, the ball is worked around the horn from corner to corner. The guard at the top of the key can choose to pass, dribble, or simply hold the ball. While the four corners offense can be played aggressively and can even be exciting to watch when carried out by athletic players slicing to the hoop and crashing the boards, Milan's spread-and-delay offense was neither. Before the advent of the shot clock, the guard with the ball often exercised the last of his three options: he held the ball. And he held it and held it and then held it a little more. Against Muncie Central in the finals, during a stretch late in the game Plump held the ball for four minutes and thirteen seconds without dribbling.

The cat and mouse, as Milan's four corners offense was called, was a perfect way to both hide Milan's height deficiencies—since it had no post player on offense—and to slow down the pace of the game. (The term could also be used as a verb, as in "They were cat-and-mousing the Tigers all night.") Milan milked the strategy, and with a little help from Plump's heroic fifteen-footer in the final moments, it put away Muncie Central, an integrated school with a front line that averaged six-foot-four, by an all-time low finals' score of 32–30. Along the way, Milan knocked off a very strong all-black squad from Crispus Attucks High School in Indianapolis that featured a phenomenal six-foot-three-and-growing sophomore forward named Oscar Robertson.

In September 1927, Crispus Attucks High School (named for the first black soldier to die in the War of Independence) opened, and almost fourteen hundred black kids headed off to class. The Klan-supported school board figured that if blacks had to get educated, it was better that they did so in their own environment, so it decided to build an all-black high school in Indianapolis. For the first school day, the Klan organized a giant parade, to either celebrate the opening of a separate (and clearly inferior) educational facility or to air its residual disdain that blacks were being educated at all or—most likely—to do a little of both while reminding the community of its influence. Crispus Attucks would eventually become a hoops powerhouse that would displace the white schools from the top of the high school basketball hierarchy.

By 1940 hoops had caught on in the black neighborhoods of Indianapolis. Basketball worked in impoverished urban areas for many of the same reasons that it worked in rural Indiana: the sport was accessible and inexpensive. In the Lockfield Projects, the Dust Bowl, a full court with two netless hoops, became the gathering place for talented black ballplayers like Robertson to hone their skills and tangle with the top competition. Once Dust Bowl basketball became a prime ghetto attraction, it was just a matter of time before basketball at Attucks took off. The Indiana High School Athletic Association (IHSAA), however, would do its best to keep black city basketball on the ground. In a blatantly racist decree, it banned Attucks from state tournament play until 1942. Attucks came of age in basketball by competing against local black schools like Gary Roosevelt and Evansville Indiana.

By the start of the 1950s, without its own gym and with players wearing hand-me-down uniforms from (ironically) Butler University (the school that had passed the tactical kryptonite onto Milan's Coach Wood), Attucks was poised for tournament greatness. In 1955, the year after the "Milan Miracle," the Attucks Tigers won the championship game against black rival Gary Roosevelt, 97–64, narrowly missing the triple digits and surpassing the scoring record for a team in tournament play by twenty-nine points. The following year, the Tigers did it again, handily beating a white team from Jefferson-Lafayette for the title and finishing the season 31-0. Crispus Attucks High School was soon to be unbeatable, but it was still beatable when it squared off against Milan High in 1954.

The Attucks boys played an explosive, full-court game. On defense they hounded the opposition out of a 2-3 zone or press, and on offense, they looked to break whenever they could. Oscar Robertson, one of the first forwards to double as a point guard, often led the attack, so the Tigers played improvisational basketball and hit the offensive boards with a vengeance. This was the essence of black basketball—up-tempo, innovative, and exciting. It is interesting that this full-court style had previously been a white tradition in Indiana and specifically at IU. Before Bob Knight's name became synonymous with Indiana University, Bloomington belonged to Coach Branch McCracken. In his twenty-four years as IU coach, McCracken won two NCAA championships and four Big Ten titles, and he compiled multiple twenty-win seasons by playing high-scoring, racehorse basketball. And the fans loved it. During his tenure the boys from Bloomington were known as the Hurryin' Hoosiers. With an abundance of top-caliber black athletes, Attucks and its coach, Ray Crowe, had the kind of players to make this brand of basketball work effectively at the high school level, and the Tigers were the decade's dominant club.

During their matchup in 1954, however, the Milan Indians successfully slowed down the Crispus Attucks Tigers. Bobby Plump was on fire that day, scoring 28 points in total, and Milan built a 7-point lead by halftime. The cat-and-mouse game closed out the second half: the cutters got some easy baskets, and stalling made a comeback logistically impossible.

From that tournament day on, the deliberate cat-and-mouse half-court set became not only the blueprint for how to best play Crispus Attucks—and indeed Attucks regularly came up against this tactic afterwards—but it also became the formula that small, all-white schools would forever use to counter fast-breaking black teams. With the desegregation of schools formalized by the Supreme Court's decision in *Brown vs. the Board of Education*, many previously all-white and mostly white high schools, having witnessed, at their expense, the magnificence of Attucks during the mid-1950s, now pursued black players and often played quick-paced black basketball. The fast-breaking approach, which had once been the flagship style of the Hurryin' Hoosiers, was recoded as a black style in the years following McCracken's departure. While the Attucks dynasty signaled an era in which all-black or mostly black squads now dominated Indiana high school basketball, plenty of basketball-crazy white schools still steadfastly resisted desegregation. Consequently, as Levine articulates, the popularity of Milan's slow-it-down approach expanded in the 1960s and into the 1970s at the remaining small all-white schools. This became the formula for schools to remain white and still have a decent shot at winning basketball games.

Both the "Milan Miracle" and the preeminence of Crispus Attucks had profound effects on the integration of Indiana high schools. The high caliber of play at Attucks during the Robertson years drove athletic directors and coaches to acquire more black students. The motivation for many schools to integrate was often a purely utilitarian desire to bolster the quality of their basketball teams. In fact, many schools had little interest in effecting social change and in some instances were downright adverse to the idea of desegregation. After all, only a few decades had passed since the Klan's grip on the state had significantly loosened. Regardless of the dubious rationale behind desegregation, several Indiana high schools both addressed the issue in the first place and came to accept integrated education because of what the Tigers had accomplished.

Yet in many communities, when the reality of integration set in, even the desire to field a dominant hoops team sometimes fizzled. Largely because of the aversion to a mixed race educational environment, Crispus Attucks didn't graduate its first integrated class until 1974. The desegregation plan for Indianapolis high schools contained two elephant-sized loopholes that often undermined the entire initiative. The first loophole allowed white kids in the neighborhoods around Attucks free passage to schools outside of the district; the second established that black students in any part of Indianapolis could cross their district lines to attend Attucks. As a result, white kids missed the chance to play for powerhouse Attucks, and the black kids from Indianapolis who could have gone to white or mixed schools enrolled, instead, at Attucks.

While the brilliance of Attucks's basketball pushed the desegregation process along, although it often moved grudgingly, the "Milan Miracle," had the opposite impact. Nurturing the hope that a second "miracle" might be on the way to their town, many smaller high schools rejected the notion of linking up with neighboring schools or consolidating into one school district, in the process shunning the opportunity for greater racial diversity. As journalist and Indiana historian Irving Leibovitz wrote in 1964, "Hoosiers want school consolidations like Indiana farmers want hoof-and-mouth disease for their livestock." Small-town folks preferred paying more for their children's education and making them continue to use the same dingy facilities than squandering a possibility for roundball glory and the statewide notoriety that came with it. In fact, entirely because of the "Milan Miracle," the IHSAA for decades elected not to convert to the multiclass system that the rest of the high school world uses, whereby schools are organized by size into different classes and compete in separate tournaments at the end of the regular season. In order to leave the door open for another miracle, up until 1998 the IHSAA organized only one monster tournament for state bragging rights.

Small towns may have resisted consolidation and integration entirely because of town pride, but one would expect that schools in urban areas would have been far less apprehensive. After all, Attucks had put Indianapolis on the basketball map and quieted the taunts from jabbering country folk who believed that basketball was still a rural game. Yet the extensive resistance to integration on the part of Indianapolis schools immediately suggests that racist attitudes—which we could assume would have been more pronounced in small-town Indiana than in the state's capital—fueled Indiana's aversion to desegregation at least as much as any hoop dreams. Indianapolis has an atrocious track record on school integration. In 1960, only 20 percent of high schools had been desegregated, compared with 15 percent in 1950. Indianapolis was so slow to desegregate that in 1968, the U.S. government sued the Indianapolis Board of School Commissioners, citing *de jure* racial segregation in the Indianapolis public schools. The government accused the board of purposeful discrimination, gerrymandering of school zones, and faculty segregation. The state of Indiana had prevented school consolidation in Marion County by keeping metropolitan Indianapolis as part of one district and its outlying suburbs as part of another. After the 1968 suit, a drawn-out court battle ensued between the Board of School Commissioners in Indianapolis and the federal government as Marion County adamantly continued to resist consolidating with urban Indianapolis. According to U.S. Supreme Court testimony, "The suburban Marion County units of government . . . [had] consistently resisted the movement of black citizens or black pupils into their territory."

As part of the social fabric of Indiana, basketball has always mirrored broader social patterns in the state. Given the context of Indiana's reluctance to adequately desegregate its high schools, the notion of containing blacks on the court by slowing down the game, stalling, and cat-and-mousing takes on deeper meaning. The educational, as well as the social and political, containment of blacks in everyday Indiana society reflects the same desire behind the effort to prevent black basketball players from, literally and figuratively, taking off. The motivation behind both forms of containment is white paranoia: What would happen if "we" let "them" go? Would "we" lose "our" schools? Would "we" lose "our" pastime?

High school sports in Indiana today are still affected by the enduring stench of racism. In Green Castle, a high school basketball team was still calling itself the Dragons—a direct reference to the White Dragons of the KKK—up through the twenty-first century. In Martinsville, another high school recently lost its accreditation to compete in league play after years of having allowed black students to be pressured off athletic teams.

Where, then, does Bob Knight fit into the story of high school basketball in Indiana? What aligns Knight with Indiana's "bygone era" and what's "purely American" about the heartland and Indiana hoops is that Knight brought the same dated, racially loaded high school style of play and thinking to prime-time college basketball in the 1970s and, with minimal tinkering, stayed with this approach throughout his IU tenure. Long after basketball had become a black man's game, in terms of both the racial composition of the player population at the top levels and the dominant mode of play, Knight still coached the brand of white basketball that had been drawn up for segregated high school hoops in the 1950s. In fact, as

Levine points out, Knight's popularity and the success of his Hoosiers helped to preserve the cat-and-mouse legacy at tiny, white Indiana high schools. Of course, for the coach of a small white high school team with limited athleticism who's pitted against a bigger, more physically gifted black team, the best option is to borrow a page from Coach Wood's book. However, what reason would the college coach of a Big Ten college powerhouse have to recruit such teams and play in such a way other than to preserve a coaching ideology and a racially coded way of basketball life?

When Knight arrived in Bloomington for his first season in 1971, memories of the Hurryin' Hoosiers promptly faded. In Knight's words, his Hoosiers "were in no hurry." The General brought a series of half-court plays from his coaching days at Army, and his players carried them out like robots. Gone was the fast break that fans had loved, as outlet passes (the passes made after a defensive player comes down with a rebound and his team switches to offense) could only be thrown to a teammate no farther than fifteen feet away. With the termination of the McCracken era now unequivocally clear and Knight's methodical half-court game the new Hoosier norm, IU's followers adjusted reluctantly and resentfully. Accustomed to faster games with high scores, fans mocked the team's low-scoring debacles and heckled from the stands. However, when the team won nine of its last ten regular season games and as Knight's technical mastery became obvious, the IU faithful started coming around. The 1971–72 squad, featuring seven white players and three African Americans, finished 17-8. By the end of Knight's second season, in which the Hoosiers captured their first Big Ten title in fourteen years, the fans were in love.

In his second year, Knight installed a half-court motion offense, scrapping the set plays used during the previous season. It was hardly an experiment in freewheeling basketball; the emphasis was still on playing under control. In this offense, the Hoosiers' point guard would walk the ball up the court, allowing the defense to set up, and then he would pass until something opened up, all the while casing the defense to see how his team was being played.

This was excellent textbook basketball, but it was also boring and highly regimented. Weary of overdribbling, Knight's teams, which would routinely practice without dribbling in order to master a passing-game offense, took pride in underdribbling. Rather than creating openings and shot opportunities through dribble penetration, the guards would pass, pass, and then pass some more. Knight's teams frequently went to the delay game to control the clock, and in turn the score, by simply retaining the ball. In his 2002 autobiography, Knight voiced his contempt for any basketball innovation that he believed "would favor the team with the most talent" or "take away some of the control I felt that I had on the outcome of the game." One rule change was the shot clock, which forced the offensive team to release a shot before forty-five seconds had expired since it had first gotten possession of the ball. Without a shot clock, a team could prevent its opponent from taking any shots by simply holding the ball, as Bobby Plump had done for over four minutes against Muncie Central in the 1954 championship game.

The roots of Knight's approach did not come from a playing career at a tiny, rural Indiana high school. Knight is an Ohio native from Orrville, and he played college ball for Fred Taylor at one of IU's rivals, Ohio State. Knight mostly sat on the bench as a member of the two-time national champion Buckeyes team, which featured future NBA legends Jerry Lucas and John Havlicek. Knight's coaching philosophy came from his mentors—coaching giants like Henry Iba, Pete Newell, and Butch Van Breda Kolff—and from his coaching experience at West Point. Much of his coaching ideology—how to play the game, how to recruit, how to organize practice, how to motivate and interact with players—grew out of his six years as the head coach of Army.

In the world of Division I hoops, West Point is barely on the map. Offering potential recruits only limited exposure; an unimpressive basketball tradition; a highly structured, demanding college experience; and a mandatory postgraduate military commitment, Army is an unlikely destination for blue-chip athletes. In the era of the Vietnam War and a draft, Bob Knight struggled to piece together teams of Division I–caliber ballplayers. Yet while Knight's guys were shorter and less talented than their Division I peers, they were also members of the U.S. Army and therefore tough as nails and thoroughly loyal. To maximize what he could get from his players and to camouflage their weaknesses, Knight had to adjust in the same way that Coach Wood had done when compensating for a Milan High front line comprised of a five-foot-eleven center and two forwards of five-foot-ten and six-foot-two. Knight mapped tightly constructed set plays, implemented a spread-and-delay offense, and, more than anything else, emphasized rugged defense. He pumped every ounce of ability out of his undersized, mostly white players—these were in effect his soldiers—and his teams finished with a remarkable overall record of 102-50.

These compliant and tough teams were the kind that Knight loved and the type of boys he wanted in his program. It's doubtful that any other coach in the history of top-level college basketball has cared less about talent—about finding it and recruiting it and having it—than Bob Knight. For Knight, basketball, like life, was a thinking man's game best played by those who could analyze situations in the moment based on a predetermined system. It was also best played by individuals who knew not only their roles but also their limitations. "What a player can't do is as important for him to know as what he can do," Knight maintained.

At Indiana, Knight sought players he felt would be committed to the program, to graduating from IU, and to doing things his way. Knight's recruits had to possess the same two essential traits found in new soldiers: loyalty and impressionability. Larry Bird's mother, Georgia Bird, reflecting upon the strong possibility that Knight's coaching could have had a profoundly negative impact on her son's game, once stated, "Bobby Knight doesn't recruit the boys for what they can do; [rather] he molds them into what he wants." Indeed, this molding is easier and more complete in a recruit who is not an exceptionally talented player. A player who needs his coach, his team, and the system he's expected to follow will play more dutifully than one who is so gifted that he sees his team's structure as more restrictive than helpful. A point guard who can break down a defense off the dribble and create shots on his own doesn't need to start the offense with a preset passing routine. Because Knight believed his system represented the best, most effective way to play basketball, his scheme required ardent followers rather than creative athletes, conformists rather than innovators.

John Feinstein, in his exposé of the 1985–86 Hoosiers' season, takes readers into the huddle and demonstrates that what Knight wanted most out of his players was obedience. During a blowout loss to Michigan for the Big Ten crown, Knight reiterated *ad nauseam* the necessity of following orders unconditionally: "Hey, we got here by doing exactly what we were told to do. The minute we deviate from that, we're going to get our ass beat. You are not good enough to not listen to us [Knight and his staff] and be any good."

It's no surprise, then, that Knight never chased the top high school talent. He looked for faithful believers sold on his system, IU's mystique, and the value of a college degree. As Albom notes, landing such dedicated "in-state soldiers" and student-athletes was never a problem for a coach with the local stature of a deity; the players came to Knight. In fact, Knight almost effortlessly recruited some tremendous college ballplayers. If they fit Knight's strict criteria, the coach scooped up the local "Mr. Basketballs" and high school All-Americans. Such recruits were sure things, and they often had very good college careers. Rarely, however, did Knight sign the sublimely talented athletes who were less predictable, perhaps because of their home life or teenage experiences or simply their style on or off a basketball court. With the exception of Isiah Thomas (who bolted after two years), Indiana's most accomplished ballplayers had limited potential that, by the time they had finished college, was maxed out. Indiana players good enough to have been drafted went on to marginal or (more often) brief and inconsequential professional careers. Aside from Thomas, none of Knight's guys ever made an NBA All-Star team. Not surprisingly, Thomas and Knight shared an often antagonistic relationship at IU because of the unnaturalness of the pairing. There's something inherently ludicrous about Knight's saying "You aren't good enough to do it your way" to one of the greatest basketball players in history.

When pressed on the race issue, Knight combatively dismisses any suggestions that he consciously pursues more white players than other coaches or that he is the only coach capable of winning without black athletes. This sort of notion is "bullsh-t" since "anyone can play basketball, black, white, blue or green." Moreover, at Texas Tech, his coaching destination after Indiana, Knight's teams have been predominantly black. Yet Knight's unbending will to both totally control his players and find athletes vulnerable and pliable enough to internalize his direction contains a definitive racial element. Precisely what makes basketball a black aesthetic—individual freedom, flash, innovation, and both one-on-one and open-court play—are the very elements that are repressed in Knight's system. In a 1980 interview with *60 Minutes*, Knight explained that in order to foster loyalty and establish a team concept, he must "take away individuality." While basketball provides an essential and highly visible space for black men to express themselves—one of a very limited number of forums—such personal sovereignty and inventiveness, viewed as destructive to team success, runs contrary to Knight's ideology.

Knight takes the need to suppress personal expression to extremes. Even the physical presentation of his athletes must convey sameness and allegiance. In addition to the nameless jerseys, there are no fancy trimmings, logos, or designs anywhere on his teams' uniforms. It's just white uniforms at home and red uniforms on the road. Wristbands, headbands, kneepads, elbow pads, and other basketball accessories are all suggestive of an insurrectionary need to assert uniqueness and are thus frowned upon and generally disallowed. Off the court, jewelry and "deviant" fashion are immediate turnoffs to Knight and red flags when he is tracking potential recruits.

The irony, of course, is that Knight denounces individualism by making his teams all about one person—their coach. From reading Feinstein's *A Season on the Brink* and Steve Alford's *Playing for*

Knight, one gets the impression that very often the Hoosiers were indeed playing for Knight—to safeguard his greatness, to avoid his wrath after losses, to follow his plan to the letter. Games were big games because they were big games for Knight. A team was playing for the General's umpteenth Big Ten championship, to preserve a win streak in a rivalry that had begun before any of the players was a freshman, to show up one of the many coaches Knight disliked, or to best one of the shady programs that didn't recruit the good guys.

Knight's systematic refusal to recruit junior college players while he was at Indiana resulted in the limited acquisition of black talent. With the exception of Courtney Witte, a white reserve forward whose circuitous path to Indiana included an unplanned stint in junior college, Knight had coached the Hoosiers for a decade and a half before reluctantly taking in his first junior college recruits. Only after the disastrous 1984–85 season, in which Knight's Hoosiers finished 7-11 in Big Ten play (Knight's first season under .500 in fourteen years) and failed to secure an NCAA bid, did Knight amend his policy and allow himself to be swayed by his only black assistant coach, Joby Wright.

The junior college circuit offers an immense pool of basketball talent, most of it African American. For Knight, dipping into the murky waters of junior college recruitment was a move with which he was very uncomfortable. For one thing, it meant pursuing a player who had exhausted part of his college eligibility and thus would not be in Knight's system for a full four years; nor would he be a four-year student-athlete at Indiana University. To his credit, Knight has stuck to his commitment to recruit ballplayers genuinely interested in receiving a college education, graduating in four years, and living up to the ideal of the student-athlete experience. (Knight feels that high school phenoms who head straight to the pros are doing college athletics a service: if they don't want to go to school, they shouldn't be there.) Junior college kids were major liabilities whose dubious academic credentials and abilities might compromise Knight's program. (Their failure to meet the NCAA's academic requirements for incoming freshmen were in many cases the reason they hadn't started college at a four-year school.) Such prospects were risky investments for other reasons as well; most likely, they were poor, ghetto-hardened black kids. These were "projects" from the projects, better suited for Georgetown and John Thompson.

Bob Knight's reaction upon meeting Keith Smart, one of the first junior college players to come to IU, is extraordinarily telling. Of course, Smart was something of a godsend for Knight. His coaching greatness had temporarily been called into question until Smart netted him a third and final NCAA championship with a sixteen-footer in the closing moments against Syracuse in 1987. Knight writes the following in his autobiography: "When I first met Smart, I thought he was going to wear himself out with all the chains and rings he had. But he is a very, very bright kid." For Knight, Smart's remarkable intellect—a quality apparently rarely found in those with a propensity for showy jewelry—ultimately compensated for whatever may have been "un-Hoosier" about his appearance or demeanor.

Before the embarrassment of the 1984–85 campaign, a season so unthinkably horrible that Feinstein dubbed the following year "a season on the brink," Knight had done the impossible: he had won consistently without an abundance of black players and without top-notch talent. Probably the most revealing moment of Feinstein's book comes when Knight gathers his staff in the coaches' locker room—"the cave," as it was called—to compile a list of all the IU players who had been recruited since 1980. Once all the names had been recalled and written down, the coaches put a check next to the names of players they *should* have recruited, an "x" next to those they *shouldn't* have, and a dash next to those in the middle. The list consisted of "very few checks" and mostly x's. Knight, who increasingly left recruiting responsibilities to his assistants, could not have been more aware that he was not recruiting top-quality athletes. Nonetheless, if it hadn't been for the horror of 1984–85 and the following year "on the brink," Knight may never have altered his recruiting strategy or policy toward junior college players. Ultimately, the policy shift was both temporary and tenuous: Knight's teams, with a few exceptions in the 1980s, had no former junior college players until 1995–96. Neither Keith Smart's forty-inch vertical nor clutch play sold Knight on the value of a junior college transfer.

Hoosier fans and white basketball fans nationwide undoubtedly reveled in the consistent successes of IU's mostly white squads, the preponderance of white college superstars—the Kent Bensons, Steve Alfords, and Damon Baileys (even though their legacies as superstars were surely confined to their college days)—and the heroics of mediocre white players over superior black players. Former Indiana guard Dan Dakich, who became an assistant under Knight before taking over as head coach at Bowling Green, enjoys to this day a cult following and a magical place in hoops history as "that white guy who once shut down Michael Jordan." As in any good fish tale, the brilliance of Dakich's performance increases the more his story is told. During the 1983–84 Hoosiers' season the slow-footed Dakich, a sometime starter, drew the unenviable task of defending against Jordan, who was then playing for the heavily favored Tar Heels of the University of North Carolina (UNC). Knight gave Dakich the game plan: play off of MJ—give him the jumper—and use every ounce of Dakich's six-foot-five, 185-pound frame to keep MJ from crashing the offensive boards. (Upon hearing of his defensive assignment, Dakich puked.) The game was a remarkable triumph for Dakich and Indiana: Jordan struggled, scoring only 13 points, and the Hoosiers pulled off a monumental upset over a great UNC team. Dakich played a very tough game, and the national media treated him like a war hero. Yet Jordan's failure to get things going was more of a testament to Knight's sound defensive strategy, combined with an off day for a young, still shakable Jordan with a still unreliable jump shot, than to Dan Dakich's talent.

Knight's ideology and approach never wavered while he was at IU. He coached the only way he knew how: with passion and emotion, through player provocation, and by brandishing absolute power. He prepared his players by putting so much mental and psychological stress on them during practice that the pressure they experienced from the opposition on game day seemed entirely manageable. Dealing literally in fear, Knight believes that if his players are afraid of what will happen to them if they make mistakes, then they will stop making them. Similarly, if his players are more afraid of him than of anyone or anything else, they will never fear their opponents. To Knight's credit, his old-school approach—which employs the full gamut of "motivating tools" (emasculation, intimidation, deception, humiliation, verbal abuse, even physical force)—often resulted in superior performances from his players, as well as an unshakable sense of allegiance.

For the most part, Knight's players served him loyally throughout his Indiana tenure. Young ballplayers, who both feared and respected Knight, went to IU to become the best they could be, and many, both white and black, believed they had attained this goal. Knight's despotism often kept players in school. His player graduation rate is excellent for an elite college program (though, according to a claim by critic Murray Sperber in 1992, it was often erroneously inflated). For his followers, Knight's coaching tenure preserved the belief that hard work and discipline (not simply top-notch talent) could still produce success, that good teams could be assembled without breaking NCAA rules, and that student-athletes should be both students and athletes.

Bob Knight was synonymous with Indiana basketball for almost three decades. He led the Hoosiers to national prominence, guiding IU to national championships in 1976, 1981, and 1987. When he left Indiana, Knight was 117 wins shy of surpassing Dean Smith's record as the all-time winningest coach in collegiate history. He won more games than any other coach in the Big Ten's storied history. To this day his reputation as a brilliant tactician and straight shooter demanding nothing less than the best from his players is staunchly defended by the majority of his former athletes and coaching colleagues, in spite of the controversy that surrounds him. Isiah Thomas, who as coach of the Indiana Pacers would offer Knight an assistant position with the organization, and Mike Krzyzewski, the coach of perennial powerhouse Duke and Knight's protégé at Army, are two of Knight's countless well-respected supporters.

So in awe were they of Knight's greatness that university officials, alumni, and fans looked the other way when Knight behaved inappropriately, and even violently, as long as Indiana continued to win. In the final six years of Knight's tenure, however, the Hoosiers declined rapidly, losing four times in the first round of the NCAA tournament. It became increasingly difficult to accept the win-at-any-cost mentality once Indiana's teams were no longer dominant and the national media began more closely to scrutinize Knight's conduct. In May 2000—not coincidentally the same year a lower-seeded Pepperdine humiliated IU in the first round of the NCAA tournament—the bombshell dropped: a videotape showed Knight with his hands around the neck of guard Neil Reed during a 1997 practice. CNN/SI was first to air the tape, and moments later it was broadcast everywhere. The event was treated like breaking news of urgent national interest when, in fact, the act caught on film was nothing more than business as usual at Indiana University. This was simply the first time the media had truly placed Knight and, in consequence, Indiana University's administration on trial. The act itself and the university's response revealed Knight's true colors first and those of IU second: Knight had been committing crimes for decades, and Indiana hadn't been about to stop him.

The old guard at IU and in the state of Indiana defended Knight. In Bloomington's *Herald Times*, Knight's deed was recorded as a benign physical gesture: the "placing of his [Knight's] right hand in the vicinity of Reed's neck." IU trustee John Walda came to a similar conclusion during the university investigation, declaring that Knight's behavior was "clearly inappropriate" but could not be called a choking.

The tape shows Knight with his left hand wrapped around Reed's neck and his right hand against his upper chest, in the vicinity of the player's Adam's apple. In his autobiography Knight would dispute that he choked Reed by calling attention to two aspects of the tape: its content and its picture quality. In regard to the former—that is, the act itself—Knight maintains that since there is only one hand entirely around Reed's neck and two are needed to apply an adequate chokehold, this was not a choking. Knight also points out that both he and Reed simply go their separate ways after the confrontation, and Reed does not make any gesture indicating discomfort. The debate over whether or not Knight's act of aggression could technically be classified as a choking avoided the real question that required answering: why was he putting his hands on one of his players? In regard to picture quality, Knight implied that some sort of doctoring had taken place. According to him, the already grainy picture was "unexplainably blurred in the central area [referring to Neil Reed's neck region]."

If there's any validity to a conspiracy theory, it lies in the curious circumstances surrounding the video's release, in addition to the circumstances of Reed's relationship to Knight and the IU program. Indeed, the tape appeared seemingly out of nowhere and precisely at a moment when many fans and sportswriters were beginning to more thoroughly question Knight's coaching abilities and the legitimacy of his tactics; it came on the heels of IU's most recent tournament lose to yet another lower-seeded team. While there is no solid evidence linking Neil Reed to the tape's sudden appearance, Reed would have had ample reason to carry out a particularly nasty vendetta against Knight. Reed, a former McDonald's High School All-American and 1994 Louisiana High School Player of the Year, watched his promising basketball career at Indiana dry up because of injury and dissension with teammates and the coaching staff. Reed had been the third-leading scorer on both the 1995–96 and 1996–97 Indiana teams, but after his junior year and a series of clashes with teammates and coaches, Reed's teammates voted him off the team. Reed resurfaced as a transfer student at unheralded Southern Mississippi and promptly faded from the prime-time college basketball scene.

A May 2000 *Sports Illustrated* cover story chronicled a pattern of violent behavior on Knight's part. News publications nationwide documented that at one time or another, the coach had beaten up much of his staff. In the 1980s, Knight's secretary, Jeanette Hartgraves, was hit by shards of glass after Knight threw a vase in her direction that smashed into a picture frame by her desk. Knight also allegedly knocked over Kit Klingelhoffer, the school's director of sports information at the time, after he had submitted a press release that Knight found unfavorable. Knight sent an assistant coach, Ron Felling, into a bookshelf when the two failed to see eye to eye. After the assault Felling was fired after fifteen years of service, and he sued both Knight and IU. He accused Indiana of negligence, negligent supervision (essentially looking the other way after Knight's hostile explosions), battery, and age discrimination. In September 2002, Knight and Felling settled after Knight agreed to pay Felling a sum of cash and sign a statement noting that he had shoved Felling in anger.

Knight's beef with Indiana after his own firing superseded any ill will he may have had toward Felling. In a strange twist, as part of the settlement in the Felling case, Knight agreed to cooperate in Felling's lawsuit against Indiana; the suit alleged that the university had been negligent because it had permitted Knight to batter Felling. Over two years after his dismissal, Knight launched an unsuccessful legal battle against the university in an effort to recoup over $2 million in "lost income" from a shoe deal and other endorsements, television and radio appearances, and his basketball camp. (Knight claimed that he was fired without cause, purportedly without an opportunity to defend himself before either the Board of Trustees or the administration.) There is no mention of "lost salary" because Indiana paid out the remainder of his coaching contract. A Monroe Circuit Court judge dismissed Knight's lawsuit without a trial.

Knight abused those around him verbally as well, publicly and privately humiliating athletic directors, assistant coaches, team doctors, players, and managers. No one was safe from his explosions. When he was angry, which was often, the term "c—ksucker" replaced people's names. Knight routinely fired staff or kicked players off the team before calming down and rehired them or allowed them to rejoin the squad during a tenuous time of peace and reconciliation. Knight would even fire himself temporarily. Rather than ending practices at a scheduled time, Knight frequently shut them down. Sudden terminations and emergency evacuations became commonplace, with sessions ending either by Knight's storming off or by his banishing those present.

Numerous books and articles have been written about Knight's in-your-face coaching style, and many have attempted to resolve the controversy and mystique of the General. John Feinstein sealed a hugely successful career after the release of *A Season on the Brink.* Knight reluctantly—and in retrospect with regret—granted Feinstein nearly indiscriminate access to his practices, coaches' meetings, and locker room, allowing Feinstein to intimately observe Knight's players, staff, and Knight himself and to conduct impromptu interviews for the duration of the 1985–86 season. The book's first chapter hits the hardest: it feels more like a secret peek inside a POW camp than a glimpse of college athletics. During practices and tape viewings that lead up to the season's start, Knight is at his ugliest. Most likely terrified by the prospect of a second consecutive losing season, he brutalizes his players. In these moments, he is neither pushing nor challenging them; he is simply mistreating them.

Knight claims in his autobiography that he put down Feinstein's book after reaching page 6, never to pick it up again. He stopped reading, he says, because he was appalled not by his own actions but by Feinstein's duplicity. According to Knight, Feinstein failed to keep his promise that he would leave the F-word out of the text. Had Knight made it to the next page, he would have read a transcript of perhaps the most acerbic verbal lashing dealt out that year. While watching a tape of practice, Knight publicly tore into Daryl Thomas for what Knight considered a lackluster effort:

> You are the worst fucking pussy I've ever seen play basketball at this school. The absolute worst pussy ever. You have more

> goddamn ability than 95 percent of the players we've had here but you are a pussy from the top of your head to the bottom of your feet. An absolute fucking pussy. That's my assessment after three years.

Emasculation is a sadistic means of pushing players, but it is commonly used by coaches at all levels. Knight, however, frequently took this brand of "motivation" to the extreme. In 1981, Knight put Tampax in a locker belonging to Landon Turner, another "soft" front-court player.

Knight's behavior in public varies little from his comportment during practices. His sideline hysterics and often violent tantrums have evolved into folkloric gems for basketball fans. One-time team doctor and all-purpose helper Tim Garl, who knew to expect anything and everything from Knight during the course of a ballgame, packed two clipboards on game day so that if Knight broke one of them, he couldn't complain about not having a firm surface on which to write. Before the Reed incident, Knight more or less accidentally head-butted player Sherron Wilkerson during a time-out in a 1994 game against Michigan State. (Wilkerson would later transfer.) In a game in 1993, Knight kicked the chair of his own son, Pat, then a Hoosier player, during a sideline outburst and responded with an obscenity when fans behind the bench booed. During the 1985–86 season, in a game against Illinois, a frustrated Knight kicked a megaphone on the way to the locker room that hit an IU cheerleader in the leg.

The event that crystallized Knight's image as a walking volcano was that of the infamous chair toss. Against conference nemesis Purdue during the 1984–85 season, Knight whipped a chair across the gymnasium floor while Purdue player Steve Reid stood at the free-throw line to shoot a technical foul that had been called against Knight. While the public looked on in horror, the Hoosier players, on some level, must have seen it coming. Based on accounts that players relayed to Feinstein, Knight's chair throw during the Purdue game was nothing compared to the time at a Hoosiers' practice that he attacked a stack of twenty chairs and tossed thirteen of them.

Knight so comfortably took massive liberties in his handling of players that he never felt compelled to adjust his behavior while off campus. A Knight player was always one of Knight's boys. During a 1984 Olympics game pitting the Knight-coached U.S. national team against France, Steve Alford reached in on a French player curling in the lane and was whistled for a foul. Alford was then treated as if he were at an IU practice. Knight called a time-out, and as Alford approached the bench, Knight, with twisted affection, grabbed a handful of Alford's hair, let go, and then popped him on the top of his head with an open hand.

Knight reigned dictatorially as coach of Indiana from the time he first arrived in Bloomington. When Athletic Director Bill Orwig gave Knight a four-year contract in 1971, he wanted a coach who could both return IU to basketball prominence and clean up the university's basketball program. Knight promptly declared himself the new sheriff in town, ready to confront the mounting debauchery in and around big-time college basketball. He was prepared to cut off any boosters or alumni of dubious character and put an end to anything that wasn't overtly kosher. During negotiations for the position, Knight had explained that if he were named coach, things would be done his way: the Hoosiers would play how he wanted them to play and the school would recruit how he wanted to recruit. There would be no interference from the university, the athletic department, the alumni, or anyone else. Indiana agreed to Knight's terms, and the precedent was set: Bob Knight would have absolute control over the basketball program. Ten years later, after more than proving himself as an elite coach and elevating Indiana basketball to new heights, Knight got a new contract, which he practically wrote himself. There would be no system of checks and balances for Knight, an individual with zero capacity to monitor himself.

The aftermath of the chair toss during the Purdue game revealed the depth of Knight's authority. The president of the university, John Ryan, chose not to reprimand Knight. Ryan, who had come to IU at the same time as Knight and had positioned himself more as a fan than an employer, was so afraid of crimping the coach's style that he simply did nothing. Instead of handling the incident as an in-house matter and showing that IU did not condone this sort of behavior, Ryan crumpled as soon as Knight made it known that he would walk if disciplined by the university. In effect Ryan let Big Ten Commissioner Wayne Duke do the dirty work for him. Knight still got off easily: Duke passed down a one-game suspension.

For years Indiana University had allowed Bob Knight to walk all over the school, and when it came time to address the Neil Reed situation, the institution responded with the same spineless tolerance. After a two-member committee of Indiana trustees had conducted a seven-week investigation, the university decided to let Knight keep his job, even in light of his horrific past abuses. His punishment was inconsequential: a three-game suspension, a $30,000 fine, and a "zero-tolerance" policy regarding physical contact with anyone at the school. In other words, he would not be permitted to rough anyone up, a basic human understanding that had now been spelled out for him. During a press conference on May 15, 2000, school president Myles Brand explained that despite evidence of abuses that were "persistent and systematic," Knight was a "man of integrity" and deserved another shot. Furthermore, Knight had never received a concrete "set of guidelines" of acceptable and unacceptable behavior. With a straight face, Brand asked the university and the public how Knight could be expected to conform to a standard of decency if one had never been set forth. The university considered its decision both fair and likely to be successful because, in Brand's words, it "established tough, specific guidelines to send a clear message that abusive and embarrassing behavior will not be tolerated." The investigation, the subsequent ruling, and Brand's explanations not only made the school look ridiculous but they also illuminated exactly how far backward IU would bend for Knight.

Knight's lack of punishment prompted *New York Times* sports columnist George Vecsey to write, "They [Indiana University] have more than two decades of behavior so crude, so grotesque, that it would get anybody else fired." Offended by Indiana's cowardice, sportswriters across the nation called for Knight's unconditional ousting. In his weekly column in *Sports Illustrated*, Rick Reilly admonished Indiana's higher-ups for hiding from Knight "like mice" and allowing "a thug [to] run your university," calling on IU to "End the Knightmare."

The irony was that the administration's course of action—a seemingly disingenuous and chicken-hearted disciplining of Knight—constituted an attempt to take a stand against him. In 1994, Myles Brand, a former philosophy professor from Brooklyn, New York, had become the president of IU. Brand was neither a Bob Knight bootlicker nor the type of president who would be content to end his tenure without leaving a mark. Brand respected Knight's interest in education and mindfulness of NCAA regulations, but he also took issue with Knight's volatility and unbridled influence at the university. After Brand's appointment, IU hired Clarence Doninger to replace Ralph Floyd as athletic director. Doninger and Knight clashed from the beginning. Indiana's athletic directors before Doninger—Floyd, John Ryan, Bill Orwig, and Tom Ehrlich—could all be classified as certifiable Knight guys. Doninger, in contrast, could not be counted as an ally.

For Coach Knight, the Brand-Doninger era represented a clear departure from the past, as well as an effort to limit his power. For Knight, the first major indication that things were different came in 1996, when Doninger fired football coach Bill Mallory. Knight's endorsement to Floyd had virtually landed Mallory the job, and the two coaches shared a close friendship. When asked for his input by both Doninger and Brand, Knight voiced a highly favorable opinion of Mallory and the job he had been doing at IU. Even after Knight had lent his support for his pal and colleague, the university terminated Mallory. He felt betrayed and never trusted Doninger and Brand again. From that point on, Knight's relationship with both men was strained and often antagonistic. Gone were the buddy-buddy days of obsequious superiors. Moreover, the days of Indiana's basketball preeminence had also passed. When the Neil Reed tape became public, neither Doninger nor Brand made any attempt to shield Knight or to hush things up. As Knight saw it, they weren't even interested in hearing his side of the story.

More than a decade before Coach Knight's dismissal, Al McGuire, Knight's old coaching comrade, had once warned Knight that if a supervisor were to come in and try to knock Knight "off the coaching pedestal he deserves," Knight's track record would inevitably do him in. "Suppose some administrator comes to Indiana and decides he's the guy to prove once and for all that he's Bob Knight's boss. If anything like that happens, Bob is going to be judged wrong no matter what he does because of the past. He deserves better than that." McGuire made it clear that once a superior chose to act as such, the case against Knight would be stacked.

After all the free passes, Brand and the university finally brought down the General in September 2000. IU dismissed Knight after he violated the "zero tolerance" agreement by grabbing a nineteen-year-old freshman, Kent Harvey, who said, "Hey, what's up, Knight?" to him when the two passed in the hall. Though he denies that there was any sort of "incident," Knight concedes that he did indeed grab Harvey's arm to pull him aside for an impromptu lecture on the importance of respecting one's elders and referring to them by their proper titles (as in "*Coach* Knight" or "*Mr.* Knight"). This act, coupled with various "uncivil, deficient, and unacceptable" offenses (such as verbally assaulting a female university administrator) that Knight purportedly committed after the "zero tolerance" agreement were the collective straws that broke the camel's back. The "zero tolerance" policy had been strangely tolerant during the seventeen weeks between its implementation and Knight's firing. Doninger and Brand were reluctant to pull the plug on Knight until they had a smoking gun. According to Knight, the two eagerly awaited a good enough reason to terminate him; once they had it, they expedited Knight's demise by promoting media coverage of the Harvey incident. Knight claims that when Harvey's stepfather contacted Brand's adviser and spokesman, Christopher Simpson, Simpson immediately called ESPN.

With the announcement of Knight's firing came massive discontent from IU students, who passionately defended their fallen hero. In one of the more dramatic expressions of dissatisfaction, a group of students hung a stuffed dummy of Harvey from their off-campus house; the mock hanging was a necessary punishment for Harvey's treason against the General. Harvey was burned in effigy as well. Student demonstrators handed out flyers with Harvey's picture, accompanied by the caption, "Wanted. Dead." His life literally in danger after such displays of hostility, as well as death threats via telephone and e-mail, Harvey fled the school and the state, along with his two brothers, mother, and stepfather. Harvey's stepfather, Mark Shaw, the host of a local radio show that had been critical of Knight (and coincidentally Larry Bird's biographer), also received death threats and accusations that he and his stepson had orchestrated the entire plan to get Knight fired.

Murray Sperber, an IU professor of English and American Studies who had expressed the view of many in the faculty that the university had been shamefully submissive in its dealings with Knight, also received threats from fervent Knight supporters and subsequently took an unpaid leave of absence. After he returned to Bloomington, campus police advised him to enroll in a self-defense class, and he was not permitted to post his office hours.

Thousands of protesters gathered outside of Brand's house, demanding his dismissal, and a support rally (which Knight attended) took place in front of Assembly Hall. School property was destroyed, and Indiana state police, sometimes struggling to keep order, monitored the demonstrations in full riot gear.

Indiana fans and alumni responded legally as well. Forty-six plaintiffs filed a lawsuit that asserted that state law had been violated when the trustees met to talk about Knight's firing without issuing advanced public notice. After the General's departure, membership in the Varsity Club—the chief booster group—declined significantly, forcing a higher minimum donation for entry into the club. Amid reports of financial troubles in the usually well-endowed athletic department, IU also went quickly through two athletic directors—Doninger, who retired as soon as the dust began to settle, and Michael McNeely, who resigned just over a year after taking the position.

For most of his twenty-nine years at IU, Knight was bigger than the entire school, as fans and the IU administration completely overlooked the facts of his tenure—the abuses, violence, and cover-ups. Moreover, Knight's departure unleashed a campus whirlwind: violent demonstrations, death threats, hate propaganda. All of this for a basketball coach?

When facts are rendered invisible and a personal history is ignored, an individual under scrutiny is no longer evaluated as a person but a symbol. What he stands for in the eyes of others and what they think he represents become far more important than what he does or what his actions imply.

Indiana University is a complicated place to go to school because the tides of conservatism and liberalism have always arrived simultaneously rather than succeeding one another. On the one hand, Bloomington is regarded as the most liberal place in a highly conservative state. In the 1960s, amid the surrounding traditionalism, IU emerged as a progressive enclave in the center of the country; it was a center of the antiwar, civil rights, and feminist movements. Academic Mary Ann Wynkoop recently detailed the impressive counterculture movement at IU in *Dissent in the Heartland: The Sixties at Indiana University*. At the same time, this period of liberalism was undermined by extensive violence on campus against civil rights groups; some of the violence was the result of the campus infiltration of the KKK.

Today IU and Bloomington are still a bundle of contradictions. Hippie communes, holdovers from the 1960s, are still popular in Bloomington. Indiana University Press publishes some of the most progressive works on social conditions. Simultaneously, the school often operates as a giant old-boys network, with a booming fraternity culture. IU, the nation's top party school in 2002 according to the *Princeton Review*, recently served as the location for *Shane's World*

No. 32: Campus Invasion, a pornographic movie filmed on campus using registered IU students. Knight critic Murray Sperber grounds much of his analysis in *Beer and Circus: How Big-Time College Sports Is Crippling Undergraduate Education* in a probe of fraternity life, cultural politics, and university bureaucracy at IU. Sperber argues that major universities put their cash and energy into pumping up a social scene centered on college sports, to the detriment of the quality of education. While schools amass tuition dollars, students are kept happily ignorant and sedated with alcohol.

The explosive reaction to Knight's dismissal and the virulence of the protests—specifically the burning and hanging of Kent Harvey in effigy—exhibit a particular type of hostility: the angry white mob mentality. This sort of response emerges to perceived threats against white solidarity and traditions. The angry white mob mentality was the force that undercut campus progressivism in the 1960s. When the first black student body president was elected at IU in the 1960s, hostile whites burned crosses on campus. In 1968, the Ku Klux Klan firebombed a black and white student hangout run by Rollo Turner, a black activist and sociology graduate student. In 1970, after the Black Student Union submitted to the school a list of demands calling for more black advisers and a broader black studies program, the KKK distributed leaflets on campus. According to an English professor at the time, during a Board of Trustees hearing attended by members of the Black Student Union, members of a white fraternity stormed the building where the meeting was being held and shot out the windows.

In such instances, blacks who were deemed dangerously insurgent have been the targets of white rage. The white Kent Harvey, by betraying a white institution and turning Knight in, became the target of such vicious hatred that it resembled racial violence in the past that had been aimed at minorities. Treacherously undermining a previously airtight solidarity and old-boys network, Harvey was charged with bringing down the embodiment of white basketball and a way of life in Indiana.

Knight's legacy also represented a symbolic sense of control over the game of basketball at a time when many believed that deference to authority had all but disappeared. Tattooed black men with oversized shorts sliding off their backsides were playing by their own rules, defying their coaches, and walking away with millions of dollars. Hip-hop god Allen Iverson was late for practice or skipped it nearly fifty times in a single season; Latrell Sprewell choked his own coach; Robert Horry threw a towel in the face of his; Nick Van Exel pushed an official; Cedric Ceballos left the Lakers to go water skiing in the middle of a playoff race after his playing minutes decreased; Shaquille O'Neal slapped Greg Ostertag across the face; Dennis Rodman kicked a cameraman in the groin. The notion of the student-athlete had become fleeting at best. Black teenaged stars were playing the system: they were skipping college entirely (making millions without a college diploma!) or converting a subsidized college education into a one- or two-year personal showcase for drooling NBA recruiters. Whatever had happened to discipline, the delay of gratification, civility, and family values?

Many fans see these specific acts of indiscretion and violence, as well as the seeming devaluation of college, as evidence of a universal moral breakdown in society and a loss of control. Fans often wonder where those in positions of power are—the fathers—to restore order, discipline the undisciplined, and teach life's fundamentals. Basketball players are, after all, young men (many of whom, ironically, already have children) who were in many instances raised in "broken" homes by their mothers. Knight was a coach who was always in complete control of his players, his "boys." He thus symbolized the stereotypically strict father who kept his kids from getting into trouble by scaring the daylights out of them; his style was reminiscent of the 1950s school of child rearing, in which discipline, the weeding out of effeminate tendencies, and an incessant demand for excellence were paramount to successful fathering. Bob Knight (whose Indiana basketball program was like the army, complete with the army's policy of short hair and no facial scruffiness), was one of the few who still believed in the value of a swift kick in the butt. And Bob Knight had become a national phenomenon because of what Americans—not simply people from Indiana—believed he stood for and epitomized.

The irony, of course, is that Knight himself—the symbol of ultimate discipline—was spiraling out of control during his entire time at IU. Where was Knight's father to keep his son's temper tantrums in check and scold him when he misbehaved? While Knight was disciplining his players and anyone else who he perceived needed a "straightening out," no one was disciplining the man most in need of discipline.

It's a complicated time at Indiana University today. After the school's successful run in the 2002 NCAA tournament, IU signed interim coach Mike Davis to a six-year contract extension. Davis's coaching ideology signified a dramatic departure from Knight's authoritarian style and his stronghold on the school.

As a coach, Davis instantly distinguished himself from his predecessor by implementing a coaching etiquette that corresponded with both the times and the basic tenets of human decency. In a local piece aptly entitled "The Quiet Man," writers for the *Indianapolis Monthly* watched Davis during a practice for Big Ten players selected to compete against European teams in exhibition play. The writers describe a relaxed instructor and motivator running an efficient practice in which drills and pointers were explained clearly and without emotional involvement or the belittlement of others.

Using an even-tempered professionalism with his IU players, Davis temporarily brought a needed sense of calm to Indiana basketball, undoing an edginess that had permeated the squad while Knight was in charge. On numerous occasions during the 2001–02 season, Davis had to tell scared players looking toward the bench after making a mistake to simply play and stop worrying about being pulled. Davis's motto: "Play loose yet hard."

Dane Fife, a gifted shooter, lost complete confidence in his outside touch during his first two years with Coach Knight, connecting on a lackluster fourteen three-pointers in his freshman and sophomore years. Fife, a loyal Knight partisan who at one point announced that he would transfer after Knight's firing, had to learn how to shoot without fear once Knight had departed. With the help of a supportive head coach, Fife rediscovered his outside shot: "Coach Davis has really pushed me to shoot the ball. . . . For the first time, I'm allowing myself to improve at the game. My mind has just been transformed."

In addition to reversing the psychological damage, Davis modernized IU's offense, trading in Knight's deliberate half-court motion for an offense predicated upon creativity. Davis's offense emphasized dribble penetration, guard play, and the exploitation of one-on-one matchups. While still an outside shooting team in the half-court, IU looked to run and push the action.

Davis pursued a completely different kind of player from the Knight archetype. Whereas Knight simply rounded up the local boys and never gave chase, Davis recruited doggedly and without geographic constraint. In many ways, point guard Bracey Wright embodied the new-school IU ballplayer. Wright was an incredibly quick and deft ball handler whose speed and creativity opened scoring opportunities for himself and his teammates. He didn't need an intricate offensive scheme to get open or to come off a pick to get a shot off. Davis had to work very hard to get Wright, a native Texan, to come to Indiana. He attended all of Wright's Amateur Athletic Union (AAU) games during the summer before his senior year in high school. (The AAU is discussed further in chapter 6.) Davis's recruits arrived from all over the country, some even fifth-year seniors from prep schools; many of them would never have appeared on campus if Knight had still been coaching the Hoosiers.

Tom Coverdale, a redheaded point guard, could feel the changes all around him. Coverdale was one of two Knight holdovers on the 2002–03 team. When Knight was fired, Coverdale threatened to transfer before he hesitantly agreed to remain a Hoosier; he then played an integral part in Indiana's 2001–02 run. Coverdale was one of Davis's favorite players. Yet Coverdale revealed to *Sports Illustrated* that "if I were a high school senior right now, I'm not sure Coach

Davis would recruit me." While Davis claimed that he'd love to land "another Coverdale," Coverdale's assertion was probably dead on given the sort of point guard Davis had recruited in Wright and the direction in which he had taken IU's offense. Coverdale was a solid player, a good passer, and an excellent shooter, but he was neither quick nor especially athletic nor particularly difficult to guard. During the 2002–03 season, Coverdale went the entire month of February—seven straight games—without taking a free throw. He was not a player with the capacity to break down the defense, create openings, and get to the rim. He was, instead, precisely the kind of guard that Knight had stockpiled during his IU tenure: a floor leader, a jump shooter, a competitor not quite explosive enough to play his own way and get away with it, and a local white guy.

Though Davis's approach to basketball may be revolutionary by Bloomington standards, his loyalty to Knight and personal politics are anything but radical. In the wake of Knight's dismissal, Davis carefully avoided stepping on any toes as speculation over Knight's successor circulated. While several players and assistant coach Pat Knight talked of leaving, Davis stated that he would do whatever Knight and the Indiana players wanted him to do. When Indiana University finally appointed Davis to the interim position, the new coach explained that his decision to stay at IU was driven largely by the fact that the players and their concerned parents clamored for him to remain with the program. Davis positioned himself as a Knight guy, pressing on like the General would have wanted him to. Regardless of his attempt to deferentially fill the sacred void Knight had left, a black head coach was hardly an easy sell for the old guard at IU. In a place where locals invest tremendous meaning and importance in a basketball coach, the *kind* of black man that Davis represented became of utmost significance.

In the movie *Hoosiers*, the local men gather at the barbershop for a community meeting with the incoming coach of Hickory High, Norman Dale, to tell him how things are done around those parts. One of the locals warns Dale that "this town doesn't like change much," so if he expects to survive, he better be the right sort of fit. The local makes his point plainly: "We trust that you're a fine, upstanding, God-fearing man, with Christian morals and principles who will set an example and a standard of leadership for our boys."

In Davis, IU landed the safest of possible black men: a quiet Southerner who fought off a stutter, a devout Christian who refused to hold practice on Sundays, and a committed family man who even brought his children to press conferences. Davis, who doesn't drink or smoke, never missed the chance to remind others of his allegiance to God. As Indiana tore its way through the competition in the 2002 NCAA tournament, Davis referenced and thanked God so much that one would've thought IU's tournament success was more the result of divine intervention than the product of a good basketball team playing its best when it mattered most.

In the aftermath of Knight's leaving, only Davis's commitment to God proved superior to his loyalty to Knight. When under subpoena in Ron Felling's lawsuit against Knight and the university, Davis gave testimony that he believed would be confidential. After an Indianapolis TV station won legal access to the testimony, it was revealed that Davis had said "yes" when asked whether he would classify Knight as a bully. Although such a response was seen by some Hoosier fans as an act of treason, Davis disclosed such disparaging information about his former supervisor only when forced to swear on the Bible and under oath.

In Davis, by virtue of color alone, Indiana may not have had a member of the old-boys network; it did, however, have a black man who was both safe and socially pleasing. His appointment represented a major first, but one tempered by calculated conservatism.

Of course winning still mattered in college basketball, and Davis would need to win consistently to keep his job. The 2004–05 season put Davis on the hot seat as the Hoosiers limped through a miserable year to finish only one game above .500 at 15-14. Things only got worse. The anti-Davis campaign gained steam as injury, poor play, and Davis's increasing frustration derailed a promising 2005–06 season. During the season, Davis began privately and later publicly questioning his fit with the team and the program while his detractors blasted away. The Web site FireMikeDavis.com, considered by some a factor in Davis's in-season decision to step down as head coach at the end of the 2005–06 season, led the attack, selling anti-Davis clothing, posting contact details for IU officials, and creating a discussion space for the disenchanted to rant. Under such pressure, Davis, likely to have been fired if he didn't decide to leave first, gave up.

Meanwhile, Knight returned to coaching and collected his 800th career win at Texas Tech University. Since the separation, Knight and Davis haven't spoken. Knight made it known through the coaching grapevine that he felt Davis had betrayed him by staying on at IU, and he refuses to talk publicly about Davis. Knight expected his assistant to go down with the ship and disconnect himself from Indiana University. Yet Knight never offered Davis a job, and Davis, a man with a family to support, had to look out for himself.

As the coach of the Texas Tech Red Raiders, Knight has raised the spirits of fans, not to mention the school's revenues. By Knight's second season in Lubbock, Texas, season ticket sales had nearly doubled, and booster membership in the Red Raider Club had leaped by almost 50 percent. In addition to ticket sales, television exposure, sponsorships, and even admissions applications have all increased significantly. Knight's arrival has initiated a golden era of sorts for Texas Tech. The basketball team, which fumbled its way to a 9-19 record the year before Knight took the coaching job, posted an impressive 23-9 finish in Knight's first year and made the NCAA tournament.

Even with all of the controversy attached to his legacy, the iconic Knight enjoys a reputation as one of the most popular and influential figures in college basketball. What's more, at Texas Tech, Knight's fame has expanded to include two new dimensions: that of a reformer of college athletics and a television celebrity. At Tech, Knight has emerged as one of the main faces of a recent reform movement in college sports that is spearheaded by Myles Brand.

Knight has spoken out against the addition of a twelfth game to the NCAA regular football season and has reiterated publicly on numerous occasions his long-held belief that for each athlete a program fails to graduate that program should lose one future scholarship in that sport. By taking on Knight at IU, Brand secured a reputation as a fearless regulator, which earned him the position of NCAA president and chief executive officer. Ironically, Brand now campaigns for higher academic standards for college athletes and other reforms that Knight first endorsed decades earlier.

Knight has also been converted into a television celebrity. After taking the Tech job, Knight saw himself played by actor Brian Dennehy in an ESPN adaptation of Feinstein's *A Season on the Brink*; then he signed on for an ESPN reality series called *Knight School*, which began in February 2006. The show chronicles a competition among sixteen students for the last roster spot on the 2006–07 Red Raiders. A buzz in the television industry ensued when TV producer Lindy Dekoven and Paramount Television shopped a situation comedy based on Knight's life and shtick.

Fittingly, Texas Tech has also witnessed a dose of Knight's trademark aggression and resistance to school authority. In the infamous salad bar showdown, a verbal altercation between Knight and Tech chancellor David R. Smith allegedly transpired at a gourmet grocery near campus. According to news reports highlighting a memo written by the chancellor, a "furious" Knight charged behind Smith "with fists clenched" after the chancellor had complimented him on his good behavior. The matter died down relatively soon, and, as if still at IU, Knight walked away without any penalty or punishment from the university.

According to Grant Wahl, a writer for *Sports Illustrated*, "there was a genius in the destination Knight selected, for few places would better appreciate him." Knight is the kind of man who meshes with the essence of life in Lubbock. He is an avid hunter, a staunch Republican, a war buff, and a disciplinarian. Texas, like Indiana, has both a distinguished history of conservatism and tremendous state pride. In the words of Dan Pope, a businessman in Lubbock, Knight is "one of us," and he thrives in Lubbock because "[it] is a place for hardy people [who are] not too caught up in political correctness."

Knight's legacy at Tech is sure to endure even after the General retires. In 2005, following a trend at schools like Oklahoma State and the University of Washington, Texas Tech signed Knight's son and assistant coach, Pat Knight, to a contract that passes on head coaching duties to the younger Knight after his father's contract runs out in June 2009. Texas Tech named Pat Knight coach-designate despite his lack of college coaching experience and a combined 22-22 record as a coach in the U.S. Basketball League (USBL) and the International Basketball Association (IBA). While none of the other schools that interviewed Knight offered him a job (these include New Mexico State and Wright State), Tech felt that it had its man. Though it may not be a politically correct place, decisions can still be political in Lubbock.

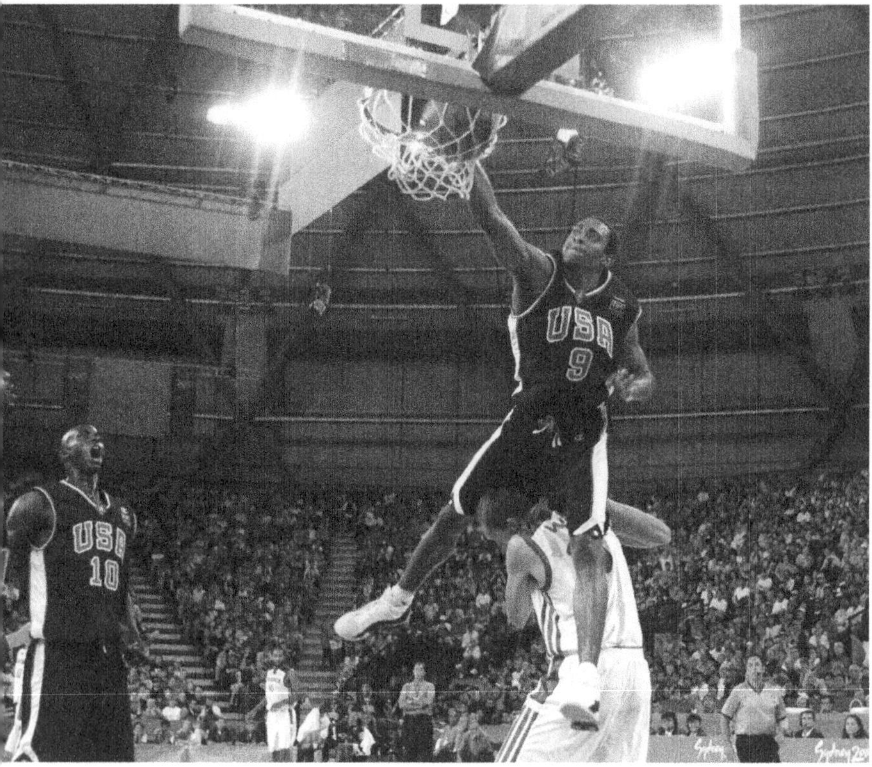

6. American guard-forward Vince Carter catapults over powerless French center Frederic Weis during Team USA's last successful campaign for Olympic gold in 2000. The dunk, humbling the Frenchman, was celebrated by smug basketball fans in the United States, who viewed foreign players as soft, earthbound, and simply not as good as their American counterparts. © imago/PanoramiC.

6 The New Globetrotters

Why the NBA Outsources Talent

In a game during the 2000 Sydney Olympic Games, Vince Carter dribbled into the lane and literally launched himself over a seven-foot-two helpless French center named Frederic Weis. The usually mild-mannered Carter, who had been playing the entire tournament with eerie edginess (perhaps brought about by recent beefs with cousin/teammate Tracy McGrady and his embezzling agent William "Tank" Black), looked like he wanted to do something awful to Weis. In mid-flight, as Carter continued to elevate, he spread his legs to clear the flat-footed giant; his groin crashed into Weis's face and knocked his head back. Carter, in completing one of the more incredible dunks in history, had succeeded in emasculating the Frenchman, only to cap off the defilement by roaring and gesturing to the crowd. In moments like these, the dunk clearly transcends its value as two points: it is performance, catharsis, and degradation. This would also be one of the last laughs that U.S. Basketball enjoyed at the expense of the international community.

In 1992 the Olympic Selection Committee voted to allow NBA players to participate in Olympics; since then the job of U.S. players has been to wantonly put the rest of the world in its place. The starting bunch of Magic Johnson, Michael Jordan, Larry Bird, Charles Barkley, and Patrick Ewing, shamelessly dubbed the "Dream

Team," was assembled to showcase U.S. world basketball dominance. That Carter robbed Weis of his manhood is all too fitting. Though changes were already under way by 2000, foreign players existed in the American imagination as the emasculated "others"—described with a mix of accuracy and jingoist exaggeration as those too weak, too soft, and too passive to compete with our boys. Foreigners were finesse players afraid of contact; they were predictable, nonexplosive athletes: when they dunked the ball, they simply placed it above the hoop and let go.

While a handful of foreign stars had emerged in the 1980s and 1990s—for example, Detlef Schrempf (by way of the University of Washington), Hakeem Olajuwon (by way of the University of Houston), Drazen Petrovic, Sarunas Marciulionis, and Toni Kukoc—the decision to draft a player from overseas into the NBA was always considered a major gamble, if not an act of treason or unjustified outsourcing given the abundance of homegrown talent. At the time of the first Dream Team in 1992, there were only twelve foreign players in the league. That year only one foreigner heard his name called on draft night, when Golden State inconsequentially used its forty-third pick on Yugoslavia's Predrag Danilovic. In 1997 not a single team ventured a draft pick on a prospect from overseas. Bitter Knicks fans remember Frederic Weis all too well as the skinny, unknown 1999 draft pick who never crossed the Atlantic to play in New York. The Knicks' management never recovered from the heat of foolishly selecting Weis over Ron Artest, a troubled but very talented forward out of LaSalle High School in lower Manhattan and St. John's University in Queens and a future All-Star.

Opinions about and the recruitment of foreign players changed quickly and dramatically in the twenty-first century. Today the hoops establishment deems it sound business to look for talent overseas, and owners and general managers increasingly invest their draft picks in foreign stock. The Italian Web site telebasket.com tracks overseas players and international hoops news in thirty-nine languages; it offers an extensive database for NBA talent scouts, complete with video highlights and webcasts of major games. The site's Superguide resource compiles statistics and profiles for thirteen thousand ballers and generates lists of players based on biographical and statistical requirements entered by the site's users. If a team needs a guy six-foot-eight or taller, younger than twenty-five, and averaging more than eight rebounds a game while shooting 50 percent or better from the field, Superguide will scan the globe to produce a list of applicable candidates.

The Houston Rockets, by selecting Yao Ming with the first pick in the 2002 draft, placed the future of the franchise in the hands of a Chinese athlete. By opening night of the 2005–06 season, more than eighty foreign players had secured spots on team rosters. The San Antonio Spurs have fielded the most consistently successful team over the last several years, and they have a nucleus of three foreign-born stars: point guard Tony Parker of France, shooting guard Manu Ginobili (from Argentina by way of the Italian pro leagues), and power forward/center Tim Duncan (out of Wake Forest University) from the island of St. Croix.

With the sweep of globalization, NBA teams no longer play for a national audience: well over two hundred countries watch the NBA. When Yao suited up for his first game with the Rockets, 600–800 million people in China tuned in. In 2005, New Line Features and NBA Entertainment released *The Year of the Yao*. In awkward yet typical NBA marketing hyperbole, the film's promo announced: "Upon his broad shoulders, and his even longer wingspan, is a bridge linking the cultural, athletic, and political divide between East and West." The NBA, readily applauding the powers of its most important international salesman, has legitimately built an international sport and cultural empire. The globalization of the NBA offers an exceptionally deep well of potential new consumers. Indeed, what incentive does the NBA have to bolster its following in local markets when the potential for growth in China and other interested countries is colossal? When a Rockets game comes on in China, more Chinese viewers tune in than the combined number of viewers in the United States watching all televised NBA games on that night.

In their home countries, NBA stars enjoy hero status and lucrative endorsement deals. Spain's Pau Gasol, the 2001–02 rookie of the year, pitches cookies and a sports drink, in addition to serving as the cover boy and spokesman for the European version of the video game NBA *Inside Drive 2003*. In Germany, Dirk Nowitzki is Nike's top dog. In one of his sneaker commercials, Nowitzki is shown shooting free throws in a driveway somewhere in suburbia. It's nighttime and Nowitzki swishes each one so as to not wake the neighbors, but then he suddenly falters, bricking a shot and startling the sleeping community. As the lights on the street go on, Notwitzki offers apologetically, "Entschuldigung!" (Excuse me!).

Accompanying this rapid revaluation of overseas players has been a new dialogue on foreign and domestic basketball. Whereas the superiority of American ballplayers is traditionally rooted in physical dominance—stronger, faster, hungrier athletes—today such physical traits, long associated with black athleticism, no longer denote basketball preeminence. In fact, this "natural" physicality is often dissociated from basketball ability, posited instead as the opposite of technical competence. Scouts, NBA management, and the press warily scrutinize the athleticism of up-and-coming black talent as a potential crutch that often masks poor fundamentals and a lack of fundamental basketball knowledge. European players, on the other hand, have mastered the basics: they box out, move without the ball, and make the extra pass. Presumed to be more coachable and less individualistic than their American counterparts, overseas ballers, on the whole, are smarter basketball players and (minus the occasional contractual difficulties) wiser acquisitions. In this backlash against homegrown talent, many believe that American basketball is increasingly flash, while foreign ball connotes substance. America's manly dunkers are now looked at as one-dimensional vertical leap specialists with slamming ability rather than basketball ability. The throwback players of the next era are more likely to come from the fractured republics of the former Yugoslavia than from farm towns in Indiana or the hard streets of Detroit.

In September 2002, the inevitable happened. The U.S. basketball team, another installment of the Dream Team, lost in international competition at the World Basketball Championships, falling not once but on three occasions. After losses to eventual champion Yugoslavia, Argentina, and Spain, the U.S. team finished in sixth place in a field of sixteen. The conspicuous absence of some top-tier NBA players was part of the reason for the team's humiliating performance. Whether fearful of injury, apathetic, or afraid of showing poorly in limited minutes or unfavorable rotations, most of the NBA elite took a pass on the competition. Without the likes of Shaquille O'Neal, Kobe Bryant, Tracy McGrady, Jason Kidd, or Allen Iverson, Team USA operated at a notch below maximum capacity, but it still possessed more than enough talent to win the event. In recent years in international play, the Americans have looked befuddled by the complicated, shifting zone defenses used against them. With zone defense only newly permissible in the NBA, in 2005, U.S. Basketball hired Mike Krzyzewski of Duke University to coach its national teams in 2006 and 2008 in the hopes that a college coach would be more comfortable coaching against the zone than were the NBA coaches generally called upon for the position. Meanwhile, fans, NBA management, and sportswriters cast major doubts on the quality of the American system and the skills, attitude, and hoops IQ of American ballplayers.

In a recent *Esquire* article on the way Europeans play basketball, the author commented: "They play the game with a kind of engineered beauty, economical, and drama-free, more like the insides of a watch than a racehorse. They play as every part of the whole." If the European game is beautiful, efficient, and free of drama, the implication is that the opposite holds true of the American game. Americans ballplayers are ugly, bungling, and high maintenance—more animal in the wild, as the second part of the quote suggests, than oiled machine.

The U.S. system of developing players pales in comparison to the thriving European model, according to many experts. Dallas Mavericks general manager Don Nelson, who travels extensively to scout and recruit overseas talent, pointed out, "You see other countries doing a lot less in the way of natural resources, a lot less in the way of the funding, a lot less in the way of talent, doing a better job of developing their young players than we are." While the United States still has an edge in the sheer natural ability of its athletes, it hasn't figured out how to mold this talent into rounded ballplayers. Rob Babcock, vice president for player personnel for the Minnesota Timberwolves, suggests that the United States needs to overhaul its entire approach: "It's at the point where we need to brainstorm and really take a look at what's gone wrong with basketball in this country." The Europeans are beating the Americans at the very game the Americans invented and enriched with innovations like the three-pointer and dunking and that they've dominated for over one hundred years.

Some in the know have blasted the players at least as much as, if not more than, the system itself. Michael Sokolove, in a piece in the *New York Times Magazine*, quips, "The NBA doesn't have a thug problem; it has a basketball problem. Its players are the best athletes in all of pro sports . . . but . . . are also the first to have devolved to a point where they can no longer play their own game." The players' outstanding athleticism and constant consumption of ESPN highlights and underexposure to quality basketball education and mentorship has facilitated this implosion. Unable to rely on even one particular groomed shot or move, they can literally do nothing but dunk. The "Big O," Oscar Robertson, voiced his outrage in the *New York Times* about the Shaq-sized holes in players' games, their limited understanding of basketball principles, and a child-like dependence on the dunk. Magic Johnson, a total showman but, like Robertson, one of the smartest and most fundamentally solid and rounded players in history, put together an instructional DVD to school youth on the basics of team play and nearly forgotten one-on-one moves like the drop step.

How did such a decline in U.S. basketball happen? And how did it happen so quickly? And is it even true that the European system better equips and more closely cares for its young ballplayers? A comprehensive look at how young players develop in this country compared to Europe, along with an examination of the industries and individuals investing in and enabling basketball futures in this country will answer these questions, as well as pose new ones.

Tom Konchalski evaluates high school players on the East Coast for *HSBI Report*, a newsletter that he sells exclusively to college coaches. Konchalski began working with the newsletter's creator, Howard Garfinkel, the founder of Five-Star Basketball Camp, in 1977 and bought it from Garfinkel seven years later. Konchalski has probably seen more amateur basketball in the last thirty years than anyone else. Whom better to ask about how the United States develops young players and how the process has changed over the last three decades?

Konchalski explains that the biggest development in amateur basketball during this time has been the rise of nonscholastic, amateur club ball, and it has been to the direct detriment of high school basketball. A player's success on his high school team is no longer the most important factor in determining where he will play after he graduates. Most blue-chip recruiting no longer takes place during the high school season. Rather it takes place during the summer in what's known, incorrectly, as the AAU circuit. (Below I'll get back to what's wrong with this title.) As a result, the late fall and winter months of the scholastic season are often the least critical to a high schooler's basketball future.

Konchalski attributes this shift in the recruiting calendar to three major changes in amateur basketball over the past thirty years. We will consider the first two changes here and the third, on the rising influence of sneaker companies, in a section below. The first change took place in 1982 with the NCAA's creation of an early signing period: an eight-day window, beginning on the second Wednesday in November, during which a high school senior could officially declare his commitment to matriculate at a particular university. The early signing period functions as an insurance policy for colleges while it takes pressure off of seniors who can decide quickly. Before this option, a Division I prospect didn't commit to a college until April of his senior year, when he would sign a National Letter of Intent (NLI). The NLI bound the player to his selected school—assuming he was qualified according to the university's and the NCAA's academic standards—and it meant that the school was committed to providing an annually renewable one-year scholarship. (There haven't technically been any four-year scholarships in over thirty years; that's why a school can just drop a player on scholarship.)

Today if a player doesn't sign an NLI in November, he isn't allowed to sign again until the second Wednesday of the following April. Because the first signing period closes just as high school games get under way, the senior year high school season plays no part in advancing the basketball futures of the many top prospects who sign in November. As a result of the early signing period, university coaches need to find, court, and secure recruits before the high school season.

The second change took place a couple of years after the implementation of the early signing period, when a sizable group of university presidents decided it was high time to reel in their increasingly independent athletic departments. The presidents' acting body, the Presidents Commission, asserting that athletic departments were inefficient, pushed through a series of NCAA regulations designed to contain spending. One cost-cutting item dealt with scouting trips for coaches during the school year. Prior to this point, a coach made one trip to see one, maybe two, prospects in a high school game and a second trip to check out another talent playing elsewhere. This was neither cost-effective nor necessary since shoe companies were already consolidating the best talent from around the country to play in various summer events. The nation's best teenagers gathered at invitation-only, All-Star tournaments and camps like the Nike All-America in Indiana and the Adidas (now Reebok) ABCD Camp in New Jersey and at top amateur team tournaments like the Adidas (now Reebok) Big Time Tournament in Las Vegas. To save time and money, the NCAA tightly limited the number of recruiting trips coaches were permitted to take during the school year; it directed them instead to two ten-day windows in July, with no restrictions on the number of games they could view. While the NCAA is now trying to reverse the trend it started, the summer became the primary recruiting season once the camp and tournament events were positioned as more significant than several months of high school ball. For kids with prime-time aspirations, an invitation to a summer tournament means more than putting together a stellar junior or senior season in a school league. Hot careers are made under the summer sun.

Coaches who are unable to get enough looks at prospects during the summer frenzy or finalize their recruiting plans can rely on crucial three-day team tournaments in the fall and spring. These tournaments, under the auspices of amateur basketball clubs, clash with a student's school agenda. Play begins on a Friday and ends on a Sunday. Students on teams good enough to compete in these tournaments miss at least one day of school (Friday) and often two (Friday and Monday).

In the 1960s and 1970s, things were simpler. College coaches completed their recruiting during the school year through existing relationships with high school coaches, information from scouting services like *HSBI Report*, and an ear for the local buzz. They dealt not with a recruit's amateur club coach or "handlers" but with his high school coach, who, as a member of the school faculty, knew about the player's academic profile as well as his off-the-ball defense. The signing of a player frequently came down to a conversation between two coaches—two educators—unaffiliated with any auxiliary basketball system or sponsoring companies. The calendar change for recruiting limits the value of the high school season and the role of high school coaches, but who is in charge of the crucial nonscholastic circuit? Since both basketball fans and those involved in the game refer to nonscholastic basketball by its better known misnomer—AAU ball—it's commonly assumed that the AAU regulates the non–high school basketball scene.

The AAU, headquartered in Orlando, Florida, holds competitions in a variety of sports for youth in different age categories, ranging from eight and under to nineteen and under. Established in 1888, the AAU first became popular in the 1950s as a track and field association that competed with the NCAA for governing rights over the sport's amateur athletes and events. In the mid-1970s, the AAU became increasingly significant in top-level boys' basketball. Today its flagship basketball event is the Junior Olympics, a national tournament for which teams must qualify through a series of city and state regional tournaments.

The AAU does not, however, organize most of the major summertime hoops events. For example, it has no involvement whatsoever in the Reebok-sponsored Big Time Tournament in Las Vegas or the Nike All-America Camp in Indianapolis. These events are sanctioned by the NCAA—that is, college coaches can attend them and view as many games as they desire—but they are not regulated by the AAU. The coaches involved in these camps and tournaments have to register online with the NCAA. The registration process includes a basic application, a criminal background check, an authorization for release of personal information, and an agreement to adhere to the NCAA's "educational component" rules. If approved by the NCAA, a coach must renew his certification every two years.

In addition to such camps and tournaments, there are traveling teams that compete in club tournaments throughout the spring, summer, and fall (the nonwinter months apart from the school season); these competitions are not sanctioned by the NCAA. Do coaches of traveling teams have to register with the AAU? Are their backgrounds checked, or are these programs accredited?

The only teams that have to register with the AAU are those competing in the very limited number of tournaments that the AAU actually hosts. Many clubs don't bother with an AAU membership. Those that join the AAU must pay a fee and complete some simple paperwork: a team's coach must submit a nonathlete membership application that asks mostly for contact information and basic details of identity. There are no questions about a coach's professional history, qualifications, relationship to the players, or motives for having a team; no question even requires a complete sentence to answer.

The only safety check is the clause in red ink that the applicant must sign to certify that the cursory information provided is correct, that the AAU conduct code described on the Web site will be followed, and that the applicant has never been convicted of a sex offense or felony. (If the applicant is a sex offender, he must apply for membership directly through the AAU national office rather than online or via regular mail.) Instead of asking probing questions about the coaches, the form has only one specific question: a yes-or-no inquiry about whether the applicant has health and accident insurance.

The AAU is popularly conceived as a regulating group that presides over a mass of club coaches, teams, and All-Star tournaments, but such an organization does not exist. There is no governing body in place. Most of what's called "AAU basketball" has nothing to with the AAU and is known generically to the NCAA as "nonscholastic basketball activity." While the AAU needs to more closely monitor the coaches it registers, the association never intended to be anything more than a volunteer-based agency that created opportunities for kids to play competitive sports. The policing powers that it doesn't have are powers that it never had or asked for. Many people, most notably parents, often blindly assume that these powers exist.

Anyone can come off the street to coach a club team, and that's often how teams are started. Of course, most coaches are good-hearted individuals who love basketball and want to offer some constructive fun for the young people in their community. But in the absence of a governing body, conniving individuals can manipulate the lack of structure. Although most coaches never get rich from sneaker company dollars, the sneaker racket has created a curiously high financial and personal incentive to coach teenagers with basketball talent. At the elite club level, a coach who can secure the best local players stands to earn a sneaker sponsorship and, in rare cases, a place on the sneaker company's payroll. And there's the possibility of "payback" should one of his promising young players go pro. Just as a career as a pro basketball player is considered so glamorous that its allure obscures the near impossibility of achieving it, many buy into the mythology of club coaching as a viable rags-to-riches pursuit. Without having to face the scrutiny of a regulating authority or be saddled with involved fathers (in most low-income neighborhoods), these coaches, who are overwhelmingly male, can pursue their own interests without having to justify their dealings or objectives to anyone.

Even a coach with innocent intentions faces an inevitable dilemma that often leads to the corruption of his program. To have a winning team with the opportunity to travel and play in significant, often invitation-only, tournaments and to cover costly operating expenses, a coach generally needs two closely connected things: talented players and a sneaker sponsorship. If he pursues the former, the latter will hopefully follow. Without a sneaker affiliation the coach loses credibility in the eyes of potential players, who see such an affiliation as not simply a status marker but also a pipeline to career advancement. A sneaker endorsement links the club program to the tournaments, camps, and colleges and college coaches sponsored by a particular brand. It also provides the gear and cash necessary to operate without constantly paying out of pocket or fundraising. A sneaker sponsorship becomes paramount to the success of an amateur program; in the process, to the natural polarity between winners and losers is added the economic split between the haves and the have-nots. While not all winning teams score sneaker deals, no losing or mediocre team is even looked at. Thus being on a non-winning team is doubly devastating: a player is both a loser and a have-not. That's a cold lesson in cutthroat business that teen players didn't have to learn twenty years ago.

Meanwhile, the focus for coaches becomes the recruitment of top talent. Understanding xs and os and developing young players matter only peripherally when a coach's worth is determined by his prowess as a recruiter or street solicitor. Too many amateur coaches come from areas like concert and event promotions, gambling, and racketeering—in other words, areas in which what's most important is getting people to believe in what the promoter can do for them—while too few have backgrounds in education, after-school programs or counseling, and formal coaching. Tony Rosa, the legendary EBC coach and founder of a club team in New York that is more than twenty years old, sums it up: "You've got clowns coaching, clowns in control of a great player's future, hangers-on . . . guys who shouldn't be dealing with kids."

The AAU has taken heat in the media and from concerned parents for failing to probe past the red-ink signing clause, and it has begun to administer its own background checks. In December 2003, the *Seattle Times* ran a story on the abuse of athletes, specifically female athletes, at the AAU and high school levels. The story revealed that thirty-eight AAU coaches and volunteers on the AAU roster of over four thousand were convicted felons. In New York City, sexual abuse allegations recently rocked the two biggest and best AAU programs for boys, at Riverside Church in Harlem and the Bronx-based Gauchos.

Rosa traces the phenomenon of what he calls "riding" a star player. Coaches in the club circuit hold an unusually high degree of influence over the child athletes they coach and often come to represent them as unofficial agents. Within the unlegislated sprawl of amateur basketball, club coaches are positioned as the enablers of a young athlete's basketball future. Coupled with the inordinate amount of time a coach spends with a player in intimate circumstances (taking long road trips, sharing meals, sleeping in the same hotels), club coaches have unique opportunities to shape a young person's life. In Rosa's paradigm, a club coach does not teach his apprentice about basketball (and life) by reprimanding him for selfishness or poor sportsmanship, prioritizing school and learning, and having him earn what he wants by setting goals and working toward them; rather, he usually cheats his student out of such lessons. Afraid that criticism may steer a player to a competing program and faced with a lack of professional credentials, club coaches frequently "ride" a talented player. In urban areas, such coaching creates a seemingly paradoxical class of young athletes: spoiled poor kids.

Instead of teaching and requiring basketball basics—like how to jab step to create distance from a defender or box out to gain a position advantage before going for the rebound—coaches simply turn a star player loose. If a kid can naturally blow by someone, that's good enough; if he can jump, he's allowed to just elevate his way to rebounds. As a result, athleticism and size—the very two characteristics that a coach can't coach—become a player's exclusive attributes. The player then gets passed to the coach in college, and the college coach's hands are already tied. He must win to keep his job; because he doesn't have time for remedial training on basic skills, he opts for the most physically marvelous, explosive recruits available and parlays these noncoachable attributes to victories.

Who really controls amateur basketball? The answer is a logo: either a swoosh (i.e., Nike) or three stripes (i.e., Adidas). With few parents around and no safety mechanisms in place, two sneaker companies are watching over the preteens and teens who play amateur club basketball in this country. (Adidas purchased Reebok in the summer of 2005.) Thus the third change in amateur basketball over the last three decades is the most powerful and the most dangerous: the rising and unmitigated influence of sneaker companies in amateur basketball.

Sneaker companies have transformed amateur basketball into a business and amateur ballplayers into product pitchmen. Shoe manufacturers have so-called "grassroots" departments concerned exclusively with amateur athletics. These departments sponsor top amateur club teams and create brand-themed teams by drafting the most talented players available, regardless of where they live or if they're already playing for another club. "Grassroots" basketball has nothing to with helping cash-poor clubs in need of free uniforms and travel money; it's about creating an association and allegiance between a sneaker brand and young talent.

The sneaker companies sponsor the All-Star tournaments and summer camps that have transformed the recruiting process. The grassroots departments determine which Division I prospects will be invited to such events, which will expose them to recruiters, scouts, and coaches from private high schools and prep schools, colleges and universities, and the pros. The sneaker companies pay all the expenses, including an opportunity for the kids to hear from famous athletes and coaches, who are paid to wear the sponsor's sneakers. If a kid is really good, the sponsor may foot the bill for a few of his friends to come as well using some of a very limited number of coveted invitations on presumably less deserving players. It is not insignificant that the kids leave with lots of free shoes and gear stamped with big logos infused with street cred. Moreover, the grassroots divisions sponsor the high school and college programs that the recruits enter, and they supply the sneakers, game uniforms, practice uniforms, workout and leisure clothing, and, often, salaries for the coaches.

Sonny Vaccaro, best known for signing Michael Jordan to his first shoe deal with Nike, came up with the concept of paying college coaches to have their teams wear a sneaker company's shoes. Prior to Vaccaro's hiring at Nike in 1978, Adidas relieved university sports budgets of sneaker costs and scored free advertising by giving away its sneakers. Without opening its checkbook, Adidas had successfully cornered the college team market. Vaccaro convinced Nike that it would have to pay to penetrate Adidas's monopoly, and so began the business of floating a small sum of cash—a surprise treat—along with the complimentary sneakers the coaches had come to expect. Iona College's Jim Valvano and the University of Maryland's Lefty Driesell were among Nike's first takers. Changes came quickly: what had been a verbal, noncash arrangement was transformed into a contractual, big-money agreement involving higher-profile coaches; among the latter was Georgetown's John Thompson, who was named to Nike's board of directors. Coaches became hired hands, and Nike was suddenly a major presence in the college game, rapidly locking up the biggest programs. The investment proved well worth the small cost for Nike (and for Vaccaro, who was now a powerful player in the sneaker game). Nike paid a fixed fee for a season-long stream of "incidental" advertising: entire teams wore Nikes on television, including the star players who were unable to sign individual deals or deviate from team dress codes because of their amateur status.

The next logical step for sneaker companies was to pay high school coaches and then club coaches to get to their players. The companies could now have a decade's worth of free advertising from individual stars traveling through the amateur ranks.

But the real score—the entire premise of the "grassroots" philosophy—is the creation of meaningful relationships between top amateurs and the sneaker companies that enable their futures. By inviting and paying for an amateur's trip to an All-Star showcase (perhaps even taking along his family and friends), funding his club team and high school basketball experience, retaining his coaches, and essentially facilitating his entire basketball advancement from grade school through college, a sneaker company hopes for and expects loyalty in return. This strategic charity will ideally be repaid when the prodigy goes pro and agrees to officially endorse a sneaker company's product. Now the company can really sell some sneakers.

Young ballplayers in this country are socialized to see themselves as VIPs, free agent guns for hire, and finished products who arrive ready to hop on the court and run with a team on a temporary basis. Bouncing around among the best-connected teams to squeeze in as many profile-building games as possible, teenagers are spread too thin, tired, overexposed, and thoroughly conditioned to think of themselves as individuals and businessmen pursuing the best deal. Elite prospects also frequently play like shameless ball hogs because their hoops futures may be determined in moments rather than over the course of a career. Top players need to impress a college coach who may be looking at them for no more than fifteen seconds as he sorts through two hundred of the best pre-collegians according to Adidas—or according to magazine and Web site scouting services that rank basketball players. As Nick Blatchford, founder of the student-athlete New Heights program in New York City, explains, before growth spurts and puberty, kids with unusual talent are socialized to see themselves as individual stars jockeying for a position in the rankings with other prodigies. At an exceedingly young age, a top-rated kid may start working out one-on-one with a self-proclaimed training guru who has a reputation for developing young talent. Blatchford considers this part of a trend in youth basketball by which kids "play nationally and then train individually" and miss out on the crucial part of practicing and developing within the context of one's team.

As a teenager, I didn't have enough game to play for the top amateur New York City teams, the Gauchos or Riverside Church, but I was good enough to run with a short-lived though successful squad, the Pacers' Athletic Club. Our coach assembled a talented, well-integrated mix of mostly white players from private schools and mostly black players from public schools—standouts like The Collegiate School's Ian McGinnis (who later led the nation in rebounding while at Dartmouth) and Manhattan Center's Aki Thomas (now a top player in Venezuela). The most impressive club tournament we entered was the Delaware Shootout, a massive court-after-court, three-day double-elimination tournament; it featured the nation's best amateur teams and was attended by hundreds of Division I coaches and recruiters. Stephon Marbury headlined the list of past tournament MVPs in the blurb that confirmed our team's registration.

The year we played, 1996, everyone was buzzing about a six-foot-ten forward from New Jersey's Paterson Catholic High School named Tim Thomas, who had the versatility and polish to play all five positions. Thomas went on to play for a year at Villanova before going pro and not living up to the extraordinary hype that was building around him. Though his potential was billed as limitless, the praise was shrewdly accompanied by criticism: the buzz was that Thomas was an aloof ballplayer prone to inconsistency; he would disappear at moments and not always play his hardest. That criticism still haunts Thomas as a professional because of its accuracy.

I was struck by both Thomas's talent and his seeming ambivalence. Whether he was bored by his less skilled peers or simply exhausted was unclear, but he didn't look like he was playing that hard. He reached in and swiped at the ball on defense; on offense the shots in the lane that he could have dunked ferociously were instead lofted up as apathetic floaters and half-hooks. He didn't have much to say to his teammates, nor did he have much time for his coach. Worse yet, he looked about as happy as a teenager working a catering job; the tournament appeared to be a weekend obligation rather than a road trip to play ball with his boys. In retrospect, I'd say that the club basketball scene probably rendered him indifferent or at least physically and emotionally spent. The hectic scheduling and traveling is tiring and isolating, estranging players from friends and family. Amateur basketball has no off-season. The pushing and pulling from all the parties interested in a player, competing for his favor and expecting things from him, can be stressful and depressing. Playing on makeshift teams for coaches who are not regulated, whose intentions are not always clear, and who are frequently better equipped as businessmen and promoters than coaches and mentors can be soulless and corrupting. Club ball offers a recipe for burnout before adulthood; it is a fast way to spoil young men as both people and basketball players. Thomas—who ironically now sponsors his own New Jersey club team, the Tim Thomas Playaz, with money earned on the several teams he's quickly passed through in the NBA—looked like a victim of a system that was not nearly as frenzied or coarse ten years ago as it is today.

It only gets worse at the college level. With even more money at stake, the big business of college basketball offers new pressures and more exploitation for its athletes. When Blatchford sends one of his New Heights players off to college, he knows better than to count on the school to protect and nurture the same ballplayers it frantically courted and to whom it offered scholarships. "We're not just going to drop [a player] off on campus and then say goodbye. We've done that and that's hurt a lot of kids. . . . We're going to have a relationship [with our kids] for . . . life." Outside of less competitive conferences, like the Ivy and Patriot Leagues, Blatchford sees time and again what elite college sports boil down to: "The graduation rates speak for themselves. There's no real interest in graduating kids from college. . . . What's expected of [them] is to win at basketball, perform on the court; anything above and beyond that is a bonus. That's the cold, harsh reality." The 2004 NCAA title game pitted two schools, the University of Connecticut and Georgia Tech, with identically miserable graduation rates for its players: 27 percent.

Tony Rosa, whose dream job would be to coach the underdog Clemson Tigers, the perennial bottom-feeders of the Atlantic Coast Conference (ACC), finds the college game disturbing for the same reason as Blatchford: "It's a dirty game all around, *especially* at the highest level, especially the ACC and the Big East and the SEC [Southeastern Conference], all the major conferences. . . . You've got [celebrated TV college basketball announcer] Dick Vitale just raving and raving about what a beautiful thing it is to play for these universities, to play for these great men. Please! It's all bullshit. Nobody's innocent. There are really good people out there—I never mean everybody—but it's not just that the AAU game is dirty."

The city kids that Rosa coaches at Rucker Park over the summers and on his club team often hit the wall hard in college. Many feel deceived and displaced. "I've got guys [former players] calling me up talking about 'Yo' Tony, I'm hungry, I don't have any money.' All the things that they [the recruiter] said were untrue."

Murray Sperber, the Bob Knight critic, writes at length about what he considers the myth of the college student-athlete. The era of the student-athlete embodied by Bill Bradley passed long ago. Today the college experience for many blue-chip athletes often can be divided into three equally ugly and morally deficient phases: entry, experience, and departure. College life often starts on a shaky footing, when an anything-goes precedent is established. The entry phase begins when improper bonuses such as cash payments and goods are offered to a top recruit and his family, commonly through a third party like a college booster, a "friend of the program," or an assistant coach. The head coach then comes to the forefront to speak with the recruit and his family about what the player can expect while on campus. The coach promises a comfortable academic and social adjustment regardless of the transitions that the teenager will have to make. These transitions are often major departures from a student's home comfort zone: he may be going from an urban environment to a rural one or vice versa; from a mostly minority student body to an overwhelmingly white population; from a small, parochial high school to an enormous public university; there are many possible changes or combinations of changes.

Once the student is enrolled, the school experience frequently proves even less certain than had been promised at the initial recruitment stage. In 1973, when the NCAA converted four-year scholarships into one-year grants with an option to renew, it transferred a great deal of power to coaches and athletic departments at the direct expense of the security of the students. College athletes now had an added pressure: the knowledge that injury, a failure to perform in the classroom, or the taking of extra semester(s) to fulfill graduation requirements could leave them without a scholarship at the start of a new semester.

Because much of a university's personality and bottom line derive from its sports teams, college teams make enormous demands on their athletes. The demands on an athlete's time are so great that his free time is nearly eliminated. Formal and informal workouts, team meetings, video sessions, and other obligations make playing college sports at the Division I level an around-the-clock endeavor. In 1991 the NCAA established the "four- and twenty-hour rule," setting a maximum of four hours a day and twenty hours a week for in-season team commitments. However, teams evade the rule by calling some activities, such as team practices, "voluntary"; at the same time, they punish players who do not participate with (for example) scorn from a team captain (mandated by the coach) or a reduction in their playing time. A player's obligations are year-round, effectively eroding the off-season. By controlling their free time and profiting financially from such a monopoly on players' lives, teams convert their athletes into unpaid laborers. As a result, they frequently foster a dynamic of guilt on the part of the school and feelings of resentment from the athletes.

Schools manage their guilt (and navigate the bureaucracy of academic requirements mandated by the NCAA) by coddling their athletes through a unique system of support that is predicated upon the extension of favors. Division I programs provide a customized academic support team for their athletes. An academic coordinator advises athletes on which courses to take and then monitors their performance in these courses throughout the year, sometimes acting as a liaison between an often absent athlete and his professor. Professors are expected to adjust to the scheduling needs of athletes who take their classes by preparing abbreviated packets to cover coursework that is often missed and offering alternative dates for exams and assignments. Tutors are on hand for all subjects. In many cases, the tutors are work-study students who are either concurrently taking the same classes as the athletes or have already taken them and done well.

Meanwhile, athletes see themselves as "special cases" appeased through privileges and entitled to every single one of them in lieu of the cash they really want. To advance their sport careers, they feel they might as well exploit the schools that are using them. The athletes who do not have a serious interest in higher education use the university as a high-exposure personal showcase for professional suitors, or they convert the college team into a *de facto* minor league team in which to develop their skills and profile. Of course, many athletes are getting a four-year degree that their basketball prowess and not their academic abilities made possible. At the highest levels, NCAA sports perpetuate a tacit arrangement of mutual exploitation between a school and its athletes, with either party ready to bail at any moment. Just as schools can choose not to renew a player's scholarship, a player can relinquish his amateur eligibility, dropping his team, teammates, and coaches, to turn pro.

In the second phase of college, athletes at Division I schools commonly float through school in a bubble within the bubble of normal college life. This second bubble keeps them even further away from the reality of the outside world. On one hand, top-level college athletes are the most privileged kids on campus. On the other hand, they are the most closely scrutinized and shamelessly exploited. If a starting cornerback gets an "F" in a class, it may put him at risk of academic ineligibility; that, in turn, could cost the school millions in potential revenues if the football team cannot make a desired bowl game because the cornerback had to sit out a pivotal game. Meanwhile, with an "F" either in the classroom or on the playing field the cornerback may lose his starting spot and eventually his scholarship. Now that's pressure! To blow off steam in a scenario such as the one described, athletes often feel that they might as well have as much fun as they can while still living on the university's dime. They party a lot, indulge in the groupie circles that form instantly, and have as recklessly good a time as possible.

Between their on-court importance, off-court status, and preferential treatment in the classroom, celebrity athletes are not seen as typical peers by their fellow students. They may be despised by resentful classmates who receive far less support from the school, or they may be beloved by idolatrous classmates who live out their own sports dreams vicariously through them. Either way, they're under the proverbial microscope: watched, gawked at, fantasized about, cursed, etc. Even a basketball good guy like Dikembe Mutombo, one of the NBA's biggest philanthropists, is notoriously talked about by his former Georgetown classmates as an unlikely gigolo in college. The celebrated story goes that the awkward seven-foot-plus African native, with a baritone voice and thick accent, walked into a party at school, threw his arms up in a provocative gesture, and asked, "Who wants to sex Mutombo?" The line is immortalized through T-shirts and Web sites.

Professors and coaches, too, may have trouble managing their personal feelings toward both the athletes and the school's star system. Some professors may repress feelings of rage and discomfort when they adjust their courses to suit certain individuals. Others will happily acquiesce, sending athletes along with a pat on the back and a feeling of self-satisfaction for doing their part in helping the university toward victory on game day. Faculty members who both teach and coach must deal with an inevitable conflict of interests. The corrupt University of Georgia father-son combo of Jim Harrick Sr. and Jim Harrick Jr. never even made an effort to reconcile the conflict between fielding a winning sports team and educating athletes academically and ethically. At Georgia, where the senior Harrick served as head coach and the junior Harrick was his assistant, Junior taught a class called "Coaching Principles and Strategies of Basketball." In a scandal that cost both Harricks their jobs at the school, Junior administered a bogus twenty-question final that would determine final grades. It asked such questions as, "How many points does a three-point field goal account for in a basketball game?" and "In your opinion, who is the best Division I assistant coach in the country?" The last question, which was multiple choice, listed four assistant coaches, including Harrick. Hangovers and all, every student got an "A" in the course.

The final phase of college for an athlete—departure—is just as disturbing as the first two. Often a top athlete never graduates. If he does, what tangible skills will he have gained in college if he isn't drafted by the pros? One of the first cases of the overt exploitation of athletes to garner extensive publicity occurred in the late 1970s. Oklahoma State graduated football star Dexter Manley, who, having scored a six out of forty on the ACT, entered the school illiterate and left the same way.

Critics of big-time college sports deem the preferential treatment of athletes both an injustice and a disservice to the athletes it allegedly benefits. A sheltering of the athletes and a lowering of expectations only sets them up for a rude awakening in the real world, where employers, unimpressed by rebounding ability, will expect independent, competent workers. It can also be argued that by not providing a system of extra assistance, the school does not protect its recruits from academic failure. If an athlete is a "special admit" who is entering college without an academic background, he is likely to drown unless he receives the help he needs to keep pace with his better-prepared peers. Schools commit an injustice when they accept a student who they know writes at a seventh-grade level and then leave him to flounder amid coursework and expectations that he cannot realistically handle.

The U.S. system of developing amateur ballplayers creates a scenario of mutual abuse by which the young athletes exploit a system that's exploiting them. Is it possible, then, to marry high-stakes, corporation-sponsored basketball with genuine concern for education? Can a student-athlete truly live up to both titles? The Europeans don't seem to think so. Their solution: rather than half-heartedly attempting to join the two, they keep school and competitive sports completely separate. School is strictly for classroom learning, and sports belong elsewhere and as far away as possible.

In Europe, elementary, high school, and college basketball do not exist. There's no sneaker-sponsored amateur scene that culminates in the summer recruiting hysteria. Without college teams, teenagers do not have to audition for coaches who are ready to lure them in with empty promises and scholarship dollars. Amateurs do not jump around from club team to club team; from high school to prep school; from secondary school to college; from college to college; from junior college to university; from college to the pros. They stay put. They play for one program, under the supervision of one set of coaches, from pre-puberty all the way through the professional ranks. What is known as club basketball in Europe is nothing like our conception of club (or AAU) basketball. In lieu of sneaker-sponsored travel teams and scholastic basketball, clubs in Europe operate as centralized academies that develop young players from the junior ranks through the pros, developing their skills and managing their basketball and business futures. The clubs function, in many respects, like a less corporate version of the sports and entertainment conglomerate IMG.

Started in the 1960s by Mark H. McCormack, IMG, with offices in thirty countries, manages athletes, writers, models, and entertainers through a network of in-house enterprises and relationships with other firms; with these tools IMG develops a client's talent, markets him, and sells him to companies who either buy his services (for example, an athlete gets a contract with a sports team) or use his name and image (in an endorsement, perhaps). Tennis players and golfers with IMG, for example, train at IMG facilities with IMG coaches, while the group's agents handle the athlete's tournament schedule, as well as his endorsement deals and other commercial interests.

Another way to think of European basketball is as an apprentice system. A ten-year-old interested in learning the game signs on for a basketball apprenticeship at a given club to learn the sport from the masters, in-house coaches who came through the same program. Retired professional players coach the senior or professional teams, and players on the senior teams coach the players on the junior teams. At the age of sixteen, the apprentice, after extensive training, is ready to move on and can turn pro. Like with an apprenticeship in a conventional trade, the elders train an apprentice to think of his sport as a craft with particular skills that have to be mastered before he can move on the next level and honor the tradition of his craft. The thinking goes that talent is not to be turned loose but is to be channeled so as to fit into the needs of a group. By mastering the skills—many of which are team skills—the apprentice affirms the original design of the game and, in turn, the craft's tradition.

Blatchford, whose family comes from Croatia, spent six months there coaching at a well-established club. In the United States, amateurs learn through playing; it is on-the-job training whereby skills and concepts come through osmosis. In Croatia, as in the rest of Europe, basketball is learned through drilling. Practice and how to most effectively use practice time are central to player development. Thinking through player development led the East Europeans to focus on plyometric training—specific workout regiments targeting the fast-twitch muscles in the legs that are responsible for jumping and quick movements—before the rest of the basketball world became serious about it. Progress in plyometrics eventually spawned a multimillion dollar industry based on a realistic (or unrealistic) fulfillment of the dream of dunking, and the industry now advertises in basketball magazines like *SLAM*. Fittingly, the best white athletes—in terms of athleticism—come from Eastern Europe.

A top athlete's ego evolves differently in Europe. While basketball occupies a smaller space in European popular culture and in the imagination of children dreaming of their futures, the Europeans flatten egos by taking the phenomenon of teenagers going pro in the United States and turning it on its head. Until the NBA imposed an age mandate for players entering the draft, American players routinely spurned college to turn pro at eighteen or nineteen because they'd seen the precious few that had successfully made the jump.

The best in Europe turn pro at sixteen. At such an early, seminal age, no matter how unusually gifted a player may be, he is still significantly developing physically, mentally, and emotionally. Facing bigger and better competition inevitably reverses some of the head-swelling that comes with being a prodigy. This deliberate throwing to the wolves is a lesson in humility that teaches players to rely on their teammates, realize their limitations, and play team ball. Physically they can't have it any other way. Those who don't get the message through this cutthroat initiation are promptly chewed out by the coaching staff. Overseas, selfish and showy play is simply not tolerated, and for that reason, it's not part of the basketball culture.

This unmistakable show of authority contrasts jarringly with the ethos of coaching teenagers in the United States. Here coaches often vie for players' approval like sad puppy dogs; they pimp out their athletes for sneaker contracts, and they emphasize one-on-one play by their teen superstars to mask nonexistent concepts of "team" and bolster their own celebrity. Ron Naclerio, who was both the club coach and the high school coach for Rafer "Skip to My Lou" Alston, became famous simply by making available a highlight tape of his most stylish player's one-on-one repertoire.

By keeping school and sports separate, Europeans never face eligibility issues, and players can stay in school while being paid to play professionally. Because turning pro is not predicated upon dropping out of school, a sixteen-year-old professional can theoretically pursue his hoop dreams and education simultaneously while earning money in the process. Such a system does not come from a greater appreciation of education; in fact, the opposite holds true. The Europeans refuse to pay even lip service to the student-athlete ideal; they make it even harder than it is in the United States for a teenager to juggle school and basketball obligations. A pro teenager in Europe who stays in school faces the same expectations as a teenager in the United States who leaves school. Like in the NBA, in the European professional leagues there are no NCAA-type restrictions on practice time, game scheduling, or team commitments. A matriculating student in Europe must manage coursework while completing as many basketball obligations as his contract stipulates. In this country, high school and college athletic programs still place restrictions on practice time and team duties, however half-heartedly they are instituted and administered.

The resulting differences in style of play are most apparent when the United States plays a team in international competition. When Blatchford watched the United States take on Lithuania in a losing effort during the 2004 Olympics, he immediately noticed a difference in how the two teams moved the ball in their respective offenses: "[When the Lithuanians have possession,] the ball moves ten times before it hits the floor, and then they get a wide-open three and they can knock it down. The ball comes down to the other end, and it hits the floor ten times before it moves." This difference in ball movement—a team collectively passing the ball to find an open shot versus a single player dribbling to create his own shot—reflects the broader difference between the more team-oriented European game and the American game, which relies more heavily on one-on-one play.

How and why did the Americans get away from the team game while the Europeans embraced it? The Dream Team's 1992 gold medal Olympic campaign in Barcelona serves as the singularly most important moment in the transfer of basketball knowledge and popularity overseas. In 1992 professionals were finally permitted to compete in the Olympics, and Team USA stocked its roster with several of the game's all-time best players. The timing was golden for U.S. basketball: not only was this arguably the best crop of talent in NBA history but even with their individual abilities and superstar profiles, these players still relished team basketball. Even Michael Jordan readily shared the ball and the limelight with his celebrity peers. Team USA blew away completely outmatched foreign teams by forty and fifty points but did so tastefully, in the spirit of team play. The players used strategy and moved the ball rather than simply taking turns sticking it to their defenders. They subbed in and out selflessly, stood and cheered for one another, and, with a couple of exceptions, bit their trash-talking tongues and curbed their swagger. Sentimental guys like Magic Johnson and David Robinson radiated gratitude, helping the rest of the guys to fully realize that not only were they a part of history but they were also fulfilling the most noble of athletic duties: playing for one's country. Thus the original Dream Team provided the model for how to play basketball at its finest level, and the foreign players and coaches took careful notes. Their heroes had just worked them through a clinic, and they couldn't have taken their beatings more gracefully. While the foreign teams got right to work on mastering team ball, basketball in the United States took a different direction.

Upon closer inspection, a fissure in American basketball could be seen within the cast of the original Dream Team. The 1992 games represented a final go-round for Larry Bird and Magic Johnson, the last ambassadors of team basketball. While Bird and Magic were only half a decade apart from Michael Jordan in their NBA tenures, the cultural gulf proved colossal, akin to a generational difference. Michael Jordan never again shared the ball or the stage like he did in Barcelona. And why would he? His individual greatness catapulted the Bulls to six titles and validated the Bulls' design template for an NBA squad: one Batman, one thoroughly deferential Robin (Scottie Pippen in the Bulls' case), and a supporting cast of loyal, self-sacrificing role players. Drastically different business orientations further separated Jordan from Bird and Magic. The NBA's popularity grew through Bird and Magic in the 1980s under the visionary eye and controlling hand of Commissioner David Stern, but Jordan made the NBA an international brand. In many ways, the split once again came down to a matter of sole.

Bird and Magic, like basically all the players before them, wore Converse. First shelling out Chuck Taylors, Converse, without any competition, easily maintained a monopoly on the feet of NBA players from the start of the league in the middle of the twentieth century. The college game was Adidas territory, Converse had the pros, and sneakers just weren't a big deal. The famously frugal Bird and a pre-businessman Magic (who wasn't yet concerned with opening movie theaters or buying up Starbucks franchises) happily took more than adequate sums of cash to put on green and white or purple and yellow Converses. But Michael Jordan and Sonny Vaccaro changed everything in the mid-1980s, creating the sneaker industry as it's understood today.

Jordan signed a long-term contract with the Bulls that represented big bucks for a newcomer but chump change for a mogul. The Nike deal that tied Jordan's earnings to sneaker sales made him filthy rich and built the Nike empire. In many ways, Jordan's loyalty was to the Nike swoosh—or more specifically the Jumpman that was created for him—rather than to the NBA or the United States. When Reebok signed to outfit the Dream Team, Jordan stood firm in his commitment to Nike. At the medals ceremony in Barcelona, Jordan, in a now famous gesture of capitalism over all, conspicuously folded over the collar on his warmup jacket to cover the Reebok logo on the neckline .

After 1992, the NBA followed a new path, one determined by individual endorsement deals, signature sneakers, and one-on-one isolation plays. Overseas it followed the paradigm crystallized by the team-spirited Dream Team. The result, as one writer on the topic put it in an almost offensive statement in *Esquire*, "We stopped making players . . . in America, the way we stopped making our own hotel maids and muscle cars." The outsourcing of basketball talent—slow at first and then rapid toward the end of the 1990s—was under way.

In the same *Esquire* article, coaching great Larry Brown reduces the geographic shift in basketball prowess to Social Darwinism: American kids from the ghetto used to be hungry for opportunities like scholarships, knew they had the raw talent but not the formal skills, and did the dirty work to break into the basketball world; they were eager to be taught the game's finer points. That same sense of urgency exists in today's foreign players while the American kids have gotten fat on a diet of pampering, sneaker company flattery, and freebies. Indeed, one can argue that many overseas players come from an even rougher, more hard-core ghetto upbringing than the underprivileged American kids. The Nets' Zoran Planinic from Bosnia-Herzegovina, for example, woke up during his childhood to air raids, went without electricity for long stretches, and ate from aid packets distributed during the war in the Balkans.

Tom Konchalski maintains that the Europeans learned from American coaching masters long before the Dream Team lessons in 1992: "we've taught the rest of the world. We sent our coaches around, and [European coaches] very diligently took down every . . . word that they spoke." Konchalski is referring to a host of distinguished U.S. college coaches, such as Bob Knight, Dean Smith, and Lou Carnesecca (the legendary former coach at St. John's), who brought their meticulous, drill-centered approach to teaching clinics for coaches and players in countries such as Spain and Italy. As far back as the late 1960s, European programs brought in coaches like Carnesecca for the purpose of modeling. Not coincidentally, arguably the highest level of basketball in Europe is played in the Spanish and Italian pro leagues.

NBA teams draft a large number of Europeans not only because of their exceptional skills but also because of the way pro teams decide whom to pick. They invest heavily in the three-day pre-draft workouts held annually in Chicago. A potential draft pick's physical attributes are measured—for example, sprinting speed, leaping ability, wingspan, and height. In addition, the candidate is run through numerous drill sessions, and the Europeans often test unusually well on these because they were raised on drills.

As touched upon above, the Europeans routinely and in a calculated manner push kids with sports potential to become professional athletes. Even before their teenage years, those who are chosen head to an academy for the singular purpose of "building" a professional athlete. In the United States, such an academy model also exits, but it's mostly accessed by aspiring tennis players rather than by prodigies in hoops or other team sports—and specifically team sports that draw large numbers of kids from lower-income households. Academies, which are basically boarding schools for tennis education, offer full-time physical and mental training that is prioritized ahead of academics. In the United States, racket-wielding wonder kids from all over the world gather at academies that are generally in affluent areas with agreeable climates, most commonly Florida. (Sunshine, money, and tennis go together just like blacktop, poverty, and basketball.) Once enrolled in an academy, youngsters work individually and in groups with coaches specializing in all facets of the game. Players develop through drilling and video analysis; they build stamina and strength through sophisticated cardiovascular exercises, plyometrics, and sport-specific weight-lifting; they achieve a psychological and mental edge through "mental toughness" classes that combine visualization and focusing techniques, meditation, and self-affirmation; moreover, a mathematical system provides a methodical way to handle each and every real game situation. Schools like the IMG-owned Nick Bolletieri Tennis Academy (where Andre Agassi started out) strive to internalize in their students an all-encompassing methodology that simplifies the game of tennis and is based upon the number 5. Bolletieri's famed System 5 divides each side of the net into five zones, the path of a groundstroke backswing into five lengths (each equivalent to the size of a racket's head), and the trajectory that a ball travels over the net into five heights (each equivalent to the height of one racket perpendicular to the ground); there are additional five-based schemes. Employing this system, a tennis player standing in zone 3, the area between the service line and the baseline, should take the racket back three racket-head lengths on a backswing and hit the ball high enough to clear the net by at least three racket lengths. Coaches at academies in Europe apply this same sort of mathematical thinking to the game of basketball.

In the United States, when an academy prospect becomes a pro, he or she is generally warmly received by both fans and the sportswriting community. Rarely does one criticize the young person for pursuing a dream and spurning an education in the process. School dropouts who opt for baseball are similarly treated. The press celebrates European basketball players in much the same way, never questioning a developmental system that doesn't even attempt to actualize the student-athlete concept. In contrast, American basketball players who leave school to turn pro tend to elicit a different reaction from the public and the sports media. The response frequently consists of disapproval for not going to college and a "told-you-so" warning that they will most likely fail or at least struggle a great deal. By not going to school and getting a bachelor's degree, they won't have something to fall back on should a playing career fall through. The main difference between American tennis players, golfers, and baseball players and American basketball players is, of course, the difference between white and black.

There's truth in attributing this double standard to racial differences. The older, more conservative end of this country generally and historically considers any perceived shortcut to success ingenuous. The assessment becomes uglier when those who are supposedly taking the easy way out are not only black but also brash and confident, newly and suddenly rich, and completely unapologetic about doing what they needed/wanted to do to get to the top. To generalize, basketball players in this country fit this description and adhere to a new ethos: work the system to get ahead. This is one of the most frequent messages in hip-hop and throughout American black popular culture. To some, it's an innovative and entirely necessary survival mechanism to combat limited resources and institutional racism, while to others it's simply a fresh reading of the American dream: we are in this country to move up, no matter what anyone says or what it takes to get there.

It is evident that the backlash against American black players fails on two different accounts. First, the backlash comes out of a sense of guilt about America's failed education system. From the unsuccessful No Child Left Behind legislation at the elementary and high school levels to the lack of support for athletes and "special admits" in college, our school system does not sufficiently care for or empower young people. Rather than an acknowledgment of this structural failure and an attempt to fix it, it's easier to blame kids for spurning school and not buying into a doomed system.

The backlash is also unfair because by not going to college or dropping out, basketball players are actually acting rationally. As described above in this chapter, the NCAA game serves the interests of schools rather than those of the players. By going to school, a basketball player signs on for an uncertain, frequently bogus educational and social experience that may not even be justified in the end with the granting of a degree. Why not just risk the insecurity of a professional career if that's the reason he's in school anyway? Skipping college is also rational on a financial level for two reasons. First, generally speaking, basketball is a high-risk sport in which the chance of career-threatening injury is always present. An injury in college could either end a player's career all together or level his potential to get drafted. Therefore, the safest move is to turn pro at the earliest possible moment and sign a guaranteed contract. Second, the human body does not permit a player to participate in the sport at a high level for a long time. Basketball primes come and go quickly, and by the early or mid-thirties a player's physical makeup leaves him on the fast track to irrelevance.

Because of the game's physical risks and because the supply of talent eclipses the demand, the average NBA career lasts less than five years. Some say the prevalence of teenagers entering the pros out of high school markedly contributes to the shortness of NBA lifespans: teenagers haven't developed sufficiently to experience productive, long-lasting careers. But the reality is that young prospects have a potentially enormous cash and security advantage by going pro while still in their teens. The salary structure of the NBA prevents young players from getting their full market value until they have played for several seasons. The first awesome, long-term contract, known as a "max deal," comes only after a player has served out his first, tightly capped contract, which, before the terms of the 2005 CBA and with an extension option, ran five years. Going pro as a teenager or going pro after college may mean the difference between a player's earning two max deals or only one, and that could mean a difference of tens of millions of dollars. A team will readily pony up a max contract to a top player in his early or late twenties, but it will rarely invest in a player who, because he spent four years in college, is up for a second max contract at the age of thirty-three or thirty-four. That's old in NBA years. A player in his mid-thirties will usually get a less lucrative "veteran exemption" rate on a shorter-term deal. The earlier one starts on the All-Star career, the better.

A blasting of individual players misses the bigger point because it channels attention away from a system that's creating and selling damaged goods. Even criticizing kids for their propensity to dunk isn't fair. The dunk, after all, is the best shot that a player can get during the course of a game; it's the highest percentage field goal. A player hears all of his life that the object on offense is to get the easiest shot possible, to get a layup. The dunk is even better than the layup. It leaves no room for error from the time the ball leaves the shooter's hands until it goes through the hoop because the ball doesn't leave his hands *until* his hand(s) enter(s) the hoop. It's the basketball equivalent of direct deposit. Dunking is problematic only when players allow its seductive lure to distract them from learning other parts of the game.

When I was a fourteen-year-old camper at Duke University Summer Camp, I listened to Quin Snyder, a Duke alumnus and former University of Missouri head coach, give one of the standard lectures on being the best you can be as a ballplayer and (more important) a person. If a young player had a certain amount of athletic ability and basketball competency, Snyder told the campers—to my surprise even then—the best thing he could do for his game was to work on his dunking. He should keep working on approach and elevation until he could dunk comfortably and consistently; this would take his game literally to new heights. Snyder was right, too. As a high school senior, I could execute a faux dunk. My dunk meant going up on the left side of the hoop, taking off on my right leg (which was stronger and springier than my left), and extending the ball over the rim and catching just enough of the rim to cause a minimal snap and some reverberation.

This was lame even by European dunking standards. Despite my specialized shoes, plyometrics, and prayers, that was the closest I ever got. Had I been able to do it cleanly and unambiguously just once, I would have earned some serious praise from my teammates and classmates. Had I been able to throw it down consistently in games, I would have been an entirely different player; my game would have been profoundly more effective.

As Michael Sokolove points out, the NCAA banned the dunk in college play in 1967 with a ruling that "the ball cannot be thrown into the basket," and for nearly a decade the dunk was prohibited. This ruling was an attempt to neutralize the sensational UCLA center Lew Alcinder, later known as Kareem Abdul-Jabbar. The seven-foot-one Abdul-Jabbar was simply too big and too good for the competition. Sokolove argues that the NCAA ruling ultimately benefited Abdul-Jabbar and the game in general because it forced him and others like him to refine different parts of their offensive repertoire. Unable to go in for dunks, Abdul-Jabbar mastered a dependable bank shot and his famed sky-hook. (The sky-hook is now an anachronism that has evolved into a jump- or half-hook and looks nothing like what it once was—a sweeping, full-motion movement that started at the waist and was powered by striding legs. George Zidek, another UCLA center and short-time pro, nearly manufactured a career out of resurrecting the full-motion sky-hook in the late 1990s.) The no-dunk rule might have helped Abdul-Jabbar in the long run, but a celebration of the ban on dunking is a celebration of a rule change with a blatant racial premise.

There are pros and cons to the centrality of the dunk in today's game and basketball culture. But to blame today's high flyers for the diminishing quality of basketball is, as a commentator on ESPN radio once put it, like blaming children for a dysfunctional family. The same is true when American players are blamed for the shortcomings that have directly come about as a result of the big-business structure of basketball in America. While the U.S. system is clearly sick, is the European system any healthier? Is the European approach to building ballplayers worthy of the massive praise it has received?

The European structure has its own merits and deficiencies. It protects young athletes from the merry-go-round of the exhausting and generally corrupting U.S. club circuit. It instills an appreciation of authority and team and positions young prospects as basketball apprentices rather than accomplished guns for hire. It is certainly less convoluted and bureaucratic, less driven by commercial interests, and more honest with the young people it trains. However, it's also highly controlling and incestuous, and it places no value on education. To a large extent, the European system produces better basketball players because these players have been trained to be more dutiful members of both their clubs and their countries. The difference is made plain when American high schoolers, learning from the pros, turn down invitations to play on a junior national team because such a commitment would overlap with a sneaker-sponsored summer tournament.

There are indications that U.S. basketball is moving in the right direction. Maybe the student-athlete concept is not entirely dead because some parties seem genuinely interested in reform. In 2004, just before the Final Four in San Antonio, NCAA president Myles Brand announced a reform mandate for college athletics known as the incentive/disincentive plan. (The plan was later approved.) Ironically the crux of the plan was just what Brand's one-time adversary, Bob Knight, had preached for decades. Under the mandate, schools with ballplayers failing to meet certain academic requirements would lose a scholarship. Schools with repeated failures could lose NCAA tournament privileges and even NCAA membership. To assess the schools that were in trouble and to take general inventory of the problem, the NCAA would implement a point system that awarded one point for each student who remained eligible during each semester and for each new student-athlete that enrolled.

The NCAA is following up on Proposition 48, which, when passed in 1983, implemented a group of eligibility requirements for incoming freshmen. Those who could play in their first year of college would need to graduate from high school with a 2.0 grade point average (GPA) and a minimum score on the SAT or ACT. Proposition 48 drew extensive criticism, as many considered it unfair on both racial and socioeconomic grounds. With fewer resources at their disposal and generally forced to attend poorer quality schools, lower-income minority students were placed at a disadvantage. In 1992, the NCAA revised Proposition 48; it instituted a sliding scale for GPA and test scores, such that a higher GPA would require a lower minimum SAT or ACT score. While the proposition as a whole was still a flawed system for evaluating student-athletes, the revision made sense and was fairer to minority athletes. Standardized testing is a less sound indicator of aptitude than cumulative GPA, and performance on the SAT or ACT exams is notoriously and dramatically influenced by a test taker's income level and, in turn, his access to preparatory materials and courses. In 1992 the NCAA also raised the total number of core courses that must be included in a student's GPA to thirteen. In the fall of 2005, the number of core courses increased to fourteen, and it will go up yet again to sixteen in 2008.

Even with all its scars, the American game is neither inferior to the European game nor devoid of great beauty or quality players. The European game moves at a much slower pace than that played in the NBA, an attribute that can be taken as a positive or a negative. On one hand, it means that the Europeans take their time to completely execute all parts of their plays—for example, passing the ball, as Blatchford noted about Lithuania. It's hard to criticize that unless we look at if from the other hand: the Europeans slow down to work through an offense because they can't fluidly go at full speed up and down the court.

We know that the European game operates in a lower gear because playing quickly and sustaining a rapid tempo generally proves to be the most difficult part of a foreign player's adjustment to the NBA. Manu Ginobili and Tony Parker of the Spurs move with unusual swiftness for any player—foreign or American—and they've excelled because they can play team basketball with dashing speed: they zip the ball rather than hold or dribble it by default, and when they have an opening, they fly through it. The majority of foreign players can't consistently play skillfully at the rapid NBA pace that Ginobili and Parker have mastered. The American game can be gorgeous because it features huge men with the agility and speed, as well as the stamina, to move quickly and deftly up and down the court, alternating from offense to defense, and capable of seemingly impossible explosions past defenders or to the rim.

American fans suffer through a sloppy regular NBA season that is twenty or so games too long to keep players interested, competitive, and healthy enough to consistently play their hardest. These fans must contend with a contemporary basketball culture rooted in an "F-you, look at me" attitude that has been enshrined and validated by the AND 1 tour. But what occurs in March on the basketball court between college teams that are playing with every ounce of passion is the best representation anywhere in the world of the sport's potential.

The 2005 NCAA tournament provided as clear an indication as any that American basketball is still first rate. Defenders cut off the baseline and challenged every shot taken; teams whipped the ball around on offense with crisp passes as they probed for an open cutter inside; teams believed in their coaches and made second-half adjustments when they fell behind in the first half. They did it all with remarkable speed, athleticism, and grace. The shooting stood out most spectacularly. Entire teams and not just a couple of guys on a squad were often brilliant, shooting at the right times with accuracy and confidence. Teams used three-point marksmanship to neutralize disadvantages in speed and size, dishearten the opposition, and overcome major point deficits. In back-to-back games in the Round of 8, Louisville bested West Virginia in a shooting showcase in which the two squads combined to net twenty-nine of fifty-five three-pointers, and Illinois then came from 15 points down with four minutes remaining to beat Arizona by shooting sixteen of thirty-six from downtown in the course of the game.

Maybe there's hope in this country after all. The NCAA is finally getting Proposition 48 right, President Myles Brand seems genuinely interested in academic reform, and basketball in March looks as healthy as it ever did. The newest big thing in the NBA, LeBron James, a product of the corrupt American youth basketball system who skipped college, has amazingly emerged from the amateur world with a team-first focus, watertight skills, and a curbed ego. Like a beefed-up, high-flying Magic Johnson, James gives kids a sound model of what an American basketball player looks like. That's more likely to affect real change than any instructional DVD.

Conclusion

Today's hoopsters hold up a middle finger to the notion of team loyalty and old-school values like sportsmanship and patiently waiting for one's turn. This attitude is learned early in the developmental process, as outstanding athletes are showered with accolades, promises, and free rides from interested parties such as club coaches and sneaker companies, the two often in cahoots or auditioning one another for a partnership. Beginning in grade school, scouting services rank kid-athletes as individuals within the team sport of basketball, alerting suitors who then promptly begin to jostle for a meaningful position in the life of a promising young athlete and his family. Their trite but always alluring message: "I'll help you make it." Such a possibility resonates at full volume for any kid, particularly those with fewer options and models of success.

As discussed above, there are only three celebrated options out of the 'hood: playing ball, making hip-hop music, or selling drugs. These three staples of contemporary black life and male vitality have been glamorized as the exclusive means to financial and social upward mobility. Obviously kids buy in, working very hard at a supposed shortcut to the "good life." To circumvent the sobering near impossibility of succeeding along any one of these illusive pathways, the dream chasers see themselves as game players in a street contest of chance, often playing their hand in any or all of the three hustles, sometimes simultaneously.

The rare players/playas who make it to the top know how to work the system. They look out for themselves with cold, steel resolve. As master individualists, they pimp out those pimping them to get what they need. In the high-stakes competition of the NBA such an approach pits each ballplayer against the other players, owners, and managers. Those with business savvy become hustlers, with a street-bred, first-hand understanding of what rap group Public Enemy calls "the game behind the game."

Individualism brandishes an aesthetic—an entire genre of style, attitude, and fashion—premised upon black male swagger and the energy of unconstrained youth. Music critic Nelson George labels it "blasculinity," and sociologist Richard Majors calls it the "cool pose," which manifests itself as bravado and hyper-confidence and is theatricality immersed in movement, dress, and style. It's what makes a dunk more than simply two points; the act of dunking becomes a virtuoso performance, a release, the public dismantling of a lesser man—of *all* lesser men.

In the post-Jordan era, NBA executives have successfully contained the "cool pose" of stars like Allen Iverson, leaving it edgy enough for some to fetishize yet adequately safe for white, middle-class consumption. While publicly chastising the bad boy superstars when they seem to reach a limit, the NBA nonetheless happily peddles their brand of attitude and flamboyance. Business is business.

The generational, racial, and cultural differences that isolate basketball players from coaches, management, and owners similarly often separate the players from the fans. Since the 1970s, basketball has changed dramatically in virtually all areas of the game, from the style of play to the racial composition of the player population to the politics, economics, and scope of the business. During this time, sneaker conglomerates have seized control of amateur hoops to the detriment of high school basketball; NBA player salaries have exploded and appear secure in their absurd excesses as players are contractually guaranteed access to *all* sources of NBA revenues; individual ballplayers have become their own commercial brands, as highlight-based sports shows like *Sports Center* allow athletes to parlay their names, one-on-one moves, and celebration rituals into patented commodities; and hip-hop culture has infiltrated and shaped the values of the game. All of these changes have remade basketball as a sport and as a financial enterprise that is tailor made for the individual athlete rather than for teams.

Consequently, over this time basketball's support base has largely polarized, creating a population of disillusioned fans, typically white and older, who tend to place the blame for the game's perceived deterioration entirely on the shoulders of the black players—their attitude, upbringing, and dubious work ethic. Such fans are frequently oblivious both to the expectations of black male authenticity and to the changing structure of the business of basketball. At the other end, younger fans, both white and black, bred on the Jordan and post-Jordan NBA, often love the product on the floor, fantasizing along with the players and living out their hoop dreams with glitzy consumerism.

For those who focus on the failure of individuals rather than on the structure of the sport, the racial and cultural traits of the players take on heightened significance, often leading to a nostalgia for the "good old days" that is predicated on a longing for a less racially and culturally varied time. The nostalgic fan makes sense of basketball in terms of symbols, and as a result, symbolic figures become representatives of types and groups. If Ron Artest symbolizes the dangerous and unstable black athlete and Allen Iverson symbolizes hip-hop decadence and incorrigibility, then Larry Bird, whose stature among fans has long outlasted his playing days, functions even today as yet another kind of symbol. In a sport redefined by the artistry and culture of black athletes, alienated white fans find in Larry Bird, the last American-born white superstar, a less physically magnificent everyman to whom they can relate and who reassures them of their continued relevance in a beloved pastime.

The Celtic legend, with his small-town shyness and everyman appeal, meshed perfectly with Boston's civic personality and sports culture. In a city that had suddenly gone from an industrial town to a center of technological and intellectual competition, the simpler, blue-collar way of life became sacred and most easily recognizable in the city's sports icons. In Larry Bird, Boston fans, like white sports buffs nationwide, reveled in the joining of two disappearing icons in one sports hero: the factory man and the white athlete.

Meanwhile, in an era in collegiate and professional basketball tarnished by vulgarity, greed, heinous behavior, and misguided black athlete millionaires acting up and even being rewarded for it (Sprewell was better off *after* he had choked Carlesimo, while the former NBA head coach is now relegated to assistant duties), what happened to the disciplinarians ready to confront the coddled athletes who were causing trouble? Where were the drill sergeants and tough-love fathers? Bob Knight, although incapable of controlling himself, knew how to control his players. While Coach Steve Fisher at the University of Michigan procured the nation's best recruits and then allowed them to flap about the court in Fab Five swagger, Bob Knight proudly stood at the other extreme. At Indiana University, Coach Knight represented despotic authority; he insisted upon short hair, anonymous uniforms, and athletes who believed in a system. Signing impressionable players instead of the best talent, acquiring faithful soldiers who would give a decent college performance rather than go on to distinguished professional careers, and playing slower, more calculated half-court hoops, Bob Knight consistently fielded mostly white teams playing "under-control" basketball. The film *Hoosiers* exposes the symbolic weight of Knight and his link to an era of segregation in high school basketball.

Bird and Coach Knight are ties to the past and to sports institutions that are still very much relevant, yet the game and its culture evolve constantly. Today an influx of players from abroad is challenging the game's purely American black-white dichotomy, creating a broader range of ethnicities and a new class of "white" ballplayers. This globalization of the NBA and the responses of fans, the media, and the league have reversed many assumptions about the masculinity quotient and physical talents of Europeans, about American hegemony, and about the solidity of our own nationalism: are we more loyal today to the flag or to the swoosh? The globalization of basketball has pointed the NBA in a new direction, focusing overseas for new talent, new markets, and new corporate partnerships.

Indeed basketball has never occupied a more central space in our culture, nor have the behind-the-scenes parts of the game ever been more compelling.

Keep an eye on what's happening under the boards!

BIBLIOGRAPHIC ESSAY

My research draws upon a variety of sources and resources. Conversations with alumni of schools such as Indiana University and Georgetown University and ardent fans of various NBA and college teams influenced my thinking throughout the book. The Museum of Television and Radio in New York provided hours upon hours of game tapes; television shows and specials; and television advertisements to reference, study, and analyze. To this end, private tape collections—mine and those of others—were also useful. As much as anything else, I have relied on my experiences, since my youth, of watching basketball, playing basketball, and listening to hip-hop music. For facts, news, statistics, and widely circulated quotes from players and coaches, I depended chiefly on respected mainstream news outlets and publications such as the Associated Press, the *New York Times*, the *Wall Street Journal, Sports Illustrated,* and *Rolling Stone.* For background information, I also consulted basketball-specific sources—namely, *SLAM*, www.databasebasketball.com (formerly basketballreference.com), and nba.com. Often my data and perspective on events simply came from following all of the twists and turns of a news story and staying with the reportage after the first couple of rounds of buzz had subsided. My father's exhaustive and dedicated article-clipping and eye for news proved tremendously helpful in this pursuit. A representative of the NBA's Team Marketing and Business Operations provided numerous explanations of NBA bureaucracy, marketing initiatives, and strategies that go into successfully promoting a sports league. Listed below are the principal sources that have informed specific topics and discussions throughout the text. I've included all works quoted at length; popular culture items (films, music, television shows, etc.); and, in relation to trends in media coverage and analysis, the articles that best represent specific patterns.

Preface

I referred to the following in my discussion of the NBA's dress code: Lorne Manly, "The Sound of the NBA's Dress Code: Ka-Ching," *New York Times*, December 12, 2005; Virginia Postrel, *The Substance of Style* (New York: Perennial, 2003); Lisa Scottoline, *Devil's Corner* (New York: HarperCollins, 2005); "NYPD's Secret Hip-Hop Dossier," www.thesmokinggun.com, October 8, 2004.

1. Can't Knock the Hustle

Excerpts at the start of the chapter are from Earle Eldridge, "Escalade Scores with Athletes, Rappers," *USA Today*, October 23, 2001, and Nelson George, *Hip-Hop America* (New York: Penguin Books, 1998). In addition to these two works, the following sources, some of which I have quoted, provided background information and essential perspective for my discussion of hip-hop, basketball, drugs, and their intersection: Todd Boyd, *Young, Black, Rich and Famous: The Rise of the NBA, the Hip Hop Invasion and the Transformation of American Culture* (New York: Doubleday, 2003); Nelson George, *Elevating the Game* (Lincoln: University of Nebraska Press, 1992); Steven D. Levitt and Stephen J. Dubner, *Freakonomics: A Rogue Economist Explores the Hidden Side of Everything* (New York: HarperCollins, 2005); Kelefa Sanneh, "Gettin' Paid," *New Yorker*, August 20 and 27, 2001; 50 Cent and Kris Ex, *From Pieces to Weight: Once Upon a Time in Southside Queens* (New York: MTV Books, 2005). Anecdotes and perspective on the Entertainers Basketball Classic at Rucker Park provided by Entertainers Basketball Classic coach and icon Tony Rosa, interviewed by the author on August 25, 2005. The following popular culture items were used to articulate the meaning and values of hip-hop, basketball, and/or drug culture and in some instances to trace the triangular relationship among the three. Films: *Above the Rim* (New Line Cinema, 1994); *Get Rich or Die Tryin'* (Paramount Pictures, 2005); *Hustle and Flow* (Paramount Classics, 2004); *He Got Game* (Buena Vista, 1998). Music videos of Jadakiss and Mike Jones. Music by rappers/rap acts: A Tribe Called Quest, Beatnuts, Jay-Z, Mobb Deep, Nas, Nelly, Notorious B.I.G., and 2Pac. Television shows: "Calvin Gets a Job at WacArnold's"; "Chappelle's Show," *Comedy Central*, January 28, 2004 (season 2, premiere episode). Video game: *Street Hoops* (Activision, 2002). I relied primarily on two sources for the history of the sneaker company AND 1: AND 1 Web site (www.and1.com) and Larry Platt, *New Jack Jocks: Rebels, Race, and the American Athlete* (Philadelphia: Temple University Press, 2002). Quotes from the Tracy McGrady interview appeared in Russ Bengtson and Ryan Jones, "Star Time," *SLAM* (November 2002). My understanding of Michael Jordan as a businessman was informed by David Halberstam's *Playing for Keeps: Michael Jordan and the World He Made* (New York: Random House, 1999). On the perilously low odds of making good on a hoop dream, the following two sources proved highly instructive: NCAA Web site (www.ncaa.org) and the author's interview with Tom Konchalski (of *HSBI Report*), September 21, 2005.

2. Peddling the Streets

My discussion of teenaged gangsta wannabes in the 1990s was aided by conversations with friends of my age and former classmates, who jogged their memories about their high school experiences and the trends of the day. Nancy Jo Sales provided an essential backdrop and supplemented our collective memories with an important cover story—"Teenage Gangland," *New York Magazine*, December 16, 1996—that made the term "Prep-School Gangsters" an enduring part of NYC vocabulary and folklore for my generation.

The idea that black fetishism on the part of white consumers of black culture extends into adulthood was supported by the following: Adrien Brody's quote in *Mass Appeal*, no. 37, 2005; David Shields's explorations in *Black Planet: Facing Race during an NBA Season* (New York: Crown, 1999); the impact of Randy Moss's comments on HBO *Real Sports* (HBO Sports, Episode 101, Story 1: Randy Moss, August 23, 2005).

For background on the murders of Biggie and 2Pac, I relied on British filmmaker Nick Broomfield's documentary *Biggie and Tupac* (Razor and Tie, 2002), as well as the investigative reporting of Randall Sullivan—specifically "The Unsolved Mystery of Notorious B.I.G.," *Rolling Stone*, December 15, 2005.

My understanding of Iverson's personal history was shaped by Larry Platt's carefully researched, analytically oriented biography *Only the Strong Survive: The Odyssey of Allen Iverson* (New York: HarperCollins, 2002), and by two *Sports Illustrated* articles: Gary Smith, "Love Story: How Allen Iverson and Larry Brown Learned to Live Together," *Sports Illustrated*, April 23, 2001, and "Southern Discomfort," *Sports Illustrated*, October 25, 1993.

For my examination and definition of "keepin' it real," I drew upon the following sources, some of which I have quoted: Todd Boyd, *Am I Black Enough for You?: Popular Culture from the 'Hood and Beyond* (Bloomington: Indiana University Press, 1997); Boyd (2003); Gar Anthony Haywood, "Stow the Lynch Rope in Allen Iverson's Case," *New York Newsday*, July 19, 2002; Richard Majors, "Cool Pose: Black Masculinity and Sports," in *Sport, Men, and the Gender Order*, ed. Michael A. Messner and Donald F. Sabo (Champaign: Human Kinetics Books, 1990); Larry Platt, *Keepin' It Real: A Turbulent Season at the Crossroads with the NBA* (New York: Avon Books, 1999).

On the marketing of hip-hop/"black" deviance as it applies in contemporary marketing and specifically in the NBA, I referred to and/or quoted from the following scholarly works: D. Downes and P. Rock, *Understanding Deviance: A Guide to the Sociology of Crime and Rule Breaking* (Oxford: Clarendon Press, 1995); John Hoberman, *Darwin's Athletes: How Sport Has Damaged Black America and Preserved the Myth of Race* (New York: Houghton Mifflin, 1997); Davis W. Houck, "Attacking the Rim: The Cultural Politics of Dunking," in *Basketball Jones: America above the Rim*, ed. Todd Boyd and Kenneth L. Shropshire (New York: New York University Press, 2000). In addition, I referred to Phil Taylor, "The Race Card," *Sports Illustrated*, December 15, 1997.

I referenced and commented on the following articles in my analysis of the media's coverage and reaction to Iverson's arrest in 1997: Ira Berkow, "Questions Follow Troubled Iverson," *New York Times*, October 28, 1997; Dave Kindred, "Some Men Behaving Badly," *Sporting News*, September 8, 1997; Peter May, "Off-Court Problems Make for an Unsettling Summer," *Sporting News*, August 18, 1997; William C. Rhoden. "A Taint That Won't Go Away," *New York Times*, August 6, 1997; Michael Wilbon, "Friends Don't Let Friends . . . ," *Washington Post*, August 5, 1997; Mike Wise, "Image-Conscious NBA Suspends Iverson and Rider," *New York Times*, October 4, 1997; Gordon Witkin, "Another Bout of Trouble," *U.S. News and World Report*, August 18–25, 1997.

In tracing certain trends in advertising, I referred to the following articles, some of which deal specifically with the marketing of Allen Iverson: Lee Hawkins Jr., "GM Seeks Chevrolet Revival," *Wall Street Journal*, December 19, 2003; Joseph Pereira and Stephanie Kang, "Phat News: Rappers Choose Reebok Shoes," *Wall Street Journal*, November 14, 2003; Richard Linnett, "Reebok Re-Brands for Hip-Hop Crowd," *Advertising Age*, January 28, 2002; Lola Ogunnaike, "Steve Stoute Would Like to Turn You into a Sneaker," *Rolling Stone*, December 15, 2005; Adolph Reed Jr., "Keeping It Real," *Village Voice*, March 11, 1997.

In considering the cultural implications of Iverson's crossover dribble, I employed Todd Boyd's (1997) example of the word "thing" transforming into "thang" in hip-hop music.

I referred to the following articles, among others, in my assessment of the press's response to Iverson's 2002 (house) arrest: Tracy Connor, "Despite Bust, It's Party Time at Iverson's," *New York Daily News*, July 13, 2002; Jere Longman, "Iverson Freed on Bond after Plea of Not Guilty," *New York Times*, July 17, 2002; Douglas Montero: "Philly in Fury at Free Man Iverson," *New York Post*, July 13, 2002, and "Allen's Getting Most Valuable Prisoner Treatment," *New York Post*, July 18, 2002; Lisa Olson, "Keeping It Unreal," *New York Daily News*, July 17, 2002.

I referred to the following two articles in addressing the media's handling of the "kid" narrative in its evaluation of Iverson: Ira Berkow, "It's Time for Iverson to Grow Up," *New York Times*, July 13, 2002, and William C. Rhoden, "A Case of Arrested Development," *New York Times*, July 17, 2002.

In comparing and contrasting Iverson with Michael Jordan, I consulted a scholarly article on the cultural meaning of Jordan: Scott Stossel, "Who's Afraid of Michael Jordan?" *American Prospect*, May–June 1997; I also consulted a more recent newspaper piece: Jere Longman and Richard Lezin Jones, "Iverson Is a Study in Contradictions," *New York Times*, July 21, 2002.

On video games, I wrote specifically on NBA *Ballers* (Midway Games, 2004). My discussion on basketball video games was informed by an article entitled "Thug Life" (*Play Station Magazine*, August 2004) and by comments on the state of contemporary professional basketball by the legendary Oscar Robertson in "NBA Markets Style at Expense of Substance," *New York Times*, February 15, 2004.

On the destructiveness of black "burlesque" in sports, I quoted Thad Mumford, "The New Minstrel Show: Black Vaudeville with Statistics," *New York Times*, May 23, 2004.

3. Power Game

On the troubled climate of the NBA, the following books and articles informed my thinking and provided examples that I cited: Jeff Benedict, *Out of Bounds: Inside the NBA's Culture of Rape, Violence and Crime* (New York: HarperCollins, 2004); Phil Jackson, *The Last Season: A Team in Search of Its Soul* (New York: Penguin Press, 2004); Jack McCallum, "The Dark Side of a Star," *Sports Illustrated*, July 28, 2003; Ian Thomsen, "Why Fans Are Tuning Out the NBA," *Sports Illustrated*, February 21, 2005; L. Jon Wertheim, *Transition Game: How Hoosiers Went Hip-Hop* (New York: GP Putnam's Sons, 2005).

For details of the Pacers brawl and its aftermath and my analysis of the response of the players in comparison to that of the NBA, I found the following news items useful: Albert Chen, "After the Brawl," *Sports Illustrated*, December 6, 2004; Mitch Lawrence, "Image Up," *New York Daily News*, November 12, 2005; Jane L. Levere, "One Way to Deflect Attention from NBA Embarrassment: Funny Ads," *New York Times*, February 14, 2005; Rudy Martzke, "ESPN Boss Makes Right Call after Announcers Blame Pistons Fans," *USA Today*, November 24, 2004; Jack McCallum, "The Ugliest Game," *Sports Illustrated*, November 29, 2004.

For the specifics of the 2005 Collective Bargaining Agreement (CBA), as well as a broader understanding of salaries and the business of basketball, the following two Web sites were very instructive: Larry Coon's *2005 NBA Salary Cap FAQ* Web site (www.members.cox.net/lmcoon/salarycap.htm) and NBA Players' Association Web site (www.nbpa.org).

I used Larry Bird's comments on today's more violent NBA from his interview with Peter Richmond—"Larry Bird Cries Foul," *GQ*, February 2005.

I cited the following investigative report on the actual outcome of disciplinary fines in various sports leagues: Jon Weinbach, "When Players Don't Pay," *Wall Street Journal*, June 17, 2005.

In evaluating how Latrell Sprewell's image has been manipulated by AND 1, newspaper writers, and Sprewell himself, I again called upon Larry Platt and his discussion of Sprewell in *New Jack Jocks* (2002).

For an academic perspective on the manipulation and selling of images of blackness—primarily on the part of the mainstream media—I consulted the following: John Gabriel, *Whitewash: Racialized Politics and the Media* (London: Routledge Press, 1998), and bell hooks, *Black Looks: Race and Representation* (Boston: South End Press, 1992).

In evaluating the coverage of and editorialization on Sprewell-Carlesimo by the mainstream press, I considered and sometimes quoted from the following articles: Peter Beinart, "Sprewell's 'Racism' Excuse Is the Civil Rights Movement at Its Worst," *New Republic*, December 15, 1997; Dave D'Alessandro, "The Sprewell Affair: First Ugly, Now Ridiculous," *Sporting News*, December 15, 1997; Jerry Green, "Detroit Blessed with Athletes Who Aren't among the Villains in Sports," *Detroit News*, December 26, 1997; Ken Hamblin, "Latrell Sprewell: Choke Artist," *Denver Post*, December 14, 1997; Pat Lambert et al., "Dee-fense," *People*, December 22, 1997; Thomas Sowell, "A New Tribalism," *Forbes*, December 29, 1997; Sam Smith, "Sprewell vs. Carlesimo Isn't about Black vs. White, It's Green," *Chicago Tribune*, December 11, 1997; Phil Taylor, "Center of the Storm," *Sports Illustrated*, December 15, 1997; Bob Wojnowski, "Sprewell Situation Becoming a Power Struggle between Players, League," *Detroit News*, December 11, 1997. I also again referred to Platt (2002).

Details on arbitrator John Feerick's ruling in the Sprewell case were provided by the NBA Players' Association Web site (www.nbpa.org).

In evaluating the coverage of and editorialization on Sprewell-Carlesimo by the black press, I looked at and sometimes quoted from the following articles: John L. Burris: "Abusive Coach Shares Guilt," *Philadelphia Tribune*, December 23, 1997, and "A Question of Respect?" *Sacramento Observer*, March 18, 1998; Kenneth Brooks, "Latrell Sprewell Isn't the Only One at Fault," *Washington Informer* [Washington DC], December 24, 1997; Jeff Dillon, "Holla If Ya Hear Me: Spree Still Ain't Free," *Sun Reporter* [San Francisco], March 12, 1998; East Bay Bureau: "Black Fans Rip Warriors, Back Latrell Sprewell," *Sun Reporter*, December 4, 1997, and "Sprewell and His Brothers Respond to White Media," *Sun Reporter*, December 11, 1997; Howie Evans, "Media Continue Their Attacks on Sprewell," *Amsterdam News* [New York], December 18–24, 1997; Charles S. Farrell, "Courtside Motivation or Abuse? Sprewell-Carlesimo Brouhaha Raises Question of Coaching Behavior," *Black Issues in Higher Education* [scholarly journal], January 22, 1998; Wiley A. Hall, "Urban Rhythms: Latrell Sprewell: A Disgrace to the Race," *Afro-American* [Baltimore], March 14, 1998; Jaime C. Harris, "Sprewell Incident Raises Sensitive Issues of Sports in America," *Amsterdam News*, December 11–17, 1997; Earl Ofari Hutchinson, "Is Sprewell Victim of Racial Double Standard?" *New Pittsburgh Courier*, December 17, 1997; Ri'chard Magee, "Sprewell's Act Reflects Attitude of Hip-Hop Era," *Philadelphia Tribune*, January 2, 1998; Andrew Rosario, "B. J. and P. J.: Golden State of Confusion," *New York Beacon*, December 17, 1997; A. Asadullah Samad, "Between the Lines: Latrell Sprewell Incident; He Was out of Line, but So

Was Penalty," *Los Angeles Sentinel*, January 7, 1998; D. L. Stanley: "Sprewell-Carlesimo Spat about Winning and Losing," *Atlanta Inquirer*, December 27, 1997; "The Case of the Pampered Athlete," *Atlanta Inquirer*, December 20, 1997; and "Tiger, Rocker, Chipper and Latrell," *Atlanta Inquirer*, October 7, 1997; Tony White, "'Vilified Sprewell' Wants Opportunity to Be Heard," *Afro-American*, December 13, 1997; "Above the Rim, but Not the Law," *Philadelphia Tribune*, December 2, 1997; "Color Does Not a 'Brother' Make," *Michigan Chronicle* [Detroit], December 29, 1997; "Firing Sprewell Correct: Suspension Too Harsh," *Skanner* [Portland, Oregon], December 17, 1997; "Golden State Warriors Terminate $32 Million Contact of Latrell Sprewell after He Attacked Coach; NBA Suspends Him for One Year," *Jet*, December 22, 1997; "Shades of Black and White in Greene Football Case," *Michigan Chronicle*, January 12, 1999.

The following piece by black culture critic Michael Eric Dyson helped fashion my thinking about the relationship between the repeated firings of black coaches during the first half of the 2003–04 season and Rasheed Wallace's controversial comments: "Some Pain, Some Gain," *Sports Illustrated*, December 29, 2003.

In my explanation of the difference between owners' money and players' money, I referenced a Chris Rock routine: *Chris Rock: Never Scared* (HBO, 2004).

4. The Last White Superstar

The insights of the following individuals, all interviewed by the author, helped inform and frame this chapter and provided insider perspectives on the Celtics, Larry Bird, and the racial climate of Boston: Jeff Cohen, former Celtics vice president, interviewed on October 30, 2002; Jackie MacMullan, *Boston Globe* columnist, former pro basketball specialist for *Sports Illustrated*, and co-author of a book with Larry Bird (*Bird Watching: On Playing and Coaching the Game I Love* [New York: Warner Books, 1999]), interviewed on October 31, 2002; Dan Shaughnessy, *Boston Globe* columnist, author of books on Boston sports teams (including *Ever Green—The Boston Celtics: A History in the Words of Their Players, Coaches, Fans and Foes, from 1946 to the Present* [New York: St. Martin's Press, 1990]), and the *Globe*'s beat reporter for the Celtics from 1982 to 1986, interviewed on October 28, 2002; Jeff Twiss, Celtics vice president of media relations, interviewed on October 29, 2002.

I also relied on guidance, feedback, and information from my communications, in person and via e-mail, with Harvey Araton, a *New York Times* columnist and the author of several books on basketball. The most relevant of the books (co-authored by Filip Bondy), *The Selling of the Green: The Financial Rise and Moral Decline of the Boston Celtics* (New York: HarperCollins, 1992), explored a history of dubious ethical practices on the part of the Celtics.

A brief e-mail correspondence with Peter May of the *Boston Globe* in October 2002 was also revealing.

On the idea of white nostalgia in sports and elsewhere, I quoted from *Chris Rock: Bigger and Blacker* (HBO, 1999).

For a perspective on the disappearance of big-name white athletes, I relied on S. L. Price, "What Ever Happened to the White Athlete?" *Sports Illustrated*, December 8, 1997.

The following sources provided background on Larry Bird's life and professional career, as well as on the history of the Boston Celtics and the experiences of the team's players: Araton and Bondy (1992); Larry Bird with Bob Ryan, *Drive: The Story of My Life* (New York: Doubleday, 1989); Lee Daniel Levine, *Bird: The Making of an American Sports Legend* (New York: McGraw-Hill, 1988); Bob Schron and Kevin Stevens, *The Bird Era: A History of the Boston Celtics 1978–1988* (Boston: Quinlan Press, 1988); Shaughnessy (1990); Mark Shaw, *Larry Legend* (Lincolnwood, Ill.: Masters Press, 1998).

The following sources provided background as well as quotations on social and economic changes in Boston and throughout the United States from 1950 on: Daniel Bell, *The Coming of Post-Industrial Society: A Venture in Social Forecasting* (New York: Basic Books, 1973); Barry Bluestone and Mary Huff Stevenson, *The Boston Renaissance: Race, Space, and Economic Change in an American Metropolis* (New York: Russell Sage Foundation, 2000); Howard Bryant, *Shut Out: A Story of Race and Baseball in Boston* (New York: Routledge, 2002); New Economy Index (www.neweconomyindex.org), created by the Progressive Policy Institute (PPI), Washington DC; Jack Tager, *Boston Riots: Three Centuries of Violence* (Boston: Northeastern Press, 2001).

Howard Bryant's meticulously researched book (2002) also helped me to link the events and player experiences of the Boston Red Sox to those of the Celtics.

On the Dee Brown incident, two articles proved valuable: Joseph P. Kahn, "The Dee Brown Incident Prompts a Quiet Suburb to Deal with Its Diversity," *Boston Globe*, April 16, 1991, and Leigh Montville, "Beantown: One Tough Place to Play," *Sports Illustrated*, August 19, 1991.

The following two illuminating, connected sources offered a great deal of information on the relatively cryptic, poorly documented history of the ABA: *Long Shots: Life and Times of the American Basketball Association* (HBO Sports, 1997) and Terry Pluto, *Loose Balls: The Short, Wild Life of the American Basketball Association: As Told by the Players, Coaches, and Movers and Shakers Who Made It Happen* (New York: Simon and Schuster, 1990).

For background on the underwatched, pre-Stern NBA of the 1970s and early 1980s, I used Armen Keteyian, Harvey Araton, and Martin F. Dardis, *Money Players: Days and Nights in the New NBA* (New York: Simon and Schuster, 1997).

I relied on Todd Boyd's (1997) discussion on the stylistic differences between the Celtics and the Lakers.

I commented on the following basketball films: *History of the NBA* (NBA Entertainment/HBO Sports, 1990); *Larry Bird: A Basketball Legend* (NBA Entertainment/Fox, 1991); *NBA Superstars* (NBA Entertainment/Fox, 1990s).

I noted Nelson George's findings in *The Death of Rhythm and Blues* (New York: Pantheon Books, 1988).

5. My Dad Was a Military Man

My conceptualization of the racial identity and style of play of certain professional and collegiate teams was stimulated by the provocative thinking and writing of Todd Boyd (1997, 2003) and Nelson George (1992).

My discussion of the difference between Indiana University and the University of Michigan in the 1990s was aided by Mitch Albom's best-selling book, from which I quoted at length: *Fab Five: Basketball, Trash Talk, and the American Dream* (New York: Warner Books, 1993).

On the history of Indiana University's men's basketball program, the IU Media Department was extremely helpful, providing excerpts from media guides and team photos from Knight's twenty-nine-year tenure. I also used another helpful book: Pete DiPrimio and Rick Notter, *Hoosier Handbook: Stories, Stats and Stuff about IU Basketball* (Wichita: Midwest Sports Publications, 1995).

I wrote extensively on the celebrated, critically acclaimed sports movie *Hoosiers* (Orion Pictures, 1986), and my understanding of the factual differences between the story depicted in the film and the actual events collectively known as the Milan Miracle was aided by Jeff Merron, "'Hoosiers' in Reel Life," ESPN*.com*; accessed March 2, 2004.

My interpretation and description of the "spirit" and way of life of the

Hoosiers (Indiana natives) was guided by the work of two authors: Irving Leibovitz, *My Indiana* (Englewood Cliffs, N.J.: Prentice-Hall, 1964), and Levine (1988). The former, ironically, was a relocated Jew from New York.

On the relationship of basketball to the history of Indiana and on race relations within the state and in its history of high school basketball, I relied on the following sources, some of which specifically explore the Milan Miracle: Nelson Campbell, ed., *Illinky: High School Basketball in Illinois, Indiana, and Kentucky* (New York: Stephen Greene Press/Pelham Books, 1990); David M. Chalmers, *Hooded Americanism: The History of the Ku Klux Klan* (Durham, N.C.: Duke University Press, 1987); Glenn T. Eskew, *But for Birmingham: The Local and National Movements in the Civil Rights Struggle* (Chapel Hill: University of North Carolina Press, 1997); Greg Guffey, *The Greatest Basketball Story Ever Told: The Milan Miracle, Then and Now* (Bloomington: Indiana University Press, 1993); Philip M. Hoose, *Hoosiers: The Fabulous Basketball Life of Indiana* (New York: Vintage Books, 1986); Levine (1988); George R. Metcalf, *From Little Rock to Boston: The History of School Desegregation* (Westport, Conn.: Greenwood Press, 1983); Mark Plaiss and Mike Plaiss, *The Road to Indianapolis: Inside a Season of High School Basketball* (Chicago: Bonus Books, 1991); Wertheim (2005).

On Bob Knight's life, coaching career, and—most important—his methods and philosophies, the following sources illuminated my thinking and writing: Steve Alford with John Garrity, *Playing for Knight: My Six Seasons with Coach Knight* (New York: Simon and Schuster, 1989); John Feinstein, *A Season on the Brink: A Year with Bob Knight and the Indiana Hoosiers* (New York: Simon and Schuster, 1986); Hoose (1986); Bob Knight with Bob Hammel, *Knight: My Story* (New York: St. Martin's Press, 2002); Joan Mellen, *Bob Knight: His Own Man* (New York: D. I. Fine, 1988).

The quote from Bird's mother on Coach Knight came from Levine's (1988) hugely helpful book.

The following articles, from some of which I quoted, offered details on Knight's legacy of abuse at IU (including the Neil Reed incident), as well as on Knight's pardoning in 2000 by IU and the media's response to and interpretation of the university's leniency: Harvey Araton, "At Indiana, the Toadies Are Shocked," *New York Times*, May 16, 2000; Joe Drape: "Few Cheers from Faculty in Handling of Knight Case," *New York Times*, April 24, 2000, and "Knight Gets 'Last Chance' to Coach at Indiana," *New York Times*, May 16, 2000; James C. McKinley Jr., "Decision on Knight Shows the Fine Line That Colleges Walk," *New York Times*, May 21, 2000; Rick

Reilly, "End the Knightmare," *Sports Illustrated,* May 1, 2000; George Vecsey, "At Indiana U., Trustees Can't Handle Coach Knight," *New York Times,* April 16, 2000; Alexander Wolff, "General Amnesty," *Sports Illustrated,* May 22, 2000.

On the specific backlash against Knight critic and IU professor Murray Sperber, I consulted Mike Rubin, "Whistling in the Dark," *GQ,* October 2003.

I referred to and in some cases quoted from the following articles to make sense of both Knight's firing and the backlash at the school, specifically against Knight's replacement, Mike Davis: Jarrett Bell, "Indiana Dismisses Knight," USA *Today,* September 11, 2000; Ira Berkow, "Degrees of Separation for Coach and Indiana," *New York Times,* September 11, 2000; Joe Gergen, "Bloomington Backlash," *New York Newsday,* September 12, 2000; James C. McKinley Jr., "At Indiana, Players Dig in over Firing of Knight," *New York Times,* September 12, 2000; Benjamin Nugent, "Helping the Hoosiers Forget Bobby," *Time Atlantic,* April 1, 2002; Kelly Whiteside, "General Court," *New York Newsday,* September 11, 2000.

The following sources offered both background on race relations specific to Bloomington and Indiana University and a sense of local politics and culture: Murray Sperber, *Beer and Circus: How Big-Time College Sports Is Crippling Undergraduate Education* (New York: Henry Holt, 2000); Emma Lou Thornbrough, *Indiana Blacks in the Twentieth Century* (Bloomington: Indiana University Press, 2000); Mary Ann Wynkoop, *Dissent in the Heartland: The Sixties at Indiana University* (Bloomington: Indiana University Press, 2002).

The following articles helped guide my analysis of Mike Davis's experiences as IU head coach during a tumultuous time and helped me to grasp the particulars of Davis's personality and coaching style: Mike DeCourcy: "Davis and Goliath," *Sporting News,* January 21, 2002, and "Transition Game," *Sporting News,* April 1, 2002; Tim Layden, "He's in Control (Really!)," *Sports Illustrated,* February 3, 2003; Rick Reilly, "As Different as Knight and Davis," *Sports Illustrated,* March 26, 2001; John B. Thomas and Valainis E. Anthony, "The Quiet Man," *Indianapolis Monthly,* November 2001.

The following articles shed light on the post-Indiana phase of Knight's legacy: Allen Barra, "Knight as Reformer? Why Not?" *New York Times,* March 23, 2003; Joe Lapointe, "The NCAA Selects Brand as Its Chief," *New York Times,* October 11, 2002; Richard Sandomir, "Coming Soon to ESPN: Bob Knight, Reality Star," *New York Times,* August 9, 2005; Phil Taylor,

"America's Best Sports Colleges," *Sports Illustrated*, October 7, 2002; George Vecsey, "At Salad Bar with Knight, Praise Only the Cherry Tomatoes," *New York Times*, February 8, 2004; Dick Weiss, "Recurring Knightmare," *New York Daily News*, February 4, 2005.

6. The New Globetrotters

On the decline of American basketball and the accompanying backlash against American players, I used the following sources: Jaime C. Harris, "Allure of NBA Lifestyle Outweighs Game for American Ballers," *Amsterdam News*, July 4, 2002; William C. Rhoden, "Trend Should Also Be a Warning," *New York Times*, June 29, 2002; Robertson (2004); Michael Sokolove, "Clang!" *New York Times Magazine*, February 13, 2005; Ian Thomsen, "World Weary," *Sports Illustrated*, September 16, 2002.

On the globalization of the NBA, I referred to the following: "FIBA Not Thrilled about NBA's Plan," *Sports Illustrated*, February 25, 2002; movie poster and promotional materials for *The Year of the Yao* (New Line Features, 2005).

On the influx and abilities of foreign players in the NBA, as well as on the media's interpretation and general celebration of foreign (mostly European) players, I referred to the following articles: Chris Broussard, "Foreign Countries Doing Better Job Prepping Players," *New York Times*, June 26, 2003; Chris Jones, "The New Black Guys," *Esquire*, February 2004; Liz Robbins, "Nets' Top Pick Learned to Play in a War Zone," *New York Times*, June 29, 2003.

I accessed the Italian database telebasket.com as a search engine for non-American players.

My discussion of the rising significance of club basketball and other changes in amateur basketball that minimized the importance of high school basketball was actively informed and framed by my interview with the very knowledgeable Tom Konchalski, publisher of the recruiting service newsletter *HSBI Report* and an authority on the history of amateur hoops.

My interviews on August 23, 2005, with Tony Rosa, founder of the Mustangs club program, and Nick Blatchford, founder and director of New Heights, were also beneficial. Some of the thoughtful responses of these two individuals are quoted in the chapter.

On the exploitative practices of sneaker companies through grassroots marketing and incestuous relationships with coaches and programs and on the history of this destructive trend, two books helped steer my analysis and provided essential background information and evidence: Ian O'Connor, *The Jump: Sebastian Telfair and the High Stakes Business of High School Ball* (Emmaus, Pa.: Rodale, 2005), and Dan Wetzel and Don Yaeger, *Sole Influence: Basketball, Corporate Greed, and the Corruption of America's Youth* (New York: Warner Books, 2000).

On the limitations of and problems with AAU and club basketball in the United States and on the history and contemporary state of New York City club basketball, I again referred to my interview subjects—Blatchford, Konchalski, and Rosa—and consulted the following sources: AAU Web site (www.aausports.org); Gauchos Web site (www.newyorkgauchos.com); Maureen O'Hagan and Christine Willmsen, "Coaches Who Prey," *Seattle Times*, December 14–17, 2003 (four-part series); Michael O'Keefe, "High and Dry," *New York Daily News*, April 24, 2004.

On the myth of the student-athlete and the mutually exploitative relationship between Division I athletes and the universities for which they play, I referred to Murray Sperber's case studies in *Beer and Circus* (2000) and to a section on teacher cheating (which specifically references the Harricks) in *Freakonomics* (Levitt and Dubner 2005).

On the celebration of Mutombo's alleged sexual conquests while he was at Georgetown, I looked at the Web site www.whowantstosexmutombo.com.

On the history of IMG, I referred to the company's Web site: www.imgworld.com.

On the incentives of amateur ballplayers to leave school early or to skip college entirely, Wertheim (2005) provided an instructive explanation.

On the cultural value and racial significance of dunking and its temporary ban by the NCAA, I relied on the following: Chris Broussard, "A Game Played above the Rim, above All Else," *New York Times*, February 15, 2004; Houck (2000); Sokolove (2005).

Lightning Source UK Ltd.
Milton Keynes UK
UKOW06f0741160615

253576UK00025B/350/P

9 780803 280533